Cookbook for Cancer

Celebrate...life is a special occasion!

A Collection of Recipes by
Julie Scott
Batavia, Ohio

*Dick Anderson
Donna Anderson)
Linda's (Pense)
Mom & Dad*

ISBN: 0-9740186-0-0

Cover photo copyright: 2003, Julie Scott
All personal stories/photos with permission
All Bible quotes from King James Version

Published by Resolve Publishing

Printed in the U.S.A. by
Morris Press Cookbooks
P.O. Box 2110 • Kearney, NE 68848
800-445-6621 • www.morriscookbooks.com

50191-gs   1

Mom Scott   *Mom*   *Mema*

Dedication

My mom and mother-in-law are survivors, and for that I am eternally grateful. My "Mema" has passed on, but I am still thankful for the time we shared. This book is dedicated to all of those who have won their battle and those who have gone on to see another day, in a better place.

Foreword

When Julie Scott, a friend and member of our church community first told me about this book, my initial reaction was "WOW!" Like all of the generous recipe contributors around the world, my family, too, has had to suffer the stunning blow of a cancer diagnosis. When my mother was diagnosed with liver cancer, all nine of us children, along with other family and friends, started cooking her favorite Lebanese foods to keep her body, as well as her spirits, nourished. Isn't that what food is about? The camaraderie, the nurturing, the sense of closeness and safety we feel when gathered around the table. My Mom always said, "Sharing food is a way of showing love." This book is Julie's way of celebrating her own family and the lives of those who have gone before her. Her endeavor is a rich tapestry of love that will be passed on.

Rita Nader Heikenfeld, CCP

Author's Note

As a stay-at-home mom who loves food, I decided to compile a cookbook. My mother and mother-in-law are cancer survivors; my "Mema" was not so lucky. I wanted to include some of their recipes, as well as those of others in my life affected by cancer. As the idea grew, I wondered if it would be possible to gather recipes from across the country – some of the proceeds could go to the American Cancer Society!

Worth a try? Well, here it is – 350 recipes from 33 states, plus 8 countries. Thanks largely in part to the internet and e-mail, individuals whose lives or loved ones have been touched by cancer have sent in their favorite recipes, plus photos, quotes, mottos and personal stories.

No matter what your cancer experience may be, it's impossible to continue on life's path unchanged. Some of those featured are still with us and some have passed on, but the one thing they all have in common is they all live/lived life to the fullest. Every day is a gift. You learn to celebrate the little things. A celebration almost always involves food, and thus was the inspiration for this book.

Throughout this project, I have read hundreds of personal experiences and met many wonderful people from across the United States and the world. The one thing that stands out from all of them is this – do not take one day for granted. Celebrate. Not just the "special occasions," but every day, because LIFE itself is a special occasion!

Enjoy!

Sincerely,

Julie

Acknowledgments

My deepest gratitude must be extended to: My husband, for his unending support, patience and sacrifice. My family and friends, who gave me guidance and helped immeasurably. The American Cancer Society for their help and support. Everyone who "passed the word" and shared my enthusiasm for this project, without all of you, this book would not have been possible.

American Cancer Society

The American Cancer Society is the nationwide community based voluntary health organization, dedicated to eliminating cancer as a major health problem through research, advocacy, patient support and education.

The ACS is the largest source of private not-for-profit cancer research funds in the US, second only to the federal government in total dollars spent. To date, the Society has invested more than $2 billion in cancer research, including funding 32 Nobel Prize winners.

Working nationwide on federal, state and local levels, the Society strives to promote beneficial policies, laws and regulations for those affected by cancer.

In addition, the ACS has a wide range of programs, offering patients, their families and caregivers, emotional and practical support.

The ACS provides a wealth of information, educational materials and support to the public. To contact the American Cancer Society, call 1-800-ACS-2345, 24 hours a day, seven days a week, or visit their web site www.cancer.org.

Author's note: Here are some additional web sites you may find helpful:

Association of Cancer Online Resources ....www.acor.org
Cancer Links ....www.Cancerlinks.org
Coalition of National Cancer
  Cooperative Groups..www.CancerTrialsHelp.org
Corporate Angel Network
  –free travel for patients..............................www.CorpAngelNetwork.org
National Cancer Institute ....www.cancer.gov
National Coalition for Cancer Survivorship...............www.CancerGuide.org
OncoLink...www.OncoLink.org
Shared Experience
  –patient experience exchange ....www.SharedExperience.org
The Wellness Community
  –patient support ....www.TheWellnessCommunity.org
Vital Options International ....www.VitalOptions.org
411cancer.com–cancer information center www.411cancer.com

---

While research is important in understanding any medical condition, the information contained in this book and the above web sites is for educational purposes only. It is not intended as medical advice, and should not substitute for consultation with a medical professional. If you have, or suspect you may have, a health problem, consult your health care provider. Please note *Cookbook for Cancer* is not responsible for the contents of any referenced web sites. ACS Screening and general information provided by the American Cancer Society.

50191-gs   4

The American Cancer Society's
Screening Recommendations

Early cancer detection is essential. For many types of cancer, finding the disease in an early, highly treatable stage can make the difference between life and death.

The ACS recommends men and women get a cancer-related checkup every year. It should include examinations of the thyroid, testicles, ovaries, lymph nodes, oral cavity and skin, as well as health counseling about tobacco, sun exposure, diet and nutrition, risk factors, sexual practices and environmental and occupational exposures.

The following are general screening guidelines. Discuss your individual risk factors with your doctor to determine when screenings will be necessary for you.

Breast Cancer
Mammogram – Annually for women age 40 and over
Clinical breast exam – Every 3 years for women ages 20-39
Annually for women age 40 and over
Breast self-exam – Monthly from age 20

Colorectal Cancer
Starting at age 50, people of average risk with no symptoms:
FOBT (fecal occult blood test) – annually and
Flexible sigmoidoscopy – every 5 years or
Colonoscopy – every 10 years

Prostate Cancer
Beginning at age 50, men should talk with their doctors about yearly screening
Two tests used to detect prostate cancer:
Digital rectal exam (DRE) and Prostate-specific antigen (PSA) blood test

Lung Cancer
Smokers are especially high risk, however, anyone with the following symptoms (which can also be signs of other illnesses) should consult a doctor: Persistent cough, shortness of breath, hoarseness, loss of appetite, chest pain, wheezing, weight loss, fever without cause, repeated cases of bronchitis or pneumonia

Be aware of your body. If something doesn't seem quite right, don't put it off, have it checked out! It might just save your life!

****

To help the ACS continue its mission,
50% of the net profits (after taxes), from the sale of the *Cookbook for Cancer*
will be donated to the American Cancer Society.

****

Table of Contents

Breakfast & Breads

Linda Robinson - Michigan

Larry Allen - Florida

Ruby Needles - Missouri

My Aunt Ruby

"Life may not be the party we hoped for, but while we're here, we might as well dance!"

-Unknown

In 1974, my favorite aunt, Ruby Needles, underwent a mastectomy for breast cancer. Back then, the surgery was more radical and treatment options were limited. I remember crying and writing her saying, I wasn't worried, because I knew she could handle this. After having had cancer myself about 20 years later, I'm not sure that was the best thing I could've said, but it was, nonetheless, totally true. She inspired everyone. She was never morose and joked when anyone else was complaining by saying, "That gets me right here in my left one!" Her left one was the breast she had lost.

The main lesson I learned from Aunt Ruby was to live every moment in faith and to the fullest. The cancer that eventually took her from us never diminished her zest for life. She loved and enjoyed her family, making each of us feel important and valuable. She always reinforced every good thing anyone did. She lived her life in such a joyous, grateful way; everyone who knew her realized one doesn't have to be stoic and rigid to be a servant of God.

After battling breast cancer and then colon cancer for a total of 19 years, Aunt Ruby was finally told in the hospital, she would not be going home...she was, in fact, dying. Her response was as inspiring as her life had been. She started to sing. As her daughter, Kathy, stood by her bedside, the lilt of "Precious Lord, Take My Hand" filled the room.

She was a shining example to me. I credit her with inspiring me to help heal myself. As Louise Hay says "Incurable only means that it must be cured from within. In curable."

Racheal Clearwater
Portland, Oregon

Find Racheal's breast cancer survival guide:
www.dreamwalksurvivor.com

Breakfast & Breads

𝓑REAKFAST FRUIT SALAD

1 apple	¹/₂ c. blue grapes
1 banana	¹/₄ of pineapple
1 orange	¹/₄ c. dates
1 tangerine	¹/₈ c. honey

Optional (may replace any of above with):

¹/₄ c. raisins	¹/₂ c. strawberries
1 kiwi fruit	¹/₂ c. cranberries
1 pear	¹/₂ c. raspberries
1 peach	¹/₂ c. blueberries
1 mango	

Chop apple, banana, orange, tangerine, grapes, pineapple. Mix in large bowl with dates. Add honey and stir well. You can add this mixture to a blender and make a smoothie. As a smoothie, this will make about 30 to 35 ounces.

Note: My average breakfast fruit salad contains 10 to 15 items, cut up in a big bowl. I find this fruit salad breakfast does a very good job of nourishing my body and I do not get very hungry the rest of the day.

Alex Fraser
Courtenay, British Columbia, Canada

$\mathcal{Q}$UICHE FROM PARIS

1 (10-in.) deep-dish already
  prepared & baked pie crust
1 double pkg. lardons (cooked &
  drained) or 10 slices cooked,
  drained & crumbled bacon
5 lg. eggs
½ c. milk
¼ c. creme fraiche (or heavy
  cream)

1½ c. Gruyere cheese (shredded)
¾ c. emmenthal (or mozzarella)
  cheese (shredded)
Salt & pepper to taste
2 tsp. noix de muscade (which is
  nutmeg)

Place the cooked and drained lardons (or crumbled bacon) on the bottom of the prepared and cooked pie crust, covering the bottom. In a large mixing bowl, whisk together the eggs, milk, creme fraiche (or heavy cream), salt and pepper to taste, and 1 teaspoon of the muscade (which is nutmeg). When well whisked, add 1¼ cup of Gruyere and ½ cup of the emmenthal or mozzarella. Pour over the lardons or bacon in the pie dish. Sprinkle the remaining cheese on the top and cover with the remaining 1 teaspoon of muscade (also sprinkled). Bake in a 350° F/180° C oven for about 45 minutes. You will need to cover the quiche with foil after about 30 minutes of baking to avoid burning the crust. Serve hot or cooled to room temperature. This makes a great dinner also when accompanied by a good salad and bread. Bon Appetit!

Note: This recipe was given to me by my French teacher who is a native Parisienne! She did not give me the exact measurements, but this recipe is as close as I've come to the mouthwatering quiche she made for me.

Amy Guisinger
Paris, France

"There are no guarantees in life, only the breath you just took, live each day like it was your last."

Ron Adams

50191-03

ℬAUERNFRUHSTUCK "FARMER'S BREAKFAST!"

4-5 potatoes
2 T. oil
¼ c. onion (chopped)
4 slices ham

¼ tsp. paprika
¼ tsp. oregano
5 eggs (beaten)
Salt & pepper to taste

Boil potatoes with skin until tender. Allow potatoes to cool, peel skin and slice. Heat oil in skillet with onions and ham. When onions begin to soften, add potatoes, paprika, oregano, salt and pepper. Let it cook until it is crusty. Pour beaten eggs in pan and let cook together with potatoes and ham until eggs are done. Eat with bread.

Silvia Raab
Raunheim, Germany

ℂHILI CHEESE EGG SQUARES

12 eggs
2 c. grated cheddar cheese

2 (4-oz.) cans Ortega chopped
  chilies (or 1 lg. (15-oz.) can)

Mix eggs, cheese, and chilies in a blender. Pour into a 9 x 13-inch pan. Bake at 375° for 30 to 40 minutes.

Note: Good for a breakfast or brunch!

Judy Kulhank
San Jose, California

ℬREAKFAST CASSEROLE

6 eggs
2 c. milk
1 tsp. salt
1 lb. sausage

1 tsp. dry mustard
1 c. grated cheddar cheese
6 slices cubed white bread

Brown, drain and cut up sausage. In large bowl, beat together eggs, milk, and salt. Add mustard and cheese. Mix well. Add sausage and bread cubes. Mix well. Bake in 9 x 13-inch casserole for 35 to 40 minutes at 350°.

Sherry Dickson
Ft. Wright, Kentucky

$\mathcal{H}$OLIDAY MORNING EGG SCRAMBLE

5 slices white bread
4 T. butter
2 T. flour
½ tsp. salt
¼ tsp. pepper

2 c. milk
12 eggs (scrambled)
6 cheese slices
8 oz. cooked sausage

Prepare the night before. Break bread slices into pieces and sauté all of the pieces in 2 tablespoons butter. Set aside. Melt 2 tablespoons butter in saucepan. Blend in flour, salt and pepper. Add milk and cheese broken into pieces. Blend well, simmer on medium heat until thickens to a soupy consistency. Set aside. Put precooked scrambled eggs in a buttered 9 x 13-inch casserole dish. Cut cooked sausage into bite-sized pieces and place over scrambled eggs. Pour the cheese mixture over sausage and egg, then top with sautéed bread. Cover and refrigerate overnight. In the morning, uncover, and bake at 350° for 30 minutes.

Marianne Cronin
Crestview Hills, Kentucky

$\mathcal{S}$WEDISH PANCAKES

6 eggs
½ tsp. salt
1½ tsp. sugar

1½ c. flour
2¾ c. milk

Beat eggs and add in salt, sugar. Slowly add in flour and milk until smooth. Mixture will be thinner than traditional pancake mix, as Swedish pancakes are very light. Pour onto a heated skillet or griddle and cook until lightly brown.

Note: Our family recipe for four generations.

Kim Andersen
Flower Mound, Texas

50191-03

ℬUMPY PANCAKES

1 lg. apple (peeled & finely
  chopped)
1 T. lemon juice
3 eggs
¾ c. milk
3 T. melted butter (or oil)

2 tsp. sugar
1 tsp. cinnamon
½ tsp. almond extract
3 c. bread cubes (5-6 slices)
⅓ c. raisins
1½ tsp. baking powder

Mix lemon juice with chopped apples (will prevent browning). Mix eggs, milk, butter, sugar, cinnamon and almond extract. Add bread cubes, apples, raisins and baking powder. Drop on greased grill or skillet. Cook pancakes until puffed and dry around edges. Turn once and press down gently. Cook until other side is golden brown.

Sister Mary Florence, SND
Covington, Kentucky

Isaiah 26:4 -- Trust ye in the LORD for ever.

COFFEE CAKE

Cake:

2 eggs (beaten)
2 tsp. vanilla extract
½ c. oil
1 c. milk

3 c. sifted all-purpose flour
1½ c. white sugar
6 tsp. baking powder
½ tsp. salt

Topping:

1 c. brown sugar
4 T. all-purpose flour

4 tsp. cinnamon
4 T. margarine (melted)

Optional:

1 c. walnuts (chopped)

1 c. coconut

Preheat oven to 350°. **Cake:** Combine vanilla extract, oil, eggs and milk. Set aside. In separate bowl sift together 3 cups flour, white sugar, baking powder and salt. Combine egg mixture with flour mixture and blend together well. Set aside. **Topping:** In separate bowl, combine brown sugar, 4 tablespoons all-purpose flour, cinnamon and margarine and walnuts/coconut, if desired. Mix well. Pour ½ of cake batter in a greased 9 x 13-inch baking dish. Sprinkle ½ of topping evenly across batter layer. Cover with remaining ½ of cake batter. Top with the rest of the topping. Bake at 350° for 35 to 40 minutes or until a toothpick inserted in the center comes out clean.

Note: In loving memory of Uncle Bob, Cousin Jeff and in honor of Aunt Delores Case.

Pat and Terry Bruce
Batavia, Ohio

"It is my firm belief that sharing a wonderful meal with loved ones is as important as any other treatment in the process of healing."
Suzanne Leider

50191-03

CINNAMON ROLLS (REDUCED FAT)

Rolls:

½ c. milk	1 (¼-oz.) pkg. dry yeast
1½ T. sugar	3 c. flour
1¼ tsp. salt	¼ c. margarine
3 T. applesauce	9 T. sugar
½ c. warm water	3 tsp. cinnamon

Icing:

¾ c. powdered sugar	1 tsp. vanilla
1 T. milk	

Warm milk; stir in sugar, salt and applesauce until sugar dissolves. Cool to lukewarm. Pour warm water into large bowl; add yeast, and stir until dissolved. Stir in lukewarm milk mixture. Add 1½ cups flour and mix until smooth. Stir in most of remaining flour, then turn out on lightly floured board. Knead until dough is non-sticky, smooth and elastic, about 8 to 10 minutes. Add more flour while kneading if necessary. Put dough in bowl, cover and set in warm place to rise until doubled in bulk (about 30 minutes). While waiting for dough to rise, mix 9 tablespoons sugar and 3 teaspoons cinnamon in a small bowl. After dough rises, knead again to squeeze out air bubbles. Roll dough into a rectangular shape. Spread with margarine. Sprinkle with the cinnamon and sugar mixture. Roll up as for jellyroll. Slice. Place side by side in a buttered pan, placing a small amount of margarine between each roll. Let rise until doubled and bake at 350° for 25 to 30 minutes. Frost hot rolls with icing.

Note: A family tradition for Christmas morning breakfast.

Judy Beardslee
Troy, Pennsylvania

"Normal day, let me be aware of the treasure you are. Let me learn from you, love you, bless you before you depart. Let me not pass you by in quest of some rare and perfect tomorrow."

Mary Jean Iron

WELSH CAKES

3 c. self-rising flour
Scant ½ c. sugar
¾ c. currants

½ c. plus 2 T. milk
½ c. butter
Optional: 1 egg (well beaten)

You will need an iron skillet or griddle. Grease pan well. Turn stove on low and thoroughly heat pan for about 10 minutes. Do not leave pan unattended. In a bowl, mix margarine, egg (optional, makes cakes richer) and flour together with fingers or mixer. Add sugar and currants. Blend with a spoon or hands, do not use mixer or it will mash the currants. Add milk and stir to make a soft consistency. Roll out to about ½ inch thickness and cut out 2- to 3-inch wide circles (use cookie cutter or drinking glass). Turn stove to medium heat. Place on greased griddle and let them cook for about two minutes, turn over (using a palette knife) and cook other sides. Continue until cake is evenly light brown.

Note: These really are delicious and a favorite of the Welsh people!

Eileen Arthur
Eregrlyn Caerphilly, Wales

BEST EVER BRAN MUFFINS

2½ c. flour
4 tsp. baking powder
1 tsp. salt
2 tsp. cinnamon
½ tsp. ground cloves
2 c. milk
2 c. All-Bran cereal

1 c. brown sugar
5 T. honey (melted)
½ c. margarine (melted)
2 eggs
1 c. raisins
1 c. chopped nuts

Mix together flour, baking powder, salt, cinnamon and ground cloves. Set aside. In another bowl, combine milk and All-Bran cereal. Let cereal soak for 5 minutes then add brown sugar, honey, margarine, and eggs. Mix well and add to the flour mixture. Blend all together and add raisins and nuts. Spray muffin pan with nonstick spray. Fill each cup ⅔ full and bake at 350° for 25 to 30 minutes.

Richard and Herta Gillies
Invermere, British Columbia, Canada

50191-03

𝒫UMPKIN BREAD OR MUFFINS

2 c. oat flour
1 T. baking powder
½ tsp. salt
½ tsp. nutmeg
2 tsp. cinnamon
¼ tsp. ground cloves
½ tsp. ground ginger

1 free range egg
½ c. natural Turbinado sugar
1 c. fresh or canned pumpkin purée
½ c. safflower oil
½ c. organic milk (or soy milk)
¾ c. organic raisins
½ c. finely chopped walnuts

Combine thoroughly the flour, baking powder, salt, nutmeg, cinnamon, cloves and ginger. Beat the egg with the sugar, then add the milk and pumpkin. Stir this mixture into the flour mixture, then add safflower oil and milk. Mix completely. Add raisins and all but two tablespoons of the walnuts. Spoon the batter ⅔ full into muffin cups, then sprinkle tops with remaining walnuts. Bake at 400° for 15 to 17 minutes, or until toothpick inserted in the center comes out clean. Let sit for 5 minutes then serve warm.

Note: This is a great recipe for those crisp fall mornings.

Cynthia Kahn
Peachtree City, Georgia

𝐵ANANA BREAD

¾ c. oil
1½ c. sugar
1 tsp. salt
1 c. flour
½ tsp. baking soda

1 tsp. baking powder
1 c. mashed bananas
½ c. milk
2 eggs

Mix oil, sugar, salt, eggs, and milk in bowl. Add flour, baking soda, and baking powder. Fold in 1 cup mashed bananas. Pour in greased and floured loaf pan. Bake for 1 hour at 350°. This will make 1 loaf of banana bread.

Jean McCarter
Edgewood, Kentucky

BANANA BREAD WITH WALNUTS

½ c. butter (softened)
1 c. natural Turbinado sugar
2 free range eggs
1 tsp. vanilla
5 tsp. milk (soy or rice milk ok as well)
¼ tsp. salt
1⅔ c. oat flour
1 tsp. baking soda
3 med./lg. bananas (mashed)
⅔ c. walnuts

Combine butter, sugar, eggs, vanilla and milk until smooth. Add flour, salt and soda. Add mashed bananas and walnuts and stir well. Pour into a loaf pan. Bake uncovered at 350° for 1 hour and 15 minutes, or until a toothpick inserted comes out clean.

Note: This is my mother's recipe that is no fail, and tastes delicious every time. Being a cancer survivor, I try to use organic food whenever possible, eliminating wheat and processed sugar.

Cynthia Kahn
Peachtree City, Georgia

BANANA BREAD

1¼ c. flour
¼ tsp. baking soda
1 tsp. baking powder
¼ tsp. salt
¼ c. sugar
2 ripe bananas (mashed)
2 T. vegetable oil
1 egg (beaten)
1 tsp. lemon juice

Mix flour, baking soda, baking powder, salt, sugar together in a bowl and make a well in the center. Set aside. Mix together bananas, vegetable oil, egg and lemon juice. When thoroughly mixed, pour into well of flour mixture. Stir only to moisten dry ingredients. Pour into a greased loaf pan and bake at 375° for 55 to 60 minutes.

Richard and Herta Gillies
Invermere, British Columbia, Canada

50191-03

$\mathcal{B}$ANANA CHOCOLATE CHIP MUFFINS

3 lg. (not mini) shredded wheat
  biscuits (crushed)
1 c. milk
1/3 c. oil
1 1/2 c. lightly packed brown sugar
2 eggs

2 c. all-purpose flour
1 T. baking powder
1 tsp. salt
1 tsp. cinnamon
2 ripe bananas (mashed)
1/2 c. semi-sweet chocolate chips

Crush wheat biscuits and cover with the milk. Set aside to soak. In another larger bowl cream together the oil and brown sugar. To the creamed mixture add the eggs and beat by hand until fluffy and light. Next add the shredded wheat mixture to the creamed mixture and stir until combined. Combine the flour/salt/cinnamon and add to the wet mixture. Stir until just moistened. Fold in mashed bananas and chips. Spoon into greased muffin tin until cups are filled almost to the top. Bake at 400° for 25 minutes. Turn muffins out onto a rack to cool. Store in an airtight container. These muffins freeze well! Makes at least 12 muffins.

Note: Bet you can't eat just one!

Valerie VanMatre
New Castle, Indiana
Donna Matthews
Hobe Sound, Florida

"Hope is the thing with feathers that perches in the soul and sings the tunes without the words and never stops at all."

Emily Dickinson

$\mathcal{P}$ASSOVER MANDEL BREAD

2 c. sugar
1 c. butter (softened)
6 eggs
2¾ c. matzo cake meal
½ tsp. salt (opt.)

¾ c. potato starch
1 (24-oz.) bag chocolate chips
1 c. chopped walnuts (opt.)
1 tsp. cinnamon
2 tsp. sugar

In mixing bowl cream sugar and margarine. Add eggs one at a time, beating after each addition. Sift together matzo cake meal, potato starch and salt. Fold into creamed mixture. Add chocolate chips and nuts and mix well. Form into 3 to 4 loaves, place on greased cookie sheet. Mix together the cinnamon and sugar and sprinkle on top of formed loaves. Preheat oven to 350°. Bake on greased cookie sheet in 350° oven for 45 minutes. Optional if you like crispy mandel bread, slice and toast further in oven until browned.

Note: This recipe is so delicious it can be used at any time not only for Passover Holiday.

Bonnie Lane
Port Washington, New York

$\mathcal{E}$ASY NO KNEAD ROLLS

½ c. margarine (softened)
¼ c. granulated sugar
½ tsp. salt
1 (¼-oz.) pkg. dry yeast
¼ c. warm water

2 eggs
4 c. flour
1 c. potato water from boiled
  potatoes

In large bowl pour ¼ cup warm water over yeast and mix well. Add margarine, 1 cup warm potato water, ¼ cup granulated sugar, 2 eggs, and mix well. Add 4 cups flour or more if needed to make a stiff dough. Beat well. Butter top with brush and cover with Saran Wrap. Put in refrigerator overnight. The next morning turn out of bowl but do not knead. Roll out dough about ¼ inch and butter top with brush. Cut with biscuit cutter and fold in half. Put in pan very close together and let raise double. Bake in preheated oven at 375° until brown.

Note: This recipe has been in my family for over 50 years. These rolls are easy to make and they are good anytime. My family all loves them and I love to make them for them.

Evelyn Adams
Barboursville, West Virginia

50191-03

ℬETTY'S DINNER ROLLS

2 (¹/₄-oz.) pkgs. yeast
¹/₄ c. warm water
¹/₂ c. Crisco
¹/₂ c. sugar
1 T. salt
1 egg

2 c. milk
5-6 c. flour
Optional: For whole-wheat rolls,
    use 3 c. white flour and 2 to 3 c.
    whole wheat flour

Dissolve yeast in water. Set aside. Heat milk, add shortening, sugar and salt. Heat in saucepan until slightly warm. Add egg and flour. Add dissolved yeast mixture. Let dough rise until double in size. On a lightly floured surface (table, counter top, etc.) roll out dough. Cut with biscuit cutter or roll by hand into balls. Let rise again. Bake at 425° for 10 to 15 minutes until light brown.

Betty Lewis
Morehead, Kentucky

Joshua 1:9 -- Be not afraid, neither be thou dismayed: for the LORD thy God is with thee whithersoever thou goest.

$\mathcal{S}$OURDOUGH BREAD BASE STARTER

4½ c. flour (divided)   4 c. warm water (divided)
2 T. sugar   1½ tsp. yeast

Combine 2 cups flour, 2 cups warm water, sugar and yeast. Put in a glass or stainless steel bowl and cover with a damp towel. Set in a warm place for 12 to 18 hours. Mixture should smell pungent or fermented, and have lots of bubbles in it. When it does, it is ready for the next step. To bubbly dough mixture mix in 2 cups warm water and 2½ cups flour. Recover with damp towel and allow mixture to bubble and ferment for about 12 hours. After the 12 hours, mixture can be stored in the refrigerator, in a sealed container for 3 to 4 weeks. This recipe will produce 2½ cups of sourdough for baking bread, rolls, etc. (the amount most recipes call for) and will leave you with 2 cups of base dough (commonly called a starter). Never use all of your dough at once or you will have to start the process all over again. A good rule of thumb is, when you take out 2½ cups of dough for a recipe, refill the starter container with 2½ cups flour and 2 cups water. Reseal container and return to the refrigerator. This way you will always have dough on hand. If left unused for a long period of time, sourdough will die. It will keep indefinitely in the freezer, but will need to be nursed back to health when thawed. Add 2½ cups flour and 2 cups water, let sit, drain off excess and repeat until full of bubbles again! Instead of making a recipe, you can split your starter batch and give half to a friend.

Note: I received my starter while stationed in Guam (1972). Since then, parts of the same batch have been around the world. It spent 3 years in a friend's freezer in Arizona and eventually made the trek to Washington where it now leads an active life!

Frenchy Corbeille
Castle Rock, Washington

50191-03

$\int$OURDOUGH FRENCH BREAD

2½ c. sourdough starter *1 c. warm water*
2 tsp. salt *5½-6 c. flour*

Stir water and salt into sourdough starter until salt is dissolved. Add flour 1 cup at a time. Stirring after each addition and scraping down the sides of the bowl. Stop adding flour when dough easily leaves the sides of the bowl. Dump onto a well floured board and knead until smooth and elastic. Add additional flour until dough will not stick to a non-floured surface. Usually takes about 8 minutes. Put dough into bowl to rise. Cover with plastic wrap to keep moisture in (will crust over if exposed). Let rise until double in volume (about 4 to 5 hours). Preheat oven to 400° (350° if convection bake) and begin to boil enough water to fill a shallow, ovenproof pan. Transfer dough to board and knead it down. Pull into 2 pieces and shape into 2 long loaves (if using cookie sheet) or 1 round ball (for a 9-inch pie pan). Place loaves on lightly greased baking pan. (**Optional:** Also sprinkle pan lightly with cornmeal.) Let rise 1 hour (1½ hours max). Take a sharp knife and slash each loaf with 3 cuts as follows. First, start at one end, cutting into loaf ¾ inch deep, and drag knife ⅔ of the way lengthwise toward the other end. Next, make a diagonal cut starting ¼ of the way from the end, across your first cut, ending ¼ of the way from the other end. Lastly, make another long cut, starting at the opposite end from the first one, and going ⅔ of the way toward the end. After slashing the loaves, brush them with water (or spray them). Place pan of boiling water on the lowest shelf, below the bread pan shelves. Bake loaves immediately after brushing with water, for 10 minutes. Remove water pan and bake for an additional 25 minutes. Turn off oven and leave loaves in for 5 minutes. When loaves are removed, brush or spray them again with water.

Frenchy Corbeille
Castle Rock, Washington

SOURDOUGH ENGLISH MUFFINS

2½ c. sourdough starter
3 T. sugar
6 c. flour (opt., 1 or 2 c. may be
  whole-wheat)

1 c. milk
2 tsp. salt

Put sourdough starter in mixing bowl, stir in milk, sugar and salt. Mix well. Add flour, one cup at a time, until dough is smooth and elastic. Put in bowl to rise, cover with plastic wrap. After it doubles in volume, knead it down, put it on a lightly floured surface and roll it out to ½ to ⅝ inch thickness. Use a 3-inch cutter to cut into muffins. A 6½-ounce clean tuna can, with both ends removed, works well. When all are cut, sprinkle lightly with cornmeal and cover with waxed paper. Let rise 45 minutes, then fry in lightly oiled uncovered electric frying pan at 325° to 350° or in a range top skillet over medium to low heat. Cook 11 to 12 minutes on each side. This makes about 25 muffins. One pan holds 9 to 10 muffins, so you're looking at more than an hour cooking time. Serve hot or, when cool, slice and freeze for future use.

Note: These toast well straight from the freezer!

Frenchy Corbeille
Castle Rock, Washington

HUSH PUPPIES

2 c. self rising cornmeal
¾ c. self rising flour
1 egg

1 med. onion
Approx. 2 c. whole milk

Mix meal, flour, egg and onion. Add just enough milk to moisten so you can drop by spoonful into hot grease. Cook until golden brown.

Glaspie Jennings
Morehead, Kentucky

50191-03

MEXICAN CORNBREAD

1 lb. sausage

Cornbread mixture:

1 c. yellow cornmeal
1 T. salt
1 c. Vitamin D whole milk
1 (15-oz.) can cream-style corn

½ tsp. baking soda
½ c. bacon grease or corn oil
2 eggs (well beaten)
1-2 tsp. jalapeño juice

Layers:

½ lb. grated cheddar cheese
1 lg. onion (chopped)

4-5 jalapeño peppers (chopped)

Brown sausage and set aside. Mix together cornmeal, salt, milk, cream-style corn. Add to mixture, baking soda, bacon grease (or corn oil), eggs and jalapeño juice. In a large, greased iron skillet, pour half of the cornbread mixture. An iron skillet will give the cornbread a crisp texture on the bottom and the sides. On top of the cornbread mixture, layer the cheese, onion, jalapeño peppers and cooked sausage. Pour remainder of cornmeal mixture on top of layers. Bake for 45-50 minutes at 350°. **To double this recipe:** Double the cornbread mixture (for oil measurement use ⅔ cup grease/oil and ⅓ cup water), but do not double the layers.

Note: This is a childhood favorite which is easy to fix. Also, like a good bowl of chili, the leftovers are always better the next day.

Mitch Pryor
Austin, Texas

"I may die one day of cancer, but I won't do it today. Today I will enjoy life."

Patty Phillips, 10 years cancer free

BROCCOLI CORNBREAD

½ c. butter or margarine
4 eggs
8½-oz. pkg. Jiffy cornbread mix
8 oz. sm. curd cottage cheese

1 med. onion (finely chopped)
1 (10-oz.) frozen broccoli
 (thawed & chopped)

Melt butter or margarine in an 8-inch square glass pan. Mix together eggs, cornbread mix, cottage cheese, onion and thawed broccoli. Pour over melted butter in the glass pan. Bake in a 350° oven for 45 to 55 minutes or until top is golden brown. Cut into squares.

Note: A great quick bread that has become a family favorite. Perfect for holiday dinners, potluck suppers and picnics. In honor of Nancy Grinonneau and husband, Bill and Tom Lyell and wife, Jackie.

June LaVernway
Roswell, New Mexico

JULIA'S CORN BREAD

3 c. corn meal (self-rising)
3 eggs
1 (8-oz.) can cream-style corn
1 c. chopped onions
½ c. grated American cheese

2 T. sugar
2 tsp. baking powder
½ c. Wesson oil
2 c. Vitamin D whole milk
1 tsp. red pepper

Preheat oven to 400°. Mix corn meal and eggs. Add cream-style corn, onions, cheese, sugar, baking powder, oil, milk, red pepper. Bake until golden brown for about 30 to 35 minutes.

Julia Kautz
Morehead, Kentucky

"Acceptance leads to understanding with patience in time."
Alex Fraser

50191-03

ℳOIST CORNBREAD MUFFINS

2 eggs
¼ c. sugar
1 c. all-purpose flour
⅔ c. yellow cornmeal
2 tsp. baking powder

½ tsp. baking soda
½ tsp. salt
1 c. unflavored yogurt
¼ c. melted butter or margarine

Combine the eggs and sugar in a bowl and beat until blended. In another bowl, stir together the flour, cornmeal, baking powder, baking soda and salt. Add flour mixture, yogurt and melted butter to egg mixture, stir batter until evenly moist. Spoon batter evenly into 12 paper-lined or well greased muffin tins (2½ inch in diameter). Bake in a 400° oven until muffin tops are lightly browned and centers are firm when gently touched, about 18 to 20 minutes.

Note: Yogurt contributes to moist and tangy flavored muffins. Good!

Doris Benson
La Conner, Washington

𝒫ERFECT CORNBREAD

1⅓ c. white flour
⅔ c. cornmeal
¼ c. sugar
1 tsp. baking soda
2 tsp. baking powder

¾ tsp. salt
2 eggs
1 c. buttermilk
¼ c. shortening

Mix flour, salt, cornmeal, sugar, baking soda and baking powder. Set aside. Combine eggs, buttermilk, shortening. Mix well. Add dry ingredients and beat until fine on low (about 3 to 5 minutes). Bake at 425° for 20 to 25 minutes.

Helen Montgomery
Morehead, Kentucky

Recipe Favorites

50191-03

Appetizers & Beverages

Edwina Burke - Ohio

Eric and Helga Edlund - Minnesota

Mike Lachtanski
California

Linda, Pense RD, MS, CD
Indiana

The Woman You Love

Nothing affects you as much as discovering the love of your life has a critical illness. I hope to help anyone experiencing this to be prepared and get through it with a positive attitude, therefore helping your loved one. I'm not a doctor, or a clergyman. I'm just an ordinary working person and the proud husband of a beautiful lady who had a mastectomy because of cancer.

When my wife first noticed a lump in her breast, we figured it was a cyst or swollen gland. At the doctor's office, we searched his face for a reassuring look. The look never came.

Cancer, the mere sound of the word is terrifying. However, we can attack it, using not only medical means, but with something cancer cannot survive - faith in God and ourselves. Her illness has proven beyond any doubt God is with us, and He gives us the strength to get through.

Don't feel you are alone, don't be afraid to cry, it's not a sign of a sissy, it's the expression of hurt, anger and fear. Remember, you cannot make things better by ignoring your feelings. Get them out. If they get the best of you, don't be ashamed. Get some qualified help.

Research treatment options. Consult those who have experienced them. Talk. Be part of the treatment decision and be prepared to support it.

You'll get angry with those just trying to be nice, but most are truly trying to help - let them. Be honest with your children. A family's strengths can conquer many problems.

Take time to adjust. It won't happen overnight. You are going to worry about her, and try to protect her from everything. Being there is the best medicine you can give. I am positive in knowing how strong the medicine of my love can be.

Chuck Svihlik
Mt. Morris, Illinois

For further details see...
www.geocities.com/chucky5741/breastcancerpatients.html

Appetizers & Beverages

*B*OURBON HOT DOGS

1 T. finely chopped onion
3/4 c. bourbon
1/2 c. brown sugar

1/2 c. ketchup
8 hog dogs

Chop onions until fine. Cut hot dogs into bite-size pieces. In large saucepan combine the onion, bourbon, brown sugar, and the ketchup. Stir all the ingredients together. Add the hot dogs and simmer for 1 hour.

Lesley Kilgore
Batavia, Ohio

*B*EST SAUCE FOR COCKTAIL MEATBALLS

1 1/2 lbs. frozen cocktail meatballs
  (thawed)
1 c. (1/2 pt.) sour cream
1 (10.5-oz.) can cream of
  mushroom soup

1/2 tsp. sugar
1/4 tsp. garlic powder
2 tsp. dill

Mix sour cream, soup, sugar, garlic powder and dill. Add meatballs and warm mixture in crockpot or serve in chafing dish.

Note: A wonderful change from typical meatball sauces. Easily doubles for larger parties.

Lisa Millikin
Corpus Christi, Texas

BACON WRAPPED SMOKIES

1 lb. uncooked bacon (your
  favorite type)
1½ pkgs. Little Smokies or 1-lb.
  pkg. hot dogs (each 1 cut into 4
  pieces)

½ c. brown sugar

Cover a cookie sheet or baking pan with aluminum foil. Cut each piece of bacon into 3 pieces. Wrap each cut piece of bacon around smokie and use a toothpick to hold it together. Lay in covered pan. When completed, sprinkle generously brown sugar over bacon wrapped smokies. Bake at 350° until bacon is done. This can be done the day before and covered until ready to bake.

Note: Mmmmm. This is a great tasting appetizer. Our family and friends love it. In remembrance of our family parties, get-togethers and Betty Jane McCullough who lost her battle on 9/28/00.

Cindy Ann Lifka
St. Louis, Missouri

BACON WRAPPED WATER CHESTNUTS

2 (8-oz.) cans whole water
  chestnuts
1 lb. bacon

1 c. soy sauce
½ c. sugar
Toothpicks

Drain water chestnuts and add to soy sauce. Cover and refrigerate for as long as possible, preferably overnight. Drain water chestnuts. Cut bacon in half widthwise. Roll water chestnuts in sugar and wrap in bacon. Use a toothpick to secure the bacon. Line bottom of roasting pan with aluminum foil to make clean up easy. Place on top of roasting rack so juices collect below. Bake at 400° until bacon is slightly crisp, about 25 minutes.

Note: Easy and quick appetizer that is impressive and delicious.

Loretta Duberow
Irvine, California

50191-03

TOMATO BACON CUPS

Filling:

8 slices bacon (crisply cooked)
1 med. tomato (seeded)
½ sm. onion
1 c. (4 oz.) grated Swiss cheese
½ c. mayonnaise
1 tsp. dry basil
1 (10-oz.) can refrigerated "flaky"
 biscuits (Biscuits must say
 "flaky" on the can and be a
 normal size, not Giant or Texas.
 Hungry Jack Flaky biscuits work
 well in this recipe.)

3 (12-cup) mini muffin pans
Optional: add 2 tsp. chopped
 green peppers or 2 tsp. chopped
 green chilies to the filling.

Preheat oven to 375°. Crumble bacon and coarsely chop tomato and onion. Mix bacon, tomato, onion, Swiss cheese, mayonnaise, and basil. Set aside. Spray mini muffin (tassie) pans with non-stick spray. Separate the 10 biscuits. Evenly divide each biscuit into 3 slices. They should peel apart easily. Dip each side of biscuit dough into flour and shake off excess. Pat dough into tassie pans. Fill each cup with a spoonful of filling. Bake 15 minutes or until brown and bubbly. Serve hot. Makes 30 cups. You can chill the pans after filling and bake later in the day; however, freezing is not a good idea.

Note: I guarantee your family and friends will love this appetizer. There's only one problem, you won't be able to make enough to satisfy your guests.

Bill Campbell
Pittsburgh, Pennsylvania

"My motto? Never surrender, that's my motto!"

Terry Healey

HOT CHICKEN STICKS

24 skewers
1/2 c. chili sauce
1 T. Worcestershire sauce
2 T. hot pepper sauce
24 (2 lbs.) raw chicken tenderloin
  pieces (you may also use chicken
  breasts & cut into 24 strips)

1/2 c. finely chopped celery
2 T. finely chopped onion
1 (8-oz.) bottle prepared blue
  cheese salad dressing

Preheat oven to 400°. Mix together chili sauce, Worcestershire sauce and hot pepper sauce in a bowl. Set aside. Thread each chicken strip on a skewer, leaving 1 inch at each end. Arrange skewers in spoke-like fashion on a round pizza pan. Brush chicken with one half of the chili sauce mixture. Bake for 10 minutes. Turn and brush with remaining chili sauce mixture and continue baking 10 minutes more. Meanwhile, prepare dipping sauce. In a bowl, mix onion and celery. Add dressing and mix well. Serve with chicken sticks.

Note: If you like it hotter, add hot pepper sauce to taste.

Jerry E. Jones
Beaver Dam Lake, Indiana

CRAB CAKES

1/2 c. butter (softened)
1 (5-oz.) jar Kraft Old English
  cheese spread
1 (6-oz.) can crabmeat (drained)

1/2 tsp. salt
1/4 tsp. garlic salt
6 English muffins

Mix butter, cheese spread, crabmeat, salt and garlic salt. Separate each muffin into two halves, resulting into 12 slices. Spread some crab mixture on each muffin. Now, cut each muffin slice into 4 equal parts. Freeze for at least one hour (can be made ahead of time and kept in freezer for up to 7 weeks). When ready to serve, place frozen cakes under broiler for 10 minutes. Makes 48 pieces.

Lois Vallandingham
Villa Hills, Kentucky

50191-03

FREEZE AHEAD CRAB APPETIZERS

½ c. butter (softened)
1 (5-oz.) jar Kraft Old English
  cheese spread
1½ tsp. mayonnaise

¼ tsp. garlic powder
¼ tsp. seasoned salt
7 oz. crab meat
6 English muffins (split)

Place your butter in a medium-size mixing bowl, then add Old English cheese, mayonnaise, garlic powder, seasoned salt and crab meat. Mix until smooth and well blended. Split your muffins into halves and top with a generous amount of crab spread. Once covered cut your muffins into quarters and place on cookie sheet and put into freezer. Once frozen, transfer into freezer-safe Ziploc bag/bags. Keep frozen until needed. **To cook:** Place on an ungreased cookie sheet and broil until golden brown (about 8 to 10 minutes).

Note: So easy, and are always a hit at parties!

Darlene Kein
Gig Harbor, Washington

CRAB CAKES

1 lb. lump crab meat
½ c. mayonnaise
2 T. chopped parsley
½ tsp. salt
1 tsp. Dijon mustard
1 tsp. white wine Worcestershire
  sauce
½ tsp. hot sauce

1 T. dried tarragon
½ c. bread crumbs
1 clean, chopped leek
½ c. chopped green onions
½ c. finely diced red bell pepper
Additional bread crumbs to coat
  cakes
Tartar sauce

Sauté leek and peppers until tender. Add onions. In separate bowl, combine crabmeat, mayonnaise, parsley, salt, Dijon mustard, white wine, Worcestershire sauce, hot sauce, tarragon, bread crumbs. Add leeks, peppers, and onions to mixture. Form into 1-inch thick patties and coat with bread crumbs. Chill until ready to cook. Sauté in nonstick pan with oil, about 3 minutes per side. Serve with tartar sauce.

Note: Great appetizer. Can be used as a main dish. Lea & Perrins makes white wine Worcestershire sauce.

Susan Beth Thomas
Highland Heights, Kentucky

STUFFED MUSHROOMS

1 lb. fresh button mushrooms (approx. 35)	1 c. Philadelphia chive & onion cream cheese spread
6 slices bacon	1 c. shredded cheddar cheese

Preheat oven to 400°. Spray a 9 x 13-inch glass dish with cooking oil spray. Remove and discard mushroom stems, and wash caps. Fry bacon and cut into 6 slices each (½-inch long pieces). Place mushroom caps in dish, fill with cream cheese (until level with top), then place a piece of bacon on top. Sprinkle cheddar cheese on top. Bake, uncovered, 10 to 14 minutes until cheese is completely melted. Serve immediately.

Lisa Millikin
Corpus Christi, Texas

BAKED ARTICHOKE HORS D' OEUVRES

½ c. chopped onion	2 drops Tabasco sauce
1 clove garlic (minced)	2 c. shredded cheddar cheese
4 eggs	1 (14-oz.) can artichoke bottoms
¼ c. dry bread crumbs	or hearts
¼ tsp. salt	Pam non-stick spray
⅛ tsp. pepper	8 x 8-in. baking dish
⅛ tsp. dried oregano	

Sauté onion and garlic. Remove from heat and transfer to bowl. Beat eggs and add to onion and garlic. Add artichokes, bread crumbs, salt, pepper, oregano, Tabasco sauce and cheddar cheese. Spray baking dish with Pam and transfer mixture to dish. Bake uncovered at 350° until set or about 25 minutes. Let cool slightly, then cut into squares. Also good at room temperature. Can be prepared the night before baking.

Christy Henry
Cincinnati, Ohio

50191-03

CINCINNATI-STYLE CHILI DIP

1 (8-oz.) pkg. cream cheese
1 (15-oz.) can Cincinnati chili
(such as Skyline chili)

1 c. shredded cheddar cheese

In a 8 x 8-inch dish, spread cream cheese evenly on bottom of pan. Spread chili evenly on cream cheese layer. Top with an even layer of cheddar cheese. Put in oven at 325° for about 10 minutes or until cheese melts. Serve warm with tortilla chips.

Note: Everyone always loves this!

John Karch
Cincinnati, Ohio

CREAM CHEESE & SAUSAGE DIP

4 (8-oz.) pkgs. Philadelphia cream
cheese
2 (10-oz.) cans Ro-Tel tomatoes
with green chilies (1 can drained)

4 T. chopped jalapeños
2 (1-lb.) pkgs. hot pork sausage
(like Jimmy Dean's)
Tortilla chips

Fry the pork sausage until done. Chop the jalapeños finely. Put all of the ingredients (cream cheese, Ro-Tel, jalapeños and sausage) into a crockpot. Heat until melted, about 1 hour, stirring occasionally. Dip tortilla chips in and enjoy!

Note: This is a huge hit, I make it every time I have company and there is hardly any left. It also heats up great the next day. Very simple to make and I've never met anyone who tasted it that didn't ask for the recipe. Thanks to Christy who gave me the recipe.

Kelly Sullivan
Florissant, Missouri

Job 11:18 -- And thou shalt be secure, because there is hope.

SPINACH JALAPEÑO DIP

1 T. chopped jalapeño (canned)	8 oz. cream cheese (softened)
2 tomatoes, chopped (about 2 c.)	2 c. shredded Monterey Jack
1 (10-oz.) pkg. frozen chopped	cheese
spinach (thawed & squeezed dry)	3/4 c. onion

Mix jalapeños, tomatoes, spinach, cream cheese, Monterey Jack cheese and onion. Pour into buttered ovenproof baking dish. Bake, uncovered, at 400° for 20 to 25 minutes. Serve with tortilla chips.

Note: Always a hit! When I take it to a party I take copies of the recipe with me, because I am always asked for the recipe!

Patty Moran
Newport Beach, California

TORTELLINI TAPAS WITH CILANTRO RANCH DIP

1 (9-oz.) pkg. refrigerated cheese-	2 c. fine dry bread crumbs
filled tortellini	3/4 c. mild salsa
1 (16-oz.) bottle Ranch-style	1/4 c. cilantro
dressing with peppercorns	2 c. vegetable oil
2 lg. eggs	

Cook tortellini according to package directions. Drain and cool. Whisk together 1 cup dressing and eggs. Add tortellini and let stand 10 minutes. Drain and dredge tortellini in bread crumbs; place on baking sheet and chill at least 1 hour. Make dip by mixing remaining dressing, salsa and cilantro. Chill in refrigerator. Fry tortellini in 375° oil until golden. Drain on paper towel, serve with dip.

Andrea Hounshell
Raleigh, North Carolina

50191-03

$\mathcal{S}$PINACH AND ARTICHOKE DIP

2 (10-oz.) boxes frozen chopped
  spinach
1 (10-oz.) box frozen artichoke
  hearts (do not use canned)
8 oz. (½ pt.) sour cream (fat free
  opt.)
1 c. mayonnaise (light or fat free
  opt.)

¾ c. shredded Monterey Jack
  cheese (opt.)
1 (1.4-oz.) box Knorrs vegetable
  soup & dip mix
Round loaf bread such as wheat,
  rye & pumpernickel

Thaw spinach and drain well, place in bowl. Cook artichoke hearts as directed on box, drain and chop. Add artichoke hearts to spinach in bowl. Add sour cream, mayonnaise, cheese and 1 envelope packet of soup mix. Refrigerate overnight to allow ingredients to absorb instant soup mix. Just before serving, hollow out the inside of the loaf of bread with a large spoon, fill in with dip. Save bread scraps for dipping. Also may be served with crackers or carrot sticks.

Note: For sarcoma angels past and those of us still fighting! Keep praying, stay strong and always smile!

Eileen Corbo
New Rochelle, New York

$\mathcal{P}$ESTO LAYERED TORTE

Cheesecloth
½ c. unsalted butter

8 oz. cream cheese
7 oz. pesto

Dampen a piece of cheesecloth and use it to line a 2-cup bowl (with fairly straight sides). Let cloth hang over edges. Mix well butter and cream cheese. Put a thin layer of cheese mixture on bottom of bowl and pat down. Follow with a thin layer of either homemade (best) or store bought pesto. Continue layering, ending with cheese mixture. Fold over cloth and refrigerate several hours. Open cloth, turn over bowl, turning out torte. Remove cloth completely and garnish if desired. Serve with crackers. Serves about 6 for hors d' oeuvres.

Barb White
Eatonton, Georgia

SWISS CHEESE DIP

8 oz. cream cheese (lite), softened
1 (6-oz.) pkg. shredded Swiss
   cheese
6 green onions, chopped (use tops
   too)

8 T. melted butter (divided)
³/₄ stack Ritz crackers (crushed),
   approx. 26 crackers
8 strips cooked bacon (crumbled)

Mix together cream cheese, Swiss cheese, green onions, 4 tablespoons melted butter. Spread mixture in oven safe pan. Top with crackers and bacon which have been mixed together. Drizzle with 4 tablespoons of melted butter. Bake for 15 minutes at 350° or microwave until warm. May be baked ahead of time and microwaved later until warm. Serve with bagel chips or Wheat Thins.

Rosie Lankisch
Ft. Thomas, Kentucky

HOT ALMOND CHEESE DIP

¹/₃ c. mayonnaise
8 oz. cream cheese (softened)
1 c. shredded sharp cheddar cheese
1 c. shredded Swiss cheese

4 scallions (minced)
Ground nutmeg to taste
³/₄ c. slivered almonds, toasted

Combine mayonnaise, cream cheese, cheddar cheese, Swiss cheese, scallions and nutmeg in bowl; mix well. Stir in almonds. Spoon into baking dish. Bake, uncovered, at 350° for 30 minutes. Serve immediately with crackers. Toasted almonds may be sprinkled over top instead of stirred into dip.

Note: Very good quick appetizer!

Chris Soranno
Flower Mound, Texas

50191-03

ℬEST PARTY CHEESE BALL

3 (8-oz.) pkgs. cream cheese
3 (8-oz.) pkgs. Buddig chipped beef
  (cut into ½-in. pieces)
1 green pepper (cut up finely)

1 onion (cut up finely)
8-oz. can crushed pineapple
  (drained very well)
1½ c. chopped walnuts or pecans

Mix cream cheese, chipped beef, green pepper, onion, pineapple well. Shape into a ball and roll in nuts, covering completely. Serve with crackers.

Note: Men love this! Great for a tailgate party.

Lisa Millikin
Corpus Christi, Texas

"𝒯HREE CHEESE" CHEESE BALL

2 (8-oz.) pkgs. cream cheese
1 (5-oz.) jar Kraft Old English
  sharp cheese
2 oz. bleu cheese

1 garlic clove (pressed) or garlic
  powder to taste
Salt to taste
1 T. Worcestershire sauce

Coating:

1 c. pecans (chopped) or parsley

Soften cream cheese, Old English cheese and bleu cheese to room temperature. Mix cheeses together. Add garlic, salt and Worcestershire sauce. Form into a ball. Roll in chopped pecans or parsley. Chill until ready to serve. Serve with assorted crackers.

Note: A real crowd pleaser!

Mary Jane Sassin
Park Hills, Kentucky

"I am only one, but I am one. I cannot do everything, but I can do something."

- Edward Everett Hale

CREAMY CHICKEN SPREAD

1½ c. cooked, chopped chicken
1 (8-oz.) pkg. cream cheese
½ c. celery (finely chopped)
½ c. mayonnaise

2 T. onion (chopped)
1 tsp. onion powder
½ tsp. salt (to taste)

Blend chicken, cream cheese, celery, mayonnaise, onion, onion powder, and salt. Refrigerate. Serve with crackers.

Harriett Schulte
Morehead, Kentucky

SASSY SALSA DIP

1 (8 oz.) cream cheese (softened)
4 oz. sharp cheddar cheese
 (shredded)
⅓ c. thick & chunky salsa

⅓ c. ripe sliced olives
2 green onions (chopped)
⅓ c. red pepper (chopped)

Topping:

2 T. cilantro (snipped)

⅔ c. salsa for top

Mix cream cheese, cheddar cheese, ⅓ cup salsa, ⅓ cup ripe sliced olives, green onions, red pepper. Spread in pan to serve and top with ⅔ cup salsa. Sprinkle cilantro across top.

Note: Perfect for parties for young and adults. In honor of our mother, Linda L. Pense, RD, MS, CD.

Zachary Pense
Brandon Pense
Indiana

Luke 1:37 -- For with God nothing shall be impossible.

50191-03

UMMUS

3 c. cooked garbanzo beans
2 T. tahini (sesame butter)
2 T. lemon juice
1 oz. minced garlic
¾ tsp. cumin

Dash olive oil
Cayenne pepper to taste
2-4 T. bean juice (or water) for
    desired consistency

Blend ingredients together in a food processor until smooth. Hummus tends to thicken after it has been refrigerated. Delicious on sandwiches or crackers.

Note: From the Heart of the Harvest Cafe cookbook. Great vegetarian treat!

Yvonne Cole
Santa Rosa Beach, Florida

KAHLUA FRUIT DIP

8 oz. cream cheese (softened)
1 c. (½ pt.) sour cream
1 c. Cool Whip

¾ c. brown sugar
⅓ c. Kahlua

Combine cream cheese, sour cream, Cool Whip, brown sugar and Kahlua. Mix well and chill. Serve with fresh fruit.

Margie Bruns
Coldwater, Ohio

"I don't believe in miracles, I rely on them."

Unknown

CINNAMON CHIPS FOR FRUIT SALSA

8 (8-in.) flour tortillas
¼ c. sugar
2 T. brown sugar

1 tsp. cinnamon
¼ c. butter (melted)
⅛ tsp. vanilla

Mix sugars and cinnamon. Set aside. Add vanilla to melted butter. Brush butter and vanilla onto tortillas. Generously sprinkle each tortilla with sugar mixture. Cut with pizza cutter into 8 triangle pieces, like you would a pie. Bake at 450° for about 5 minutes, until crisp. May need to make additional sugar mixture to coat all well. I generally double this recipe.

Note: I have made this often and everyone seems to really like it!

Fruit Salsa:

2 Granny Smith apples (chopped)
1 c. crushed pineapple (drained)
½ pt. (mounded) strawberries
  (chopped)
½ pt. (mounded) raspberries

1 pear (chopped)
3 kiwi (skinned & chopped)
2-4 T. apple jelly
Juice & zest of 1 orange

Mix apples, pineapples, strawberries, raspberries, pear, kiwi, orange juice, and orange zest. Set aside. Heat apple jelly in microwave until it starts to dissolve. Mix in with fruit. Chill until ready to serve. This will last a day or two in the refrigerator. Serve salsa with cinnamon chips for dipping.

Anna Weber
Ft. Wright, Kentucky

RASPBERRY CHAMPAGNE PUNCH

2 (10-oz.) pkgs. frozen red
  raspberries in syrup (thawed)
⅓ c. ReaLemon lemon juice from
  concentrate
1 (750 ml) bottle red rosé wine
  (chilled)

1 qt. Borden raspberry sherbet
1 (750 ml) bottle Asti Spumante or
  champagne (chilled)

In blender, purée raspberries. In large punch bowl, combine puréed raspberries, lemon juice, sugar and wine. Stir until sugar dissolves. Chill. Just before serving, scoop sherbet into punch bowl, add champagne. Stir gently. Makes about 3 quarts.

Sister Mary Florence, SND
Covington, Kentucky

50191-03

CRANBERRY/LEMON SLUSH

32 oz. cranberry juice cocktail
  (Ocean Spray)
20 oz. ginger ale

12 oz. frozen pink lemonade
  concentrate
1½ c. bourbon

Mix cranberry juice, ginger ale, lemonade concentrate, and bourbon. Place in plastic container and freeze 24 hours. **To serve:** Spoon into glass, pour additional ginger ale over top to reach drinkable consistency, stir and enjoy!

Note: Many have asked me for this recipe, so here it is!

Eileen Gruber
Hebron, Kentucky

SUNSHINE SLUSH

3 c. water
1 c. sugar
2 ripe bananas
2 (12-oz.) cans unsweetened
  pineapple juice

1 (6-oz.) can frozen orange juice
1 (6-oz.) can frozen lemonade or 2
  T. concentrated lemon juice
1½ c. rum or vodka

In a saucepan combine water and sugar, bringing to a boil. Stir until sugar is dissolved. Boil gently for 3 minutes. Remove the saucepan from the heat and let the sugar mixture cool. In a blender, combine the bananas and half the pineapple juice. Blend until smooth. Stir into cooled syrup (sugar mixture). Stir in the rest of the pineapple juice, the orange juice, and the lemonade, (which all should be thawed). Stir in the rum or vodka. Freeze in a container. Needs to be prepared at least a day in advance if you will use it for a party. Serve in a glass by putting a scoop of the frozen mixture with some 7-Up or any other lemon lime soda. The size glass usually used is about 10 ounces.

Note: Tastes great in the summer especially, but good for any kind of party.

Lesley Kilgore
Batavia, Ohio

APLE EGGNOG

1 (32-oz.) can Borden eggnog
 (chilled)
¾ c. Cary's Vermont Maple
 Orchards or MacDonald's pure
 maple syrup

¼ c. rum (opt.)
Nutmeg for garnish

In large pitcher, combine eggnog, syrup and rum. Chill thoroughly. Stir before serving and garnish with nutmeg if desired. Refrigerate leftovers.

Sister Mary Florence, SND
Covington, Kentucky

ORANGE BANANA PUNCH

6 c. water
4 c. sugar
5 ripe med. bananas (mashed)
2 (12-oz.) cans frozen orange juice
 concentrate (thawed)

2 (6-oz.) cans frozen lemonade
 concentrate (thawed)
5 L. 7-Up

Mix water, sugar, bananas, orange juice concentrate, lemonade concentrate. Pour in plastic container and freeze for 8 hours. Take out of freezer and let thaw for 30 minutes. Mix in 5 liters 7-Up.

Note: In honor of my brother-in-law, Robert Marcuccilli.

Gail Gorrell
Haines City, Florida

"Love while you've got love to give. Live while you've got life to live."
Piet Hein

50191-03

CHEMO SHAKE

½ c. orange juice
2 T. flax oil
1 pasteurized raw egg (opt.)
3 T. (heaping) protein powder
1 T. (heaping) brewer's yeast

1 banana
½ c. plain yogurt
½ c. any additional fruit you may
   like (blueberries are good &
   make it an interesting color!)

In a blender, combine orange juice, flax oil, pasteurized egg (optional), protein powder, yeast, banana, yogurt, ½ cup extra fruit. Blend well. If mixture is too thick, more orange juice may be added. Enjoy!

Note: This was often the only thing that appealed to me while on chemo, and it is very easy to make. Best of all, it packs a lot of nutrition into one drink!

Debra Rooney
Vancouver, British Columbia, Canada

VERY BERRY SMOOTHIE

⅔ c. orange juice
½ c. blueberries (fresh or frozen)
⅓ c. raspberries
1 c. strawberries
½ banana

1½ c. crushed ice
Optional: Add protein powder,
   vitamin powder, or other
   supplement powders as desired.

Place orange juice, blueberries, raspberries, strawberries, banana, crushed ice and optional powders if desired. Blend on high for 15 seconds or until liquified. Tilt blender while holding the top on securely to help mix the ingredients more thoroughly. Pour and serve. This recipe makes 26 ounces of smoothie, enough for 2 people or as meal by itself.

Note: This is an excellent meal alternative when eating becomes tough. It tastes good and goes down easy. By mixing in protein powders and vitamins, it becomes a complete meal by itself. It kept me going during treatment when I could not eat any solid food.

Michael Lachtanski
San Jose, California

Recipe Favorites

50191-03

Soups & Salads

Suzanne Leider - California

Brain Stuedeman (right) and parents - Minnesota

Barbara Ann Dixon - Mississippi

Susan Dansereau - Ohio

Making a Difference

At 25, Suzanne Leider became a nurse - a confident, compassionate nurse who made her patients feel special and cared for in the most fundamental way. Then, at 26, diagnosed with synovial cell sarcoma, she became a patient herself. Following surgery and radiation, she enjoyed almost four cancer-free years. In 1996, the sarcoma metastasized to her lung, and she underwent the first of many invasive thoractomies. Each time she rebounded, defying the odds, because she had so much more to do.

Because sarcomas are rare (less than 1% of all cancers) Suzanne found herself in a group often overlooked by other support organizations. To fill the void, she founded the Sarcoma Alliance in 1999 to provide support, education and guidance to the sarcoma community. An avid cook, she published a collection of favorite recipes, Sage Cuisine, to fund the Alliance's initial operations. She developed extensive resources for the Alliance's website and gave the organization an essential ingredient: human warmth. In person, over the telephone and via email, she comforted and empowered fellow sarcoma survivors, their families and caregivers. She brought people together in support groups, chat rooms, online bulletin boards and her own living room. The Alliance became a home and a voice for people living with sarcoma. Suzanne's infectious enthusiasm drew family, friends, and casual acquaintances into the Alliance's circle, thereby ensuring that it would thrive long after she left us in 2002.

Suzanne is a vivid example of how one person can make a difference. She also demonstrated that a cancer diagnosis need not stand in the way of enjoying a vibrant and fulfilling life. We remember her radiant smile, her open arms, the wonderful aromas wafting from her kitchen and her gift for bringing comfort and joy to all whose lives she touched.

Stephanie Leider
Sausalito, California

To visit the Sarcoma Alliance see: www.sarcomaalliance.com

Soups & Salads

CORNUCOPIA SALAD

1 head red leaf lettuce
3 green onions (chopped)
1 Granny Smith apple (peeled &
  chopped)
1 avocado (peeled & chopped)

½ c. dried cranberries
¼ c. blue cheese (crumbled)
¼ c. sliced almonds
1 T. sugar

Dressing:

¼ c. vegetable oil
2 T. red wine vinegar

2 tsp. sugar
Salt & pepper to taste

Salad: In skillet, combine almonds with 1 tablespoon sugar. Stir frequently over low/medium heat until sugar is dissolved and almonds are lightly browned. This may take about 15 to 20 minutes. Watch carefully so almonds do not burn. Remove from heat and allow to cool. In large bowl, combine lettuce, onions, apple, avocado, cranberries, blue cheese, and cooled almonds. Set aside. **Dressing:** Combine vinegar, sugar, salt and pepper. Add oil and mix well. Pour over salad and toss. Serve salad on a platter.

Note: Excellent salad that everyone will love and very easy to make!

Chris Soranno
Flower Mound, Texas

Psalm 23:4 -- I will fear no evil: for thou art with me; thy rod and thy staff they comfort me.

*S*UZANNE'S SENSATIONAL SPINACH SALAD

Salad:

1 c. pecan halves
1½ lbs. sm. leaf spinach
  (washed & dried)
2 Red Delicious apples (thinly
  sliced)

½ c. Muscat raisins (lg., brown,
  fruity-tasting raisins)
½ c. scallions (chopped)

Chutney Dressing:

½ c. vegetable oil
4 T. mango/ginger chutney
1 tsp. curry powder

1 tsp. dry mustard
½ tsp. salt
2 tsp. fresh lemon juice

Preheat oven to 300°. Place pecans on baking sheet and toast in oven for approximately 12 minutes. Place prepared spinach, apples, pecans, raisins, and scallions in a large salad bowl. **For Chutney Dressing:** Place oil, chutney, curry powder, dry mustard, salt and lemon juice in a bowl and whisk all until well mixed. Drizzle dressing over salad and toss gently until all the ingredients are coated. For a beautiful presentation, do not toss salad with dressing until immediately before serving.

Note: The Leider family is contributing this recipe on behalf of their dear Suzanne, who died this past August after battling synovial sarcoma for a decade. Suzanne made this recipe a Leider family favorite and a Thanksgiving essential.

Suzanne Leider
Mill Valley, California

"Reach for the stars, go for your dreams, and don't settle for anything less than what you want out of life."

Cindy Lifka, saying passed on to her by her mother Betty J. McCullough

50191-03

JOY'S FANCY SALAD

Salad:

Lg. head Bibb lettuce or other
  fancy lettuce of your choice
1 bag Ocean Spray Craisins
1 (15-oz.) can mandarin oranges
  (drained)

1 red onion (sliced into rings)
½ c. chopped walnuts

Dressing:

1 c. sugar
½ c. olive oil
½ c. tarragon vinegar

1 T. poppy or sesame seeds
1 tsp. Worcestershire sauce

Salad: Mix lettuce, craisins, mandarin oranges, red onion and walnuts and set aside. **Dressing:** Blend sugar, vinegar, poppy or sesame seeds and Worcestershire sauce. Mix well until sugar has dissolved. Add olive oil. Toss salad in dressing just before serving. Serving spread out on a platter works better than a bowl.

Joy Bricking
Florence, Kentucky

BROCCOLI SALAD

1 med. bunch broccoli (cleaned &
  chopped)
1 (15-oz.) can kidney beans
  (drained)

1 pkg. Italian dressing (prepared)
1 sm. red onion (finely chopped)
½ c. finely chopped mushrooms
1 c. grated cheese

Mix broccoli, kidney beans, dressing, onion, mushrooms and cheese. Serve.

Judy Kulhank
San Jose, California

BROCCOLI-CAULIFLOWER SALAD

1 bunch broccoli (broken into
  florets)
1 head cauliflower (broken into
  florets)
1/3 c. grated Parmesan cheese
1/3 c. granulated sugar
2 c. mayonnaise
1/2 c. onion (chopped)
1 (6-oz.) jar Bacos

Combine broccoli, cauliflower, Parmesan cheese, sugar, mayonnaise, onion and Bacos. Mix well with a spoon. Refrigerate (best if overnight). Serves 4 to 6.

Note: Good quick dish. Can be made ahead several days. I am a breast cancer survivor!

Cathy Davis
Homosassa, Florida

TABBOULEH-MIDDLE EAST FAVORITE

3 bunches of green parsley,
  plucked (well washed, dried &
  chopped finely)
2 stems green onion (chopped
  finely)
1/4 c. cracked wheat (soaked in
  water for 30 min.)
1 lg. tomato (diced sm.)
1-2 sm. cucumbers (peeled, cut &
  diced sm.)
1 head romaine lettuce (leaves
  washed & separated)
Salt to taste
Dash cumin
Black pepper to taste
Dash of oregano (or dried mint
  leaves)
1/4 c. olive oil
1/4 c. lemon juice (to taste)

Mix parsley, onions, tomatoes, and cucumbers. Strain cracked wheat to squeeze water out and add to vegetable mixture. Mix well. Add salt, cumin, black pepper, and oregano (or mint). Mix well again. Add olive oil and lemon juice and mix well again. Spread tabbouleh mixture with a spoon on romaine lettuce leaves. Fold lengthwise and eat and enjoy healthy eating.

Note: This Middle East recipe is widely used as an appetizer or a salad. In honor of my sister, Therese Khabbaza Moussalli, who died of cervical cancer, at the age of 54, in Australia where she lived.

Mary Ansara
Sudan

50191-03

TABOULEH

1 c. bulghur wheat
6 tomatoes (chopped)
1 lg. bunch green onions (white &
  green parts, chopped)
1 bunch parsley (minced)
1-2 cucumbers (chopped)
1 lg. bell pepper (chopped)
2-3 tsp. cumin (or to taste)
Basil leaves (fresh or dried, to
  taste)

Mint leaves (opt. to taste, but
  good)
Approx. ¼ c. canola oil (to taste)
Fresh squeezed juice of 1 lemon
  (not needed if vegetables are
  straight from your garden)
Salt & pepper to taste

Place wheat in bowl and rinse under cold water three times, leaving about ½ inch water after the third rinse on top of the wheat. This softens it. Let sit for at least 15 minutes or until water is absorbed. Squeeze with hands to remove residual water and set aside. Add wheat to tomatoes, onions, cucumbers, and bell pepper. Mix well. Add oil, parsley, cumin, basil, mint (optional), lemon juice (optional), salt and pepper. Toss until thoroughly mixed. Can serve on wild grapevine leaves (the traditional way) or on leaf lettuce. Let guests use the leaves as a scoop to pick up the filling or simply serve as a side dish.

Note: My Lebanese mom, Mary Nader, died from liver cancer. She was THE best cook and for this used our garden fresh tomatoes and herbs. As kids we waited eagerly for a taste! Bulghur wheat is wonderful, it lowers cholesterol and has lots of fiber/complex carbs.

Rita Heikenfeld
Batavia, Ohio

"Life may not be the party we hoped for, but while we are here, we might as well dance."

Unknown

WINTER FRUIT SALAD WITH LEMON POPPY SEED DRESSING

Salad:

1 lg. head romaine lettuce (torn
  into bite-size pieces, about 10 c.)
4 oz. (1 c.) shredded Swiss cheese
1 c. cashews

¼ c. sweetened dried cranberries
1 unpeeled apples (cubed)
1 unpeeled pear (cubed)

Dressing:

½ c. sugar
⅓ c. lemon juice
2 tsp. finely chopped onion
1 tsp. Dijon mustard

½ tsp. salt
⅔ c. oil
1 T. poppy seed

Dressing: In a blender or food processor bowl with metal blade, combine sugar, lemon juice, onion, mustard and salt. Put on lid and process until blended. With machine running, add oil in a slowly steady stream, processing until thick and smooth. Add poppy seed; process a few seconds to mix. **Salad:** In a large serving bowl, combine lettuce, Swiss cheese, cashews, cranberries, apple and pear. Toss to mix. Pour dressing over salad a little bit at a time. Toss to coat in between. You will probably only need ⅓ to ½ the dressing. This recipe makes a large batch of dressing.

Note: This is a wonderfully "different" salad. It's a change from the standard salad with Ranch dressing.

Karin Deti
Des Moines, Washington

CIDER AND APPLE SALAD

1 (3-oz.) pkg. instant lemon Jello
2 c. boiling cider
1 c. diced unpeeled apples (I prefer
  tart apples)

1 c. diced celery
½ c. finely chopped nuts (pecans
  or walnuts)
2 tsp. diced pimento

Dissolve Jello in hot cider. Let cool until partially set. Add apples, celery, nuts, pimento. Chill until set.

Judy Kulhank
San Jose, California

50191-03

MANDARIN ORANGE SALAD WITH DRESSING

1/4 c. slivered almonds
1 T. plus 1 tsp. sugar
1/2 head Bibb lettuce (torn)
1/2 head romaine lettuce (torn)

1 c. chopped celery
3 green onions (thinly sliced)
1 (11-oz.) can mandarin oranges
   (drained)

Cook and stir almonds and sugar in a skillet on low heat until sugar melts and nuts are covered (watch closely, takes a while, but can burn easily at the end if you don't keep an eye on it). Cool on wax paper, break apart and set aside. Place Bibb and romaine lettuce, celery and onions in a plastic bag. Fasten bag securely and refrigerate. Pour dressing and oranges into bag 5 minutes before serving. Fasten bag securely and shake until all is well coated. Add almonds and shake again.

Note: Easily doubled. A wonderful melange of flavors.

Mandarin Orange Salad Dressing:

1/4 c. vegetable oil
2 T. white vinegar
2 T. sugar
1 T. snipped parsley

1/2 tsp. salt
Dash of pepper
Dash of hot pepper sauce

Mix vegetable oil, white vinegar, sugar, parsley, salt, pepper and hot pepper sauce in a tightly covered jar. Refrigerate at least one hour.

Joni Leo
Pompano Beach, Florida

PISTACHIO SALAD

1 (3-oz.) box instant pistachio
   pudding mix
1 can (2 1/2 c.) crushed pineapple
   (undrained)
1 c. mini marshmallows

1 (8 oz.) Cool Whip
1 tsp. lemon juice
1/2 c. chopped nuts (walnuts or
   pecans)

Mix pudding mix, pineapple, marshmallows, Cool Whip, lemon juice and nuts together and chill for at least 2 hours or overnight.

Judy Kulhank
San Jose, California

STRAWBERRY JELLO SURPRISE

½ (15½-oz.) bag pretzels (broken)
2 T. sugar
½ c. butter (melted)
1 (8 oz.) cream cheese (softened)
1 c. sugar

1 (8 oz.) Cool Whip (thawed)
1 (6 oz.) strawberry Jello
1 c. boiling water
1 (16-oz.) pkg. frozen strawberries

First layer: Spread pretzels in 9 x 13-inch pan. Sprinkle with sugar and drizzle ½ cup butter over top. Bake at 400° for 8 minutes. Cool. **Second layer:** In bowl, combine cream cheese, 1 cup sugar, Cool Whip and mix with electric mixer. Spread on cooled pretzels. **Third layer:** Dissolve Jello in boiling water, add frozen strawberries. Pour over cream cheese layer. Chill until set.

Note: Can use any combination of Jello and fruit.

Wanda Gardner

CREAMY ORANGE JELLO MOLD

1 (6-oz.) pkg. orange (or lime)
Jello
32 reg. size marshmallows (10-oz.
pkg. yields 45)
1 (8-oz.) pkg. Philadelphia cream
cheese (reg. or ⅓ less fat), cut
into sm. pieces

3 c. water
1 (8-oz.) can crushed pineapple
(undrained)

Put Jello in large pan. Add marshmallows, cut up cream cheese, and three cups of water. Heat and stir to near boil to completely dissolve marshmallows and cream cheese. Cool a bit and add crushed pineapple. Put in 4-cup ring mold, if desired, and refrigerate. Best made day before needed.

Note: Creamy and refreshing! In honor of our daughter, she loves this. We are very proud of her.

Judy Cleves
Cincinnati, Ohio

50191-03

DRY JELLO SALAD

1 (12 oz.) lowfat or nonfat cottage cheese
1 (8 oz.) reg. whipped topping
½ (3-oz.) pkg. Jello gelatin powder (any flavor)

1-2 (20-oz.) cans chunk pineapple (drained)
1-2 (11 oz.) mandarin oranges (drained)

Optional:

½ c. nonfat yogurt   1 c. mini marshmallows

Gently mix cottage cheese and whipped topping. Fold in Jello powder. Fold in pineapple and mandarin oranges. May add yogurt and mini marshmallows. Chill for 8 to 12 hours before serving.

Harriett Schulte
Morehead, Kentucky

SUGAR FREE CREAMY ORANGE SALAD

1 (8-oz.) container sugar free Cool Whip
1 sm. (3-oz.) box orange gelatin (instant & sugar free)

1 (16-oz.) container cottage cheese
1 (11-oz.) can mandarin oranges
½ c. pecans (optional)

Combine Cool Whip, gelatin, cottage cheese, oranges, and pecans (optional). Chill until ready to serve.

Debbie Hodge
Crescent Springs, Kentucky

"Each of us has a unique treasure to share -- at any given time in our lives it might be simply being present when we are needed."
Mike White

CRANBERRY GELATIN MOLD

1 (6-oz.) pkg. strawberry Jello
2 c. boiling water
1 can whole cranberry sauce
1 (15-oz.) can crushed pineapple in
  juice (undrained)

1 (11-oz.) can mandarin oranges
  (drained)
½ c. chopped walnuts

Rinse a 10-cup mold or fluted pan with cold water. Have ready a large bowl half filled with ice and water. Put gelatin in medium metal bowl. Add boiling water and stir 2 minutes or until gelatin dissolves. Stir cranberry sauce in can to break up. Stir into gelatin. Add pineapple, orange segments and nuts. Set metal bowl into bowl with ice. Stir until consistency of egg whites. Pour into mold, cover and refrigerate 24 hours to 3 days.

Note: In honor of my friends, Frances Edwards and Nancy Wright.

Sandra Thomas
Glasgow, Kentucky

CHICKEN APPLE ALMOND SALAD

6 cooked chicken breasts
1 c. celery, chopped
3 green onions, chopped
½ carrot, grated (for color)
1 c. slivered almonds

2 Granny Smith or Fuji apples
  (unpeeled)
1 c. white raisins or Craisins
1 c. mayonnaise (or to taste)

Chop cooked chicken, and apples in ½-inch cubes in thin slices and green onion in small slices. Add grated carrot, almonds, raisins and mayonnaise and mix well. Serve over salad greens or on a good sliced bread as a sandwich filling.

Note: This is to take to group buffets with a large bowl of salad greens or a loaf of great bread.

Yvonne Albritton
Renton, Washington

50191-03

CURRIED CRANBERRY CHICKEN SALAD

3/4 c. mayonnaise
2 tsp. lime juice
3/4 tsp. curry powder
2 c. cooked, cubed chicken
1 med. apple (cut into 1/2-in. chunks)

3/4 c. sweetened dried cranberries
1/2 c. thinly sliced celery
1/4 c. chopped pecans
2 T. thinly sliced green onion

Combine mayonnaise, lime juice and curry powder in a large mixing bowl. Stir in chicken, apple, cranberries, celery, pecans, and green onion. Cover and chill. Best prepared and served within 8 hours. To make a day ahead of time, wait until 3 hours before serving to add the cranberries, pecans and green onion. Serve with pita bread. Makes 5 cups.

Note: I absolutely love this. It's delicious!

Karin Deti
Des Moines, Washington

MANDARIN CHICKEN SALAD

4 c. cubed, cooked chicken
2 T. minced onion
2 tsp. salt
1 (7-oz.) pkg. macaroni shells or rings
2 c. grapes (if using canned grapes, drain)
2 c. pineapple chunks (drained)

2 c. mandarin oranges (drained)
2 c. salad dressing (ie. Miracle Whip)
1 1/2 c. slivered almonds
1 pt. whipping cream (whipped) or Cool Whip
Optional: 1 1/3 c. celery (finely chopped)

Mix chicken, minced onion, salt and refrigerate for several hours. Cook macaroni shells according to package. Drain and chill. When chicken mixture and macaroni have chilled, add grapes, pineapple, oranges, salad dressing. Mix all and chill for several hours or overnight. Before serving, add almonds, whipping cream, and (optional) celery.

Note: Have used this recipe for many years and everyone loves it.

Virginia Lundgren
Shoreview, Minnesota

FETA AND BALSAMIC VINEGAR PASTA SALAD

1 pkg. tri-colored spiral pasta
1 purple onion
1 bunch green onions
4 oz. feta cheese
1/4 c. balsamic vinegar

1 T. extra virgin olive oil
1/4 c. salt free sunflower seeds
Fresh ground black pepper, to
  taste

Cook pasta according to package directions; drain and coat with olive oil. Slice purple onions in thin rings, then cut rings in half and add to pasta. Chop green onions in small pieces and add to pasta mixture. Add feta, balsamic vinegar, fresh ground pepper and sunflower seeds.

Note: This salad is different every time I make it. I add whatever herbs I have growing that suit my fancy (basil and marjoram are my favorites.) My sister, Charlene, said when she was going through her treatments, not many dishes appealed to her, but this did!

Kimberly Boyer
Kent, Washington

ITALIAN PASTA SALAD

1 lb. cooked thin spaghetti (broken
  into 3-in. pieces)
1 sm. green pepper (chopped)
15-20 cherry tomatoes (cut into
  halves)
Sliced pepperoni to taste
Ripe olives to taste

1 (8-oz.) bottle Zesty Italian
  dressing
1/2 env. Zesty Italian salad
  dressing mix
1/2 (2.6-oz.) bottle McCormick
  Salad Supreme spice

Break and cook spaghetti. Rinse under cold water, drain well. Add pepper, olives, pepperoni, dry dressing mix and Salad Supreme. Pour bottle dressing over all. Marinate 24 hours in refrigerator. Add tomatoes before serving.

Janet Scheuneman
St. Paul, Minnesota

50191-03

RAINBOW ROTINI SALAD

½ lb. rainbow rotini macaroni
2 c. sliced pepperoni
1 c. cubed cheese
1 c. sliced broccoli flowerets
1 c. sliced cauliflowerets

1 c. sm. pitted ripe olives
4 sliced green onions
1 med. carrot (grated)
1 c. Italian salad dressing

Prepare rotini as directed on package. Drain. Combine rotini, pepperoni, cheese, broccoli, cauliflower, olives, onions and carrot. Toss mixture with salad dressing. Cover and chill. Before serving gently toss salad again. Makes about 6 servings.

Note: In memory of my son, Brian Robert Stuedeman, 5/22/76 to 3/2/01, who battled cancer for 11 years. He liked this dish because it can be tasted while on chemo. He was an ACS scholar and represented the Children's Cancer Research Fund. His faith and courage inspired us all.

Linda Jean Stuedeman
Young America, Minnesota

TORTELLINI SALAD

2 (9-oz.) pkgs. stuffed tortellini
   from refrigerator case (any
   variety)
1 (14-oz.) jar artichoke bottoms or
   hearts (chopped)
1 tomato (chopped)
½ c. black olives (sliced)

½ c. walnut pieces
1 red bell pepper (chopped)
1 yellow bell pepper (chopped)
8-oz. pkg. mushrooms (chopped)
½ c. crumbled feta cheese
(Note: You can add more veggies
   if you prefer.)

Dressing:

½ c. olive oil
¼ c. balsamic vinegar

3 crushed garlic cloves
Fresh basil and dill to taste

Cook and drain tortellini according to package directions. Add artichoke, tomato, olives, walnuts, red pepper, yellow pepper, mushrooms, and cheese. Toss together. Prepare dressing separately by combining vinegar, garlic, basil and dill. Mix well. Add oil. Mix well and pour over tortellini. Chill. Refrigerate until ready to serve.

Note: A great summer salad with veggies and herbs from the garden.

Christy Henry
Cincinnati, Ohio

FIVE BEAN SALAD

1 (15-oz.) can chickpeas or
  garbanzo beans (drain & rinse)
1 (15.5-oz.) can red kidney beans
  (drain & rinse)
1 (15-oz.) can lima beans
1 (14.25-oz.) can cut yellow beans
  (drain & rinse)

1 (14.25-oz.) can cut green beans
  (drain & rinse)
1 c. celery
1 green pepper (cut up)
1 red pepper (cut up)
1 sliced white onion

Dressing:

Dash of dill weed
Dash of salt
1⅓ c. white sugar
1 c. vegetable oil
1⅔ c. vinegar

1½ tsp. celery seed
½ tsp. dry mustard
1 tsp. thyme
1 (17-oz.) bottle Zesty Italian
  salad dressing

In a large bowl, combine garbanzo beans, kidney beans, lima beans, yellow cut beans, cut green beans, celery, green pepper, red pepper and onion. **Dressing:** In a saucepan, combine dill weed, salt, sugar, oil, vinegar, celery seed, dry mustard and thyme. Boil this just until sugar is dissolved, cool well. Add bottle of salad dressing. Pour over bean mixture and mix well. Put in glass jars and cover. Make sure dressing covers beans. Store in refrigerator.

Note: This bean salad is great and makes a big batch. Lots of fiber!

Richard and Herta Gillies
Invermere, British Columbia, Canada

Psalms 31:24 -- Be of good courage, and he shall strengthen your heart, all ye that hope in the LORD.

50191-03

Indian Bean Salad

1 (15-oz.) can kidney beans
1 (15-oz.) can garbanzo beans
  (chickpeas)
1 (15-oz.) can black-eyed peas
2 lemons
2 T. olive oil
1 red onion

4 jalapeño peppers
3 tsp. roasted cumin
1 tsp. coriander
1 tsp. salt
1 tsp. fresh ground black pepper
1 tsp. garlic powder

Drain and rinse beans. In large bowl, stir beans with finely chopped peppers and red onion. Mix together all dry spices (cumin, coriander, salt, pepper and garlic powder) in small bowl. Add to bean mixture. Cut lemon in half. Squeeze juice over beans, then drizzle olive oil and mix all ingredients gently. One lemon may be enough so give a taste before adding more. Cover and refrigerate and let the spices marinate for an hour or so. Delicious!

Note: We have a very dear friend (Frank Bach) from our college days who kept us eating healthy while I was going through chemo this past year. This is his recipe, chock full of antioxidants, vitamins and proteins! Thanks Frank for being a friend and the green tea!

Lynn Leuschner
Rochester, New York

Potato Salad

6 med. potatoes
1/4 c. finely chopped onions
1 tsp. salt
1/4 tsp. pepper
3 hard-cooked eggs (chopped)

1/4 c. prepared Italian dressing
1/2 c. mayonnaise
1/2 c. chopped celery
1/2 c. pickle relish

Peel and cut potatoes into small cubes. Boil until tender. Drain and cool, then put in refrigerator. In separate bowl, mix onions, salt, pepper, mayonnaise, celery and pickle relish. One hour before serving, add Italian dressing to mayonnaise mixture, mix well and pour over potatoes. Coat thoroughly. Sprinkle hard-boiled eggs on top. Makes 4 to 6 servings.

Sr. Jeanne Francis Cleves, SND
Morehead, Kentucky

CALIFORNIA POTATO SALAD

8 med. red potatoes (cooked with
  skin on, cubed or sliced)
2 tsp. sugar
1 T. celery seed
½ c. sweet relish

2 hard-boiled eggs (chopped)
¾ c. mayonnaise
2 celery ribs (chopped)
⅓ c. onion (chopped)
Paprika & parsley, garnish

Place potatoes in bowl. Sprinkle with sugar and celery seed. Stir in sweet relish. Add eggs, celery and onion. Gently fold in mayonnaise. Sprinkle top with paprika and parsley.

Note: In honor of Jane's sister and Ashley's aunt, Linda L. Pense, RD, MS, CD.

Jane A. Widmer
Ashley Widmer
Indiana

GERMAN POTATO SALAD

5 potatoes
1 stick of celery (chopped fine)
1 white onion (chopped fine)
A sprinkle of garlic powder
A sprinkle of dill weed

2 T. vinegar
2 T. vegetable oil
¼ c. warm water
Salt & pepper to taste
4 slices bacon (crumbled)

Boil potatoes in skin, when cooked, cool to lukewarm and peel. Slice very thin. Combine potatoes, celery, onion, garlic powder and dill weed. In separate jar, mix vinegar, water, salt and pepper; shake well. Add vegetable oil and shake again. Pour jarred mixture over potato mixture so that all is coated thoroughly and salad is very moist. Brown and crumble bacon, sprinkle over salad.

Richard and Herta Gillies
Invermere, British Colubia, Canada

50191-03

SAUERKRAUT SALAD

2 lbs. sauerkraut (washed & drained)
1 c. green pepper (chopped)
1 c. onion (diced)

1 c. cucumber (chopped)
½ c. vinegar
1 c. sugar
½ c. oil

Mix sauerkraut, green pepper, onion and cucumber together. Mix vinegar, sugar and oil. Pour over sauerkraut, onion and cucumber. Let stand overnight.

Note: Great for parties. Always a big hit. Tastes better the longer it stands.

Marianne Svihlik
Mt. Morris, Illinois

CORN BREAD SALAD

1 (8½-oz.) pkg. Jiffy or Martha White jalapeño cornbread mix (bake cornbread according to pkg. directions and crumble)
1 (15.25-oz.) can yellow corn (whole kernel)
1 (15-oz.) can chili beans
1 c. (½ pt.) sour cream

1 c. mayonnaise
1-oz. pkg. dry Ranch salad mix
1 med. bell pepper (diced)
4 green onions (chopped)
3 med. tomatoes (chopped)
2 c. grated cheddar cheese
1 lb. bacon (cooked & crumbled)

Divide corn bread crumbs in half. Place half in bottom of a deep dish or bowl. On top, layer corn and then beans. In separate bowl, mix together sour cream, mayonnaise, and dressing mix. Pour over top of corn bread mixture. Add remaining corn bread crumbs on top. Next layer the peppers, onions and tomatoes, one on top of the other. Finish with cheese and bacon. Let set overnight in refrigerator. Serve chilled.

Note: One of my favorites!

Kathy Flynn
Pensacola, Florida

BREAD SOUP BOWLS

Serve soup in a fresh bread bowl. Buy small round loaves of a hearty bread such as Italian. Slice off the top and remove the inside of the loaf leaving a shell about an inch thick. Place on a plate or bowl and fill with soup.

Yvonne Albritton
Renton, Washington

TOMATO BASIL BISQUE SOUP

1 onion, chopped	2 bay leaves
2 cloves garlic, crushed	1/8 tsp. ground cloves
1 T. butter	1 tsp. salt
1 c. carrots, chopped	1/2 tsp. pepper
1 c. celery, chopped	2 T. brown sugar
2 (15-oz.) cans chopped tomatoes	1 pt. (2 c.) cream or half-and-half
2 T. fresh basil, chopped	1 c. milk

Sauté the onion and garlic in butter. Add chopped carrots and celery and sauté until softened. Add tomatoes, basil, bay leaves, cloves, salt, pepper and brown sugar, simmering for one or two hours. Remove bay leaves and purée mixture in a blender. Push mixture through a large strainer with a spatula or the back of a spoon. Return mixture to the stove and heat adding cream and milk. Watch carefully as not to scald soup. Serve garnished with fresh basil and croutons in a bread soup bowl.

Note: This has been a hit for me, everyone I have made it for raves about it. The secret ingredient is cloves. Can be made with fresh summer tomatoes, parboiled and skinned.

Yvonne Albritton
Renton, Washington

"Don't spend your life planning for tomorrow, live your life for today."
Jeannie M. Bilodeau, cancer survivor

50191-03

$\mathcal{H}$EALTHY CARROT SOUP

1 (3-lb.) bag carrots	1 tsp. sea salt
1 whole bulb garlic	Approx. 2 c. soy milk
1 fist-sized gingerroot	

In a large pan add the following: carrots (sliced very thin), entire bulb of garlic (use garlic press), gingerroot (sliced into very thin, small slices) and enough soy milk to cover the bottom of the pan and provide moisture for steaming. Cover and put on low heat until carrot chunks are tender. Transfer mixture to blender, a blender full at a time, and liquify, adding soy milk (approximately ½ cup at a time) as you do to get the desired consistency, a fairly thick slurry. Refrigerate entire batch. Can be poured out a little every day, heated and consumed. More soy milk as needed to be added each day, to individual bowls, for desired consistency. Makes approximately 5 to 6 bowls.

Note: Not something you'll find in a fine French restaurant but a GREAT way to get a lot of good stuff into your body at lunch time.

Bob Norcross
West Vancouver, British Columbia, Canada

"To appreciate the beautiful sunshine, we must first had experienced a thunderstorm."

Mary Silver

*W*LD MUSHROOM SOUP WITH THYME

2 T. light butter
1/3 c. shallots, minced
1 1/2 lbs. fresh wild mushrooms
  (such as shiitake, oyster &
  crimini), coarsely chopped
1 T. fresh thyme, minced or 1/2 tsp.
  dry
3 garlic cloves, minced
Madeira, to taste

8 c. (approx.) canned low salt
  chicken broth (divided)
1 lb. russet potatoes, peeled & cut
  into 2-in. chunks
1/4 c. dried porcini mushrooms,
  brushed & cleaned of any grit
1 box wild rice, cook as
  directed & add towards end of
  cooking

Melt butter in heavy large pot over medium-high heat. Add shallots; sauté for 1 minute. Add fresh mushrooms; sauté until tender, about 5 minutes. Add thyme and garlic; sauté until mushrooms are golden, about 8 minutes. Stir in 6 cups broth, potatoes and porcini. Bring to boil. Reduce heat, cover and simmer until potatoes are very tender, about 25 minutes. Working in batches, purée soup in blender. Return soup to pot. Mix in Madeira and enough chicken broth to thin soup to desired consistency. Add cooked rice. Season with salt and pepper. Bring soup to simmer and serve.

Note: This soup can be made ahead and refrigerated for up to 2 days ahead. It also freezes well.

Kimberly Boyer
Kent, Washington

Jeremiah 30:17 -- For I will restore health unto thee, and I will heal thee of thy wounds, saith the LORD.

50191-03

DREAMY CREAMY 3 MUSHROOM SOUP

8 oz. shiitake or button
  mushrooms (mushroom lovers
  may want to use both!)
6 oz. sm. oyster mushrooms
1/3 c. chopped shallots
2 T. butter
2 T. all-purpose flour

1/2 tsp. salt
1/4 tsp. coarsely ground black
  pepper
1 (14 1/2-oz.) can chicken broth
2 c. (1 pt.) half-and-half
1/8 tsp. ground saffron or saffron
  threads

Remove tough or woody stems from mushrooms. Chop shiitake/ button mushrooms. Cut oyster mushrooms into large pieces. In a large saucepan, cook mushrooms and shallots in melted butter, uncovered over medium heat for 5 minutes or until tender, stirring occasionally. Stir in flour, salt and pepper. Add broth. Cook and stir over medium heat until slightly thickened and bubbly. Cook and stir one minute more. Stir in half-and-half and ground saffron. Heat through. Ladle into bowls and garnish with additional saffron threads if desired. Makes 6 (side dish servings).

Note: You may want to make this a day ahead if for company, as it is wonderful served fresh, but even better the next day! This soup is so delicious I always double the recipe to ensure leftovers.

Cathy Scheffter
Owensville, Ohio

TOMATO ZUCCHINI SOUP

2 T. margarine
2 c. onion (sliced)
4 c. chicken broth
4-6 c. zucchini (cubed)
5 med. tomatoes (peeled & cut
  into chunks)

1/4 tsp. oregano
1/4 tsp. basil
1/4 tsp. dried dill weed
1/2 tsp. celery flakes
1 tsp. sugar
1/2 tsp. salt

Sauté onion in margarine until clear and soft. Add broth, zucchini, tomatoes, oregano, basil, dill weed, celery flakes, sugar and salt. Bring to boil. Reduce heat. Cover and simmer 25 to 35 minutes. Makes 9 to 10 cups.

Note: Can use (28-ounce) can of diced tomatoes when fresh tomatoes are not in season.

Janet Scheuneman
St. Paul, Minnesota

EAN SOUP

1 (16-oz.) bag navy beans	1 med. onion (diced)
1 (16-oz.) bag northern beans	2 med. potatoes (diced)
1 lg. ham bone with meat (can	1 (8-oz.) can tomato sauce
buy extra ham pieces)	2 T. baking soda

Wash and soak navy and northern beans overnight in 16 cups of water, plus 2 tablespoons of baking soda. Next day, rinse beans and put in large pot with 10 cups of water. Add ham bone with meat, onion, and potatoes. Simmer with lid tilted for about 2 hours. Remove bone and cut any usable meat from bone. May add additional ham pieces if desired. Add meat to pot. Add tomato sauce and cook for about 30 more minutes. Can serve immediately or let sit and warm up later. Great to freeze and serve at another time.

Note: Great to give your grown kids as a surprise dinner. They will always save a ham bone for you!

Judy Cleves
Cincinnati, Ohio

ZESTY PUMPKIN SOUP

¼ c. butter	⅛ tsp. crushed red pepper
1 c. chopped onion	3 c. chicken broth
1 garlic clove (crushed)	1¾ c. solid packed pumpkin
1 tsp. curry powder	(15-oz. can)
½ tsp. salt	1 c. (½ pt.) half-and-half
¼ tsp. ground coriander	Sour cream & chives for garnish

Melt butter in large saucepan; sauté onion and garlic until soft. Add curry powder, salt, coriander, and red pepper; cook 1 minute. Add broth; boil gently, uncovered for 15 to 20 minutes. Stir in pumpkin and half-and-half; cook 5 minutes. Pour into blender container. Cover and blend until creamy. Serve warm or reheat to desired temperature. Garnish with dollop of sour cream and chopped chives, if desired.

LuAnn Miltenis
Flower Mound, Texas

50191-03

CORN CHOWDER

1 (10.5-oz.) can cream of
  mushroom soup
1 soup can of whole vitamin D
  whole milk
1 (15-oz.) can whole kernel corn
  (drained)

4-6 link sausages
2 T. diced onion
Grated cheese to garnish

Brown link sausage lightly in frying pan or in microwave. Cut into
½-inch link pieces. Combine soup, milk, drained corn, onion and sausage. Heat gently until nearly boiling. Garnish with a bit of grated
cheese. Serve hot.

Note: As a cancer survivor, I appreciate this recipe from my sister
Joan who died of lung cancer in 2001. She made this for my kids when
she visited us.

Kathy Biesheuvel
Broadus, Montana

POTATO SOUP

1 lb. bacon
1 bunch green onions
3½ c. chicken stock
½ c. butter

¼ c. flour
½ c. heavy cream
1 c. shredded cheddar cheese

Brown bacon in the large pan you will use for soup. Remove bacon
and crumble. Remove most of the grease from pan and add onions.
Sauté for 3 minutes. Add potatoes and cook 3 minutes. Add chicken
stock and cook until potatoes are done. Melt butter in saucepan and
add flour, cook 3 minutes. Add to boiling potato mixture and stir until
thick, add cream and cheese. You can use already baked potatoes if
you like. I sprinkle a little additional green onion and cheese on top.

Note: Great! Cornbread is good with this soup. Easy to double for
large families. Given to me by my sister, Joyce, in Ironton, Ohio.

Bev Clay
Coal Grove, Ohio

$\mathcal{B}$AKED POTATO SOUP

4 lg. baking potatoes
2/3 c. butter or margarine
2/3 c. all-purpose flour
6 c. milk
3/4 tsp. salt
1/2 tsp. pepper
4 green onions (chopped & divided)

12 slices bacon (cooked, crumbled & divided)
1 1/4 c. (5 oz.) shredded cheddar cheese (divided)
1 (8-oz.) ctn. sour cream

Wash potatoes and prick several times with a fork. Bake at 400° for 1 hour or until done. Let cool. Cut potatoes in half lengthwise and scoop out pulp. Melt butter in a heavy saucepan over low heat; add all-purpose flour, stirring until smooth. Cook 1 minute, stirring constantly. Gradually add 6 cups of milk. Cook over medium heat, stirring constantly, until mixture is thickened and bubbly. Add potato pulp, salt, pepper, 2 tablespoons green onion, 1/2 cup bacon and 1 cup of cheese. Cook until thoroughly heated. Stir sour cream. Add additional milk, if necessary, for desired thickness. Garnish and serve with remaining onion, bacon and cheese. Yields 10 cups.

Note: This takes a lot of time but is worth it! Recipe from 1991 Southern Living annual recipe book.

Joe and Kitty Cleves
Covington, Kentucky

"My motto is 'make a difference' "

Carolyn Corey

50191-03

CABBAGE AND NOODLE SOUP

2 lbs. beef short ribs
2 T. oil
1 (28-oz.) can diced tomatoes
1 lb. broad noodles

1 sm. head cabbage (core removed, then sliced)
2 c. beef broth (may add more)

Brown the short ribs in the bottom of a heavy large pot in 2 tablespoons of oil. Add tomatoes and 2 cups of broth. Bring to a boil then cook on medium-low for 1 to 2 hours with lid on, until short ribs fall from bone. When the meat is fork tender, remove from broth, remove bones and fat. While preparing meat, put the cooled broth into the freezer. When fat is solidified on top of broth, skim fat and discard. Bring broth to a boil, add noodles, cook as directed on noodle package. Add cabbage and cook for 5 to 10 minutes until cabbage is just tender. Add additional broth or water to make as thick as you like it. Salt and pepper to taste, remembering that the canned broth is already salted.

Note: This hearty soup was a specialty of my grandmother. To make it even better, make your own noodles as my grandmother did.

Marlene Dickman
Park Hills, Kentucky

ITALIAN VEGETABLE SOUP

1 lb. ground beef
1 c. diced onion
1 c. sliced celery
1 c. sliced carrots
2 cloves garlic (minced)
1 (16-oz.) can tomatoes
1 (15 oz.) red kidney beans
  (undrained)
4 c. water
5 tsp. beef bouillon granules

1 T. dried parsley
1 tsp. salt
$1/2$ tsp. oregano
$1/2$ tsp. sweet basil
$1/4$ tsp. black pepper
2 c. zucchini (cubed)
1 c. green beans, cut in 1-in. pieces
  (frozen or fresh)
$1/2$ c. sm. dry elbow macaroni

Brown beef in a large kettle, drain fat, add onion, celery, carrots, garlic, tomatoes, red kidney beans, water, bouillon, parsley, salt, oregano, basil, pepper, green beans, macaroni. Bring to boil, lower heat and simmer 20 minutes, add zucchini, simmer 5 minutes more. If you want thinner soup, add more water at this time. Enjoy!

Doris Benson
La Conner, Washington

DAD'S VEGETABLE SOUP

2-lb. round steak (cubed sm.)
1 (64-oz.) can tomato juice
64 oz. water
1 lg. onion (chopped fine)

1 (16-oz.) bag frozen vegetables
    (your choice, any will work)
3 lg. potatoes (chopped)
Salt & pepper

In a large stock pan pour tomato juice in pan, fill can with water, pour into pan, add chopped onion and round steak, salt and pepper, bring to a boil then lower heat. Cook for about 3 to 4 hours, just until the meat is tender; then add potatoes and cook until the potatoes are tender, about 45 minutes. Then about 30 minutes before serving add the frozen vegetables.

Recipe Note: Best with a fresh loaf of homemade bread, just like Dad used to do. Can be done in the crockpot also.

Mickie Weber
London, England

MOM'S MARVELOUS MINESTRONE

1 lb. Italian sausage (mild)
1 T. olive oil
1 clove garlic (minced)
1 c. sliced carrots
1 tsp. basil
2 sm. zucchini (sliced)
1 (16-oz.) can chopped tomatoes
    (undrained)

3 Wyler beef bouillon cubes
1½ c. water
2 c. shredded cabbage
1 tsp. salt
1 (15½-oz.) can northern beans

Brown sausage in oil. Add garlic, carrots and basil. Cook 5 minutes. Add zucchini, tomatoes with liquid, bouillon, water, cabbage and salt. Boil soup. Reduce heat and simmer, covered for 1 hour. Add beans and liquid and cook 20 minutes longer. Makes 8 servings.

Note: My crafty, musical, witty lovely mother had more zest for life at age 70 than I do at 38! My husband described his "ice cream eating buddy" with simply one word - NIFTY. She was just nifty!

Patricia Mohr
Indianapolis, Indiana

50191-03

CHICKEN VEGETABLE STEW

1 (2- to 3-lb.) chicken
6 T. margarine (melted)
2 onions (chopped)
2 carrots (sliced thin)
2 celery stalks (chopped)
10 fresh mushrooms (chopped)

6 c. chicken broth (homemade or
canned)
2 T. bread crumbs
2 eggs (lightly beaten)
Salt & pepper to taste

In Dutch oven add margarine, onions, carrots, celery and mushrooms. Cook for about 5 minutes until vegetables are cooked and well coated. Add chicken pieces and broth. Increase heat to boil. Reduce heat to simmer, cover and cook for about 1 hour, until chicken is done. Remove chicken pieces and set aside to cool. Add bread crumbs and eggs. Mix well and continue cooking on low. When chicken cools, cut into bite-size pieces and add to stew. Mix well and heat through.

Margie Bruns
Coldwater, Ohio

MAKE A MEAL SOUP

1 lb. smoked sausage (thinly
sliced)
1 onion (chopped)
1 tsp. oil
3 c. water
2 chicken bouillon cubes
1 tsp. salt
$1/4$ tsp. pepper
1 bay leaf
$1/2$ tsp. thyme

3 cloves garlic
3 carrots (sliced)
3 celery stalks (sliced)
$1/4$ head cabbage (cut into 1-in.
cubes)
2 tsp. uncooked rice
1 (18-oz.) can tomato sauce
1 (15-oz.) can kidney beans
1 (28-oz.) can whole tomatoes
(chopped)

In a large pan, brown onion in oil until tender. Add sausage, water, bouillon cubes, salt, pepper, bay leaf, thyme, garlic, carrots, celery, cabbage, uncooked rice, tomato sauce, kidney beans, whole tomatoes. Bring all to a boil and then simmer for 30 minutes or until vegetables are tender.

Note: Best to always serve with cornbread.

Bev Clay
Coal Grove, Ohio

CLAM CHOWDER

½ c. diced onion
½ c. diced celery
2 T. butter plus ¼ c. butter
1 (8-oz.) jar minced clams
   (undrained)
4 c. chicken broth
1 c. diced, peeled potatoes

½ c. milk
1 c. (½ pt.) half-and-half
Dash thyme
Dash salt
Dash pepper
Dash curry powder
3 T. flour

In a 3-quart saucepan, sauté onion and celery in 2 tablespoons melted butter until transparent. Add liquid from clams, broth and potatoes. Simmer until potatoes are tender. In a separate pan, melt ¼ cup butter and stir in flour until smooth. DO NOT BROWN. Stir gently until thickened. Add chopped clams, milk and half-and-half. Stir gently until thickened. Add thyme, salt, pepper and curry powder. Makes 6 servings.

Judy Kulhank
San Jose, California

MOCK TURTLE SOUP

2½ lbs. uncooked ground beef
2 qt. water
½ tsp. salt
2 lg. carrots
½ bunch celery
½ bunch parsley
½ (1¼-oz.) box pickling spice
½ lemon

⅓ c. Worcestershire sauce
½ c. vinegar
2 lg. onions
1 (46-oz.) can tomato juice
1 (14-oz.) bottle ketchup
1 (28-oz.) can whole tomatoes
4 hard-boiled eggs (chopped)
¼ lb. gingersnaps (crushed)

Grind carrots, celery, parsley, onions, tomatoes and the lemon (leave on the peel). Put 2 quarts of water in a large pot and add ground beef, salt, Worcestershire sauce, vinegar, tomato juice, ketchup, and ground vegetable mixture. Put the pickling spice in a small cheesecloth bag or metal tea steeper, and place it in the pot. Cook approximately 3 hours over low heat. Add the chopped eggs the last 10 minutes of cooking time. At the very last minute, add the crumbled gingersnaps.

Note: Recipe submitted to me by Firemen many years ago.

Rose Lankisch
Ft. Thomas, Kentucky

50191-03

MOCK TURTLE SOUP II

1 lb. lean ground beef	2 tsp. salt
1 lg. onion	Generous grinding of black
1 (14-oz.) bottle catsup	peppercorns
1½ qt. water	1 T. packed brown sugar
1 (10.5-oz.) can beef or mushroom	1 T. vinegar
gravy	10 whole cloves
2 tsp. Worcestershire sauce	10 whole allspice
¾ c. cold water	1 bay leaf
¾ c. browned flour (in some	2 hard-cooked eggs (diced)
grocery stores or you can make	8 paper-thin lemon slices
your own, see directions)	Dash of sherry (opt. but great
1 T. beef soup stock concentrate	flavor addition)
(or 3 beef bouillon cubes)	

In a heavy kettle, aluminum or stainless steel Dutch oven, start browning the beef on medium heat (do not add fat) with onions. Stir occasionally for 2 to 3 minutes, or until red color is out of meat and onions slightly soften. Add catsup, 1½ quarts water, beef or mushroom gravy, Worcestershire sauce. Bring to boil, then reduce heat so mixture simmers gently. In separate pan, stir browned flour with ¾ cup cold water to a smooth paste. Use more water if you need it. ***Browned flour can be purchased in 1-pound bags in some stores. To make your own, measure about 1½ cups all-purpose flour into a skillet. Place on medium heat and stir almost constantly with a straight-end spatula until flour has browned to "cream in your coffee" color. You start with somewhat more flour than you need, as some shrinkage occurs in the browning process. Watch carefully during the browning. You want browned flour, not scorched flour. ***Pour flour mixture into the simmering gravy mixture and stir well. Use a straight end pancake turner or spatula for stirring to occasionally scrape the bottom of the kettle and prevent scorching. Add bouillon cubes or beef soup concentrate, salt, pepper, brown sugar, and vinegar. Put the whole cloves, allspice, and bay leaf into a metal tea ball or tie them in a small square of clean cheese cloth, and add to soup. Cover the soup and simmer, stirring occasionally, for about two hours. Remove spices. Best if cooled, uncovered, and then covered and refrigerated overnight or longer for flavors to blend.

(continued)

To serve: Reheat to boiling the amount you plan to use. In the last 5 minutes of heating, add the chopped hard-cooked eggs and paper thin lemon slices. Float the lemon slices on each bowl for garnish. Add a dash of sherry wine to each serving. If reheating the entire amount at one time, add ¼ to ½ cup sherry to total amount. Makes about 3 quarts of soup.

Mary Busse
Alexandria, Virginia

HERTA'S HAMBURGER SOUP

1 lb. ground beef
1 (10-oz.) can sliced mushrooms
  (drained)
1 onion (chopped)
4 c. chicken broth (can be made
  with water & 4 tsp. chicken
  bouillon)

7 T. pot or Scotch barley
4 carrots (peeled & sliced)
4 sticks celery (sliced)
1 (28-oz.) can tomatoes
1 (10.5-oz.) can tomato soup

Brown ground beef and drain off fat. Add mushrooms, onion, chicken broth and pot barley. Simmer for 20 minutes. Add carrots, celery, tomatoes, and tomato soup. Simmer for 20 additional minutes.

Note: This is a meal in a soup and freezes very well. May substitute pearl barley for pot/Scotch barley, but pearl barley will cook a bit faster.

Richard and Herta Gillies
Invermere, British Columbia, Canada

"Nothing great was ever achieved without enthusiasm."
Ralph Waldo Emerson

50191-03

$\mathcal{D}$EE KICILINSKI'S ALBONDIGAS SOUP

1½ lbs. ground beef
1 sm. pkg. Jimmy Dean reg.
   sausage
½ lg. chopped onion
2 sm. minced garlic cloves
2 eggs
½ c. uncooked white rice
¼ c. flour

3 qt. water
1 lg. finely chopped carrot
⅓ c. white rice
1 (16-oz.) can tomato sauce
½ c. coarsely chopped cilantro
Sourdough or French bread
Salad

Thoroughly mix ground beef, sausage, onion, garlic, eggs, ½ cup rice, flour, cumin and salt to taste. Heat 2½ to 3 quarts water with carrot, ⅓ cup white rice and tomato sauce in a large pot until water boils. Turn heat down to simmer, add the meatballs (uncooked) and cook covered about 1 hour or until done. Add cilantro just prior to serving. Accompany with toasted sourdough or French bread and salad of choice. Serves 4 to 6 persons.

Red Wynn
Las Vegas, NV

$\mathcal{C}$HICKEN CHILI

6 chicken breasts
Salt & pepper
4 lg. onions
10 cloves garlic
4 T. vegetable oil
4 (12-oz.) cans beer
4 tsp. dried oregano
½ c. chili powder

4 T. cumin
12 chicken bouillon cubes
½ c. water
2 (15-oz.) cans tomato sauce
2 (16-oz.) cans kidney beans
   (drained)
1 (15-oz.) can pinto beans
   (drained)

Preheat oven to 350°. Place chicken skin side up in a shallow pan and add ½ inch water. Cover with a buttered sheet of waxed paper, buttered side down, tuck in edges. Bake for 20 to 30 minutes. When cool, tear into 1-inch pieces. Set aside. In large pan, sauté onions and garlic in oil until soft. Add beer, oregano, chili powder, cumin, bouillon, water and tomato sauce. Bring to a boil and then reduce heat to low and simmer uncovered for 1½ hours. Stir in beans and simmer 30 more minutes. Stir in cooked chicken.

Note: This is as delicious as the picture in the cookbook made it look. It makes a huge batch, so I usually cut the recipe in half.

Karin Deti
Des Moines, Washington

VEGETARIAN CHILI

1 tsp. vegetable oil
1 c. onion, chopped
1 c. green bell pepper, chopped
3 fresh serrano peppers, seeded &
  diced
3 cloves garlic, minced
1 T. chili powder
1 tsp. ground cumin
1/2 tsp. dried whole oregano
1/2 tsp. ground red pepper

1/3 c. masa harina or cornmeal
14 oz. no salt added whole
  tomatoes
14 oz. no salt added beef broth
12 oz. beer
3 cans low-sodium kidney beans,
  drained & rinsed
3/4 tsp. salt
1/2 tsp. hot sauce
1 T. white vinegar

Coat a large Dutch oven with vegetable oil and place over medium-high heat. Add onion, bell pepper, serrano pepper, and garlic; sauté 5 minutes or until tender. Add chili powder, cumin, oregano, and red pepper and stir well. Sprinkle mixture with masa harina or cornmeal and stir well. Add tomatoes, broth, beer, kidney beans, salt, hot sauce and bring to a boil. Reduce heat, and simmer, partially covered, about 30 to 45 minutes. Add vinegar, and simmer, partially covered, about 30 minutes. Serve.

Kimberly & Jim Boyer
Kent, Washington

"Sanity is relative -- Just none of mine!"

Bruce Paul

70

50191-03

*T*HE BEST CHILI

8 cloves garlic (finely diced)
1½ white onions (diced)
2½ lbs. ground turkey
4 (28-oz.) cans stewed, peeled
  tomatoes
5 (14-oz.) cans black beans
  (including liquid)

5 (14-oz.) cans corn (drained)
1 (6-oz.) can tomato paste
3 T. ground chili pepper
3 T. red pepper flakes
2 tsp. cumin seed
Salt & pepper to taste
2 T. olive oil

Toppings:

Sour cream
Shredded cheddar cheese

Diced purple onion

In a large fry pan, sauté diced onion in olive oil. When onions soften and are transparent, add garlic and sauté until golden. Add turkey to fry pan and cook until done, breaking up into small bite-size pieces as it cooks. Salt and pepper turkey as it cooks. In large stockpot, crush by hand the canned tomatoes and begin to cook over medium to low heat. Add turkey mixture to pot and then continue to add the other ingredients in this order: black beans, corn, tomato paste, chili pepper, red pepper flakes, cumin seed. Salt and pepper additionally if needed, to taste. Let simmer without a lid until hot throughout or ready to serve.

Note: This fantastic chili recipe makes a very large batch. Perfect for parties and/or large family gatherings.

Susan Dansereau
Cincinnati, Ohio

Mark 5:36 -- Be not afraid, only believe.

 MY MOM'S CHILI

1 lb. ground chuck
1 lg. onion (chopped)
2 (28-oz.) cans of diced or crushed
  tomatoes
2 (20-oz.) cans Bush's chili beans

1 (1.37-oz.) container of chili
  powder
1¾ c. water
Salt to taste

Cook onion and ground chuck in skillet until done, then drain and set aside. Place tomatoes and beans in a large stockpot, add water, salt to taste. Bring mixture to boil. Add ground chuck and onion along with chili powder to pot. Once again salt to taste. You may also add more chili powder if desired. Reduce heat, let simmer for 1 to 1½ hours, stirring and tasting periodically. Serve with saltines.

Note: This chili is full of fire and love, just like my mom. For without her gift of steady work ethic and "get up and go", accompanied by the saving grace of Jesus Christ, my Savior, my battle with cancer most certainly would have had an unhappy ending.

Ron Adams
Lawrenceville, Georgia

Recipe Favorites

50191-03

Vegetables & Side Dishes

Donna Mulinski - Michigan

Barbara Bagley (right) - Texas

Linda West - Indiana

Joyce Kennedy - Indiana

A Second Chance

"For I will restore health unto thee and I will heal thee of thy wounds, saith the Lord."

-Jeremiah 30:17

I had always been fit as a fiddle! That is until I hit middle age. I was a smoker, over 40 years, and my smoking slowly began taking its toll.

In 1996, after being hospitalized for the second time with acute bronchitis, I realized "It's time to quit smoking!" Doctors checked me out and mistakenly proclaimed me cancer free.

I committed to living a healthier life-style and for a while I felt better, both physically and mentally. I thought I had my life under control. Wrong!

One year later, I couldn't put my finger on the problem; I just knew I didn't feel 100%. Then one afternoon, I coughed up blood. All of the tests (THIS time I got a second opinion) that followed, confirmed - I had stage 1 non-small cell lung cancer. I consider that afternoon's coughing episode a blessing. Without it I would have ignored feeling a bit "off" and would not have gone to the doctor - resulting in a late diagnosis, which could have been disastrous.

At a hospital in Houston, surgery was performed successfully and no chemo or radiation was necessary! Recovery after intensive surgery is the pits. I found it would be 12 months before I was completely back to my old self.

I believe things happen for a reason! My cancer brought me to the realization that I needed to change my life-style and attitude. My energy level is back and my mental attitude is no longer consumed with my illness. I again have a sense of well being about my life and future. God has given me back my health - He has given me back my life!

Each day is a gift! I am grateful for each and every one of them!

Barbara Bagley
San Antonio, Texas

Vegetables & Side Dishes

SUMMER SCRAMBLE

2 T. butter
½ c. onion, chopped
1 sm. clove garlic (crushed)
¼ c. snipped parsley
1 tsp. salt
1 tsp. seasoned salt
Dash of pepper

Dash of thyme
1 med. head of cauliflower (broken
  into sm. flowerets)
3 lg. tomatoes (diced) or 14½-oz.
  can diced tomatoes (undrained)
2 sm. zucchini (sliced)

In large saucepan, melt butter; cook onion and garlic until tender, not brown. Add parsley, salt, seasoned salt, pepper, thyme, cauliflower, tomatoes and zucchini. Cover tightly. Simmer 15 to 20 minutes, uncover and cook 10 minutes longer. Serve in bowls with juice. Makes 10 servings.

Note: Family favorite, young and old!

Mary Jane Sassin
Park Hills, Kentucky

"Life is a journey short or long, so live everyday to the fullest."
Katie Lifka

*V*EGETABLES ROMA

4 med. size fennel bulbs (about 2
  lbs.) or 2 sm. bunches celery
1/2 c. water
1 c. salad oil (divided)
1 chicken-flavored bouillon cube
  or env.
2 3/4 tsp. salt (divided)
Med. eggplant (about 1 1/2 lbs.)
3 lg. red or green peppers (cut into
  1/2-in. thick slices)

2 med. size onions (thinly sliced)
1 clove garlic (minced)
1 tsp. sugar (divided)
3 med. zucchini (cut into 1/2-in.
  thick slices)
1 T. minced parsley
1 lb. med. sized mushrooms
3 T. cider vinegar
1/4 tsp. pepper
1/4 tsp. marjoram leaves

About 2 hours before serving or early in the day: Cut off root end, and tough stalks, from each fennel bulb. Cut each bulb lengthwise in half, then into 1/2-inch wide sticks. Rinse fennel with running water; drain. (If using celery, cut into 3 x 1/2-inch sticks.) In 3-quart saucepan over medium heat, cook fennel in 2 tablespoons of hot oil, until lightly browned, stirring occasionally. Stir in water, bouillon, and 1/4 teaspoon salt; over high heat, heat to boiling. Reduce heat to low, cover and simmer 5 to 10 minutes until fennel is tender, stirring occasionally. Remove saucepan from heat. Meanwhile, cut eggplant lengthwise in half, then cut each half into 1-inch wide sticks. In 12-inch skillet over medium-high heat, in 1/3 cup oil, cook eggplant, peppers, onions, garlic, 1 1/4 teaspoon salt, and 1/2 teaspoon sugar until vegetables are tender, stirring frequently. Remove vegetable mixture to medium bowl. In same skillet over medium-high heat, in 2 tablespoons oil, cook zucchini and 1/4 teaspoon salt till tender crisp, stir frequently. Remove zucchini to another bowl; sprinkle with parsley. In same skillet over medium heat, heat mushrooms, vinegar, pepper, marjoram, 3 tablespoons oil, 1 teaspoon salt and 1/2 teaspoon sugar to boil. Reduce heat to low; cover and simmer 5 minutes or until mushrooms are tender, stirring occasionally. Remove skillet from heat. Serve warm or cold, 12 servings, 180 calories per serving. Put everything onto large platter next to each other and serve.

Note: In honor of my dearest friend Stephanie Saraco who amazes me everyday with her inner strength and determination to survive.

Carole Leone
Port Washington, New York

50191-03

CELERY ROOT WITH ALMOND SAUCE

2 lbs. celery root
½ c. almonds (or hazelnuts)
2 cloves garlic
¼ c. fresh lemon juice

1 T. water
½ tsp. salt
½ c. olive oil
Snipped parsley

Pare celery root and cut into ¼-inch strips and place in bowl. Place almonds and garlic in food processor and blend until finely chopped. Add lemon juice, water and salt. Cover and begin blending, adding olive oil while blender is running, until sauce is smooth. Toss celery root with almond sauce. Cover and refrigerate at least one hour. Serve on lined lettuce plates and garnish with parsley and Greek olives, if desired. Makes approximately 12 servings.

Note: I adapted this Turkish recipe to meet our dietary restrictions, and it's still great.

Dorene Campbell
Vancouver, Washington

ZUCCHINI AND MUSHROOM CASSEROLE

5 zucchini (each about 8 in. long)
1 lb. mushrooms (sliced)
3 T. fresh rosemary (minced)
2 T. butter

Salt & pepper
3 oz. feta cheese (rinsed & minced)
3 c. grated white cheddar cheese

Cut each zucchini into 4 (2-inch long) pieces. Stand each piece on end and cut it into 12 to 16 little sticks. Put them in a large pan and sprinkle with a bit of salt/pepper and 2 tablespoons rosemary. Heat until the water has come out of the vegetables and is in the pan. Drain and discard water. Set zucchini aside to cool down. If you don't let it cool, it will be difficult to mix in the cheese. Cook mushrooms in melted butter with a dash of salt/pepper and 1 teaspoon rosemary. When all of the liquid has reduced and only butter and mushrooms are left, continue to cook mushrooms until they are golden to dark brown. Drain excess butter and set mushrooms aside to cool. Mix the cooled zucchini and mushrooms with feta cheese and then mix in 2 cups cheddar cheese. Place mixture in a greased 9 x 13-inch baking dish. Sprinkle 1 cup cheddar cheese on top. Bake at 350° until top has browned.

Emily Whaley
Stone Mountain, Georgia

*O*VEN ROASTED CAPONATA

2 med.-lg. red bell peppers (sliced)
1 sm. eggplant (cubed)
1 lg. red Spanish onion (sliced)
4-5 fresh Roma tomatoes
Extra virgin olive oil (to coat)
Coarse sea salt
3 T. red wine vinegar
1 T. brown sugar (or sugar substitute)
¼ tsp. hot pepper sauce (or to taste)
½ c. pitted Kalamata or Greek black olives
2 T. chopped parsley
1 T. chopped fresh basil leaves (1 tsp. dried)

Preheat oven to 500°. Wash eggplant. Trim ends and cut into 1-inch cubes. Place in a large, shallow roasting pan, large enough to accommodate all of the vegetables when arranged in a single layer. Cut red peppers in half, lengthwise. Remove seeds and cut into small strips. Add peppers and sliced onions to pan. Cut tomatoes in half, lengthwise and place skin side down in pan with other vegetables. Drizzle a light coating of olive oil over the vegetables. Lightly stir to coat. Sprinkle with coarse sea salt. Place pan in the preheated oven. Roast for 6 minutes. Stir vegetables and roast for an additional 5 to 6 minutes. Remove from the oven, when slightly cooled, take peeling off tomatoes and coarsely chop. In a separate bowl, stir together vinegar, sugar and hot pepper sauce and heat in the microwave (a little at a time, stir frequently) to dissolve the sugar. Toss with vegetables. Add olives, basil and parsley. Serve at room temperature or well chilled with whole-wheat pita bread.

Note: If you've never tried eggplant, try this recipe! You'll love it! Great also with a meatless meal. Thanks to Marilyn Harris for this wonderful recipe!

Cathy Scheffter
Owensville, Ohio

"*There is no such thing as false hope.*"

Barbara Labadie

50191-03

ARTICHOKE CASSEROLE

1 (14-oz.) can artichoke hearts
(drained & chopped)
2 (10-oz.) pkgs. frozen chopped
spinach

8 oz. cream cheese
½ c. butter

Line a buttered casserole dish with artichoke hearts. Thaw spinach and squeeze dry. Mix together cream cheese and butter. Mix in spinach. Spread spinach mixture over artichoke layer and bake at 325° for 20 minutes or until bubbly. Serves about 6.

Barb White
Eatonton, Georgia

CABBAGE CASSEROLE

1 med. head hard cabbage
(coarsely chopped into about
2-in. pieces)
½ c. butter or margarine, sliced
into 24 pats
1 sleeve saltines, crushed (approx.
37 crackers)

1 c. milk (minus 2 T.)
Salt & pepper
2½-qt. casserole, greased with
butter

Preheat oven to 350°. Boil chopped cabbage in pot of water until tender (probably 15 to 20 minutes). Drain very well. Layer the cabbage, cracker crumbs and butter into the casserole in thirds starting with ⅓ of the cabbage, covered with ⅓ of the saltine crumbs, dotted with ⅓ of the butter (about 8 pats for each layer). Sprinkle each layer rather significantly with salt and pepper. Repeat for two more layers. Drizzle the milk all over the top. Bake, uncovered, for 40 minutes until lightly browned on top.

Note: Also known as cabbage pudding, this generations-old family recipe is based upon a traditional old Kentucky favorite.

Deb Rieselman
Erlanger, Kentucky

BROCCOLI CASSEROLE

2 (10-oz.) pkgs. chopped frozen
  broccoli
2 eggs (beaten)
1 c. mayonnaise
1 (10.5-oz.) can cream of celery
  soup

8 oz. (2 c.) grated cheddar cheese
1 T. chopped onion
Salt & pepper to taste

Topping:

½ c. butter (melted)
1½ stacks Ritz crackers (approx.
  52 crackers), crushed

Prepare broccoli according to directions and drain. In large bowl, mix eggs, mayonnaise, soup, cheese, onion, salt and pepper. Add broccoli mixture. Set aside. **For topping:** Mix butter and crackers together. Pour broccoli mixture into greased 9 x 13-inch pan. Sprinkle topping over and bake at 350° for 30 minutes.

Rosemary Huntsman
Morehead, Kentucky

MERLE'S CORN CASSEROLE

2 (15-oz.) cans cream-style corn
2 eggs (beaten)
1 c. yellow cornmeal
1 tsp. garlic salt

6 T. vegetable oil
½ c. shredded hot pepper cheese
1½ c. shredded mild cheddar
  cheese

Mix cream-style corn, eggs, cornmeal, garlic salt, vegetable oil, hot pepper cheese, and mild cheddar cheese and pour into a 2-quart baking dish. Bake at 350° for 45 minutes or until top is firm.

Donna Melick
Sweetser, Indiana

50191-03

VEGETABLE CASSEROLE

1 (15.25-oz.) can white shoe peg
  corn
1 (15.25-oz.) can green beans
½ c. celery (chopped)
½ c. green pepper (chopped)
½ c. onion (chopped)
1 c. shredded cheese (any flavor)

1 c. (½ pt.) sour cream
1 (10.5-oz.) can cream of celery
  soup
½ c. butter
1 sleeve Ritz crackers (approx. 35
  crackers), crumbled
½ c. almonds

In large bowl combine corn, green beans, celery, onion, green pepper, cheese, sour cream and celery soup. Mix well. Spread into 9 x 13-inch pan. Bake 45 minutes at 350°. Remove from oven and cover with Ritz cracker crumbs and almonds. Melt butter and drizzle over the top of the casserole. Brown 10 to 15 minutes.

Note: Great for get togethers. Lots of flavor with little fuss.

Brenda Adams
Barboursville, West Virginia

BEAN AND CORN DISH

3 c. fresh green beans
3 c. corn (cut off cob)
2 c. ham (cut into sm. pieces)
1 (10.5-oz.) can cream of
  mushroom soup

5.25 can water (½ soup can)
3 oz. French-fried onions (½ of a
  6-oz. can)

Mix beans, corn, ham, soup and water together and put in a crockpot. Place French-fried onions on top. Put crockpot on high for 2 hours and then low for 1 hour. Enough for 8 to 10 servings.

Sr. Jeanne Francis Cleves, SND
Morehead, Kentucky

"Change your thoughts and you change your world."
Norman Vincent Peale

CALICO BEANS

1 lb. ground beef (browned)
1-2 T. olive oil
1 lb. cooked bacon (chopped)
1 med. yellow onion (chopped &
 sautéed)
½ c. sugar
½ c. brown sugar
2 tsp. vinegar

1 tsp. dry mustard
½ c. ketchup
1 (16-oz.) can kidney beans
 (drained)
1 (16-oz.) can butter beans
 (drained)
2 (16-oz.) cans baked beans

Brown the ground beef and onion in a little bit olive oil (approximately 1 to 2 tablespoons). Spray casserole dish or 13 x 9 x 2-inch baking dish with non stick spray. Combine beef, bacon, onion, sugar, brown sugar, vinegar, mustard, ketchup, kidney beans, butter beans and baked beans. Spread in sprayed dish and bake at 350° for 45 to 60 minutes.

Note: Wonderful side dish for a barbecue!

Chris Soranno
Flower Mound, Texas

CURT'S FAMOUS COWBOY BEANS

2 (16-oz.) cans pork & beans
1 (16-oz.) can chili hot beans
1 lg. chopped, fresh green pepper
 (or 2 med.)
1 med.-lg. chopped onion
1 lb. ground beef (browned &
 drained)

1 c. ketchup
1 c. Hunt's barbecue sauce
 (original recipe, rich & creamy)
½ lb. brown sugar (1⅛ c. firmly
 packed)
Salt & pepper to taste

In a crockpot, combine pork and beans, chili beans, green pepper, onion, browned ground beef, ketchup, barbecue sauce, brown sugar and salt and pepper. Cook on low for 8 hours, uncovered.

Note: My husband is "famous" for this dish and is expected to bring it to every get together. We always bring copies of this recipe for those having this for the first time, because it's always requested!

Vivian Moore
West Harrison, Indiana

50191-03

CHUCK WAGON CASSEROLE

½ c. chopped onion	¾ c. barbecue sauce
½ c. green bell pepper	½ tsp. salt
1 lb. lean ground beef	1 (8½-oz.) pkg. corn muffin mix
1 (15½-oz.) can mild chili beans in sauce	1 (11-oz.) can Mexican-style corn (drained)

Preheat oven to 400°. In non-stick skillet, cook and stir ground beef, onion, salt and bell pepper over medium heat 8 to 10 minutes or until beef is no longer pink; drain. Stir in chili beans, barbecue sauce and salt. Bring to a boil. Spoon into a baking dish. In a bowl, prepare corn muffin mix according to package directions; stir in corn. Spoon over meat mixture. Bake 30 minutes or until golden brown.

Note: If you like it hot, use hot chili bean sauce.

Jerry E. Jones
Beaver Dam Lake, Indiana

SCALLOPED SWEET POTATOES AND APPLES

3 med. sweet potatoes	½ tsp. salt
2 med. tart apples, peeled & sliced (equaling 1½ c.)	4 T. brown sugar
	2 T. butter

Cook sweet potatoes until just tender. Peel and slice. Set aside. Mix salt, brown sugar and butter. In an oven safe dish (with lid) place a layer of potatoes and sprinkle with a bit of brown sugar mixture. Now add a layer of apples, sprinkling with brown sugar mixture as well. Keep alternating layers (sprinkling each layer with part of the brown sugar mixture) until all ingredients have been used. Bake, covered, at 350° for 50 minutes or until apples are tender. Remove cover the last 15 minutes to brown.

Note: My children learned to love sweet potatoes by eating this super dish.

Virginia Lundgren
Shoreview, Minnesota

YAM YUMS

2 baking apples (peeled & sliced)
1/3 c. chopped pecans
1/2 c. brown sugar (packed)
1/2 tsp. cinnamon

2 (17-oz.) cans yams (drained)
1/4 c. butter or margarine
2 c. mini marshmallows

Toss apples and nuts with combined brown sugar and cinnamon. Alternate layers of apple mixture and yams in 1½-quart casserole dish. Dot with butter and cover. Bake at 350° for 35 to 40 minutes. Sprinkle marshmallows over uncovered yams and apples and broil until lightly browned. Serves 6 to 8 people.

Note: Great with pork, turkey or ham. Serve with a slotted spoon. Serves 6 to 8. A wonderful fall or winter dish!

Mary Jo Karch
Cincinnati, Ohio

SWEET POTATO CASSEROLE

3 c. cooked & mashed sweet
  potatoes
1 c. sugar
2/3 c. coconut (opt.)

1 c. butter or margarine
2 eggs (beaten)
1 tsp. vanilla extract
1/2 c. vitamin D whole milk

Topping:

1 c. ground or chopped nuts
  (pecans, walnuts, etc.)
1 c. light brown sugar

1/2 c. flour
1/3 c. butter (melted)

Mix potatoes, 1 cup sugar, coconut, 1 cup butter, eggs, vanilla, and milk. Put in a large casserole dish. **Topping:** Combine nuts, brown sugar, flour and 1/3 cup melted butter. Sprinkle on top of potato mixture and bake at 350° for 25 to 30 minutes or until brown.

Note: This freezes very well.

Carole L. Tennant
Weir, Mississippi

50191-03

$\int$WISS SCALLOPED POTATOES

2 T. butter
2 T. flour
1 tsp. salt
1 c. milk
1 c. (½ pt.) sour cream
1½ c. grated Swiss cheese

1 T. dill weed
½ c. sliced green onions
3 c. cubed ham (opt.)
7-8 c. peeled, sliced, cooked
  potatoes

Topping:

1 c. grated Swiss cheese
½ c. butter (melted & cooled)

½ c. bread crumbs

Preheat oven to 375°. Spray 2-quart casserole dish with non-stick cooking spray. Melt butter in medium saucepan. Stir in salt and flour. Cook over medium heat for one or two minutes, until thick and bubbly. Stir in milk. Cook over medium heat, stirring constantly, until mixture thickens, approximately 5 to 7 minutes. Remove from heat and stir in sour cream. **For a main dish meal:** Stir in ham. In medium bowl toss 1½ cups Swiss cheese with dill weed and green onions. Layer ⅓ of potatoes, ½ of the sour cream mixture and ½ of the cheese mixture. Repeat layer. Layer remaining ⅓ of potatoes. Mix the remaining 1 cup of Swiss cheese, melted butter and bread crumbs (if you do not let the butter cool after melting, it will melt the cheese). Spread topping evenly over last layer of potatoes. Bake for 35 to 45 minutes, until topping is evenly browned.

Note: These are a huge hit everywhere I serve them. The recipe is always requested from folks trying them for the first time!

Molly Zahn
Oxford, Ohio

Job 17:7 -- Blessed is the man that trusteth in the LORD, and whose hope the LORD is.

SCALLOPED POTATOES

6 med. potatoes (peeled & sliced thin)
Approx. 3-4 T. flour (divided)

Salt & pepper to taste
Approx. 2½ c. milk
2 strips uncooked bacon

Line the bottom of a 2-quart casserole dish with one layer of potato slices. Sprinkle layer with 1 tablespoon flour. Lightly sprinkle salt and pepper. Add another layer of potatoes, cover with 1 tablespoon of flour. Again, lightly sprinkle with salt and pepper. Repeat process until all of the potatoes have been used. Cut bacon strips in half and lay on top of potatoes. Pour enough milk over all until the top layer of potatoes is covered. Cook in oven, covered, at 350° for 45 minutes. Uncover and cook an additional 15 minutes to brown bacon.

Andrea McAllister
Conyers, Georgia

BAKED POTATO CASSEROLE

8 potatoes (peeled, diced & cooked)
1 lb. American cheese (cut into strips)
1 c. mayonnaise

½ c. chopped onion
Salt & pepper to taste
½ lb. bacon (partially fried & chopped)
¼ c. sliced stuffed olives (opt.)

Combine potatoes, American cheese, mayonnaise, onion, salt and pepper. Grease a 9 x 13-inch pan. Spread potato mixture in pan. Top with bacon and (optional) olives. Bake at 325° for 1 hour.

Note: Great with or without the olives. I took this to a "gourmet" dinner party and EVERYBODY asked for the recipe!

Gayle Cogan
Cincinnati, Ohio

"There is life after breast cancer. As a 16 year cancer survivor, I am living proof. In time, there will be a cure, let's continue to support research!"
Cheryl Shaver

50191-03

OTATO BOATS

2 lg. Idaho or russet potatoes	¼ tsp. cumin (opt.)
1 lb. banana or butternut squash (approx. ½-¾ c.)	1 tsp. sea salt or seasoned salt or salt free seasoning
¼ c. plus tsp. butter (melted), divided	Sweet Hungarian paprika to sprinkle

Bake potatoes in preheated 425° oven until soft, about 60 minutes. While potatoes are baking, cut skin from squash. Cut squash into small cubes and place in vegetable steamer, covered, over boiling water for 15 minutes or until very soft. Cool potatoes slightly. Cut them in half while still warm and gently scrape pulp from skin, taking care not to tear skin. Combine squash, potato pulp, ¼ cup melted butter, cumin, and sea salt with potato masher or in food processor until you have a creamy yellow purée. Heap potato/squash mixture into empty potato shells. Brush with 2 teaspoons melted butter and sprinkle with paprika. Place under broiler for 10 minutes or until lightly browned. Serves 2 to 4, depending on size of potatoes.

Note: This is a very nourishing feast and delicious.

Alex Fraser
Courtenay, British Columbia, Canada

CREAMY HASH BROWNS

36 oz. frozen hash browns (partially defrosted)	½ c. chopped onion
½ c. butter	1 (10.5-oz.) can cream of chicken soup
1 tsp. salt	1 c. (½ pt.) sour cream

Topping:

2 c. crushed cornflakes	¼ c. melted butter

Mix butter, salt, chopped onion, cream of chicken soup, sour cream in pan on stove top until all blended and hot. Mix in large bowl with hash browns. Spread mixture evenly in 9 x 13-inch pan. **Topping:** Stir cornflakes together in bowl with melted butter. Spread evenly over mixture. Bake 45 minutes at 350°.

Note: Can be made ahead of time and frozen.

Pat Blaisdell
Shoreview, Minnesota

TEXAS POTATOES

2-lb. pkg. frozen hash browns
1 c. chopped onion
1 tsp. salt
1 (10.5-oz.) can cream of chicken
  soup
8 oz. extra sharp cheddar cheese
  (shredded)

1 c. margarine (melted & divided)
1/4 tsp. pepper
2 c. (1 pt.) sour cream
2 c. crushed cornflakes

Combine hash browns, onions, salt, soup, cheese, 1/2 cup melted margarine, pepper and sour cream. Stir well. Grease a 9 x 13-inch pan. Spread mixture in pan evenly. In separate bowl, mix cornflake crumbs and 1/2 cup butter. Spread over potato mixture. Bake dish at 350° for 1 hour.

Note: This can be made the day before and refrigerated until ready to bake.

Marianne Cronin
Crestview Hills, Kentucky

CHEESY SHREDDED POTATOES

1 (16-oz.) pkg. refrigerated
  shredded potatoes
1 (16-oz.) container sour cream
  (1 pt.)

1 (10.5-oz.) can cream of chicken
  soup
2 c. shredded cheddar cheese
9 x 13-in. pan

Combine potatoes, sour cream, soup and cheddar cheese. Mix well. Spray baking dish with non-stick spray. Place mixture in baking dish and bake at 350° for about 45 minutes. Top of potatoes will be slightly brown when done.

Note: Great to mix ahead of time and just pop in the oven when ready.

Amy Lovejoy
Fairborn, Ohio

50191-03

$\mathcal{P}$OTATO CASSEROLE

$3^1/_2$ lbs. russet potatoes or all-
  purpose potatoes (peeled &
  boiled)
$^1/_4$ tsp. onion salt
6 oz. cream cheese (softened)
$^2/_3$ c. sour cream
$^1/_4$ c. milk
$^3/_4$ tsp. salt
1 T. additional butter (melted) for
  topping
Paprika

Mash potatoes. Add onion salt, cream cheese, sour cream, milk and salt. Spread in a greased 9 x 13-inch pan. Drizzle butter over top and sprinkle with paprika. Refrigerate overnight. Let stand at room temperature for 30 minutes before baking at 350° for 30 minutes.

Harriett Schulte
Morehead, Kentucky

$\mathcal{D}$O AHEAD POTATOES

8-10 potatoes (peeled, cubed &
  boiled)
8 oz. cream cheese (softened)
1 c. ($^1/_2$ pt.) sour cream
1 tsp. garlic salt
1 tsp. onion salt
$^1/_4$ c. butter
Paprika

Boil potatoes and drain. Beat in cream cheese until fluffy. Blend in sour cream, garlic salt and onion salt. Dot with butter and sprinkle with paprika. Bake at 350° for about 40 minutes until puffy and warmed through. Can do ahead and refrigerate for 24 hours.

Barb White
Eatonton, Georgia

"A mind is like a parachute, it works best when it's open."
Unknown

HOMEMADE MACARONI AND CHEESE

8 oz. rotini noodles or elbow
  noodles

3 c. grated cheddar cheese

Sauce:

1/4 c. butter
1/4 c. flour
2 c. milk

1 tsp. salt
1/8 tsp. pepper

Preheat oven to 375°. Cook noodles following the directions on the box and drain the noodles. In 1½-quart shallow baking dish alternate the macaroni with 1¼ cups of grated cheese, do two layers of each ingredients. Set aside and prepare the sauce. **Sauce:** Melt the butter in a medium saucepan. Remove from the heat. Blend in the flour; gradually stir in the milk, then the salt and pepper. Bring to a boil, stirring for one minute. Pour sauce over the macaroni and cheese. Top with remaining cheddar cheese and bake for 15 to 20 minutes, or until cheese is melted and golden brown.

Note: This was given to me by my mother, who under went a breast biopsy a few years ago. The biopsy came back negative, thank goodness. This dish is good as a main course with a side salad also.

Lesley Kilgore
Batavia, Ohio

"THREE CHEESE" MACARONI AND CHEESE

2 c. ricotta cheese
2 c. fresh grated Parmesan cheese
2 c. grated mozzarella cheese
1 c. (½ pt.) heavy creamy
2 eggs

1 T. salt
Black pepper to taste
14 oz. elbow macaroni, cooked
½ c. dried bread crumbs
1/4 c. melted butter

In large bowl combine ricotta, Parmesan, mozzarella cheese, cream, eggs, salt and pepper. Add cooked macaroni. Press mixture into buttered 9 x 13 x 2-inch pan or Pyrex dish. Sprinkle with bread crumbs. Drizzle with melted butter. Bake in 400°oven, uncovered, for 40 minutes or until golden brown. Let set for 10 minutes.

Note: Very tasty! Great heated up next day in microwave.

Janet Scheuneman
St. Paul, Minnesota

50191-03

REDUCED FAT MACARONI AND CHEESE

12 oz. elbow macaroni
1 T. margarine
1 lg. onion (chopped)
2 c. low fat milk (divided)
2 T. flour
½ tsp. salt

¼ tsp. pepper
6 oz. sharp cheddar cheese (grated)
16 oz. low fat cottage cheese
2 tsp. Dijon mustard
¼ c. grated Parmesan cheese
1 T. dried bread crumbs

Preheat oven to 375°. Coat pan (9 x 13 inches) with cooking spray. Cook the macaroni in boiling water following package directions. Drain and rinse with cold water. Melt butter in saucepan and add chopped onion. Cook until soft. Combine ½ cup of the milk and the 2 tablespoons flour. Whisk with a fork or put in blender until mixed well. Stir into the onions and melted butter until mixed. Add remaining 1½ cups of milk all at once. Cook over low flame and stir until thickened. Remove from heat and stir in grated cheddar cheese. Purée cottage cheese with mustard in blender until smooth (or use small curd cottage cheese and mix well with a fork!). Gradually stir into cheddar cheese sauce. Combine the cheese sauce with the macaroni and spoon into prepared pan. Combine Parmesan cheese and bread crumbs and sprinkle over macaroni mixture. Bake for 35 minutes uncovered, or until bubbly, and serve warm.

Note: Macaroni and cheese is one of my all time favorite "comfort" foods and who needs comfort more than when you're going through the battle of a lifetime! And this recipe is so good for you! High in B vitamins and calcium and so easy going down! Hope you enjoy!

Lynn Leuschner
Rochester, New York

"If you can only guess the outcome, guess it will be a good one."
Sheryl Eisenbarth

MACARONI AND CHEESE

1½ c. uncooked elbow macaroni
   (about 6 oz.)
¼ c. butter
1 sm. onion, chopped finely
   (about ¼ c.)
½ tsp. salt
¼ tsp. pepper

¼ c. all-purpose flour
1¾ c. milk
4 oz. sharp cheddar cheese, cubed
4 oz. American cheese, cubed
½ c. bread crumbs for garnish
5 slices American cheese

Cook macaroni as directed on package. In a saucepan, cook and stir butter, onion, salt and pepper over medium heat until onion is tender. Blend in flour. Cook over low heat, stirring constantly, until mixture is smooth and bubbly. Remove from heat and stir in milk. Return to heat and heat to boiling, stirring constantly. Boil and stir 1 minute and remove from heat. Stir in cheese until melted. Place macaroni in an ungreased 1½-quart casserole dish, pour cheese mixture over and stir together. Place slices of cheese over the top and sprinkle with bread crumbs. Bake in 375° oven for 30 minutes. Makes 5 servings.

Esther Albritton
Tukwila, Washington

RICE PILAF

2 T. butter
1 crumbled coil vermicelli
   (approx. ½ c.)
1 c. rice
1 (14.5-oz.) can chicken broth
1 (10.5-oz.) can cream of chicken
   soup

1 c. water
1 env. onion soup mix
2 boneless chicken breasts
   (partially cooked & cut into
   pieces)

In skillet melt butter. Add vermicelli and rice. Brown all. Add chicken broth and cream of chicken soup. Mix well. Add chicken pieces, water and onion soup mix. Cover and steam until rice is tender.

Judy Kulhank
San Jose, California

50191-03

$\mathcal{G}$REAT GRANDMA'S BREAD STUFFING

1½ loaves white bread (cut or
   torn into cubes), divided
1 c. butter
2 c. minced onions
2 c. chopped celery (stalks &
   leaves)

Salt & pepper to taste (may need
   more salt if using unsalted
   butter)
Chicken broth, opt. (for moisture,
   according to preference)

Melt butter in large skillet. Add onions and celery, cook until yellow. Add 2 cups of bread cubes to skillet. Stir to prevent excessive browning. Fold into deep bowl with remaining bread cubes and mix lightly. Cool. Place in refrigerator. Use to stuff 12-pound turkey right before it is cooked. May bake stuffing alone at 325° for about 1 hour. **Optional:** Stir in chicken broth before baking for more moisture, according to preference.

Note: Enough to stuff a 12-pound turkey. Recipe has been in our family for 60 years.

Joel Karch
Celina, Ohio

Recipe Favorites

Recipe Favorites

50191-03

Main Dishes

Burt Keeble (right) and son - Oregon

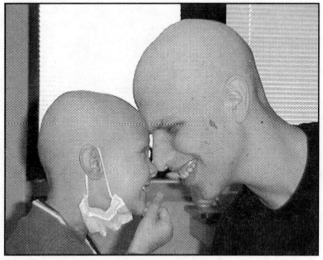

Arielle - New Jersey and Seth - Florida

Cancer and Christ

My childhood wasn't easy. Alcoholic parents. I witnessed my father's suicide. Sometimes we lived in tents, sometimes in our car.

But at 14, I came to know Christ and became very active in the church. When I was 18, I got married. We had two children.

Then Mom died, my brother disappeared and my marriage failed.

Just as things were changing (I had my Master's degree, married a fellow teacher and had two more children) I began to feel tired, achy and feverish. I found a lump in my breast while nursing my son. I was thirty-eight.

"God" I prayed, taking a breath in my soap opera life, "you couldn't possibly give me cancer." With money tight, and no medical benefits, there wasn't time to get sick.

God answered my prayer, but not as I had expected. Jesus never promised we wouldn't suffer - He himself endured pain for our sakes and then rose in new life, proving beauty can come at the end of suffering.

I had non-Hodgkin's lymphoma, intermediate grade, Stage 1 - very rare to show up in the breast, but actually good news. My oncologist called me "one in a million." I felt special.

Besides the nausea and the hair loss, I actually felt pretty good through the chemo, much better than while sick with the cancer.

Six years later, I still feel well. I speak at health fairs. I'm writing a sequel to my cancer survival book, "Crossing the Chemo Room" called "I Saw You in the Moon," which covers five years of post chemo recovery.

God has richly blessed us. No one is guaranteed a long life-span. Sometimes I'm afraid I'll find another lump. Then I remember Apostle Paul's words, "For God has not given us a spirit of fear, but of power, and of love, and of a sound mind."

Lonna Williams
Lake Arrowhead, California

Sample Lonna's books, visit www.lonnawilliams.com

Main Dishes

GRILLED SALMON

| 1-lb. salmon steak | 3 T. sugar |
| 5 T. kosher salt | Honey |

Mix salt and sugar in a zip lock bag. Add salmon. Seal bag and toss to coat. Leave salmon in mix for one hour prior to grilling. Rinse. Place on grill until fish turns without sticking (about 7 minutes). Turn and grill for another 2 minutes. Drizzle with honey. Grill 1 additional minute and remove.

Libby Cleves
Ft. Wright, Kentucky

GRILLED SALMON WITH ORANGE GLAZE

½ c. orange marmalade	1 garlic clove (minced)
2 tsp. olive oil	3 T. white vinegar
1 tsp. soy sauce	4 salmon fillets
½ tsp. ginger	

Combine marmalade, oil, soy sauce, ginger, garlic and vinegar thoroughly. Brush over salmon fillets. Grill over hot coals or on indoor grill about five minutes on each side. Serve on a bed of jasmine rice and garnish with sesame seeds and/or thinly sliced scallions.

Note: I like to fix this for my husband, who is a lung cancer survivor, because the healthy oils in salmon are good for the lungs.

Lee Ann Smith Ward
Huntington, West Virginia

GINGER SHRIMP AND VEGETABLE STIR FRY WITH RICE

½ lb. uncooked med. shrimp
  (peeled, deveined & thawed)
1 T. grated gingerroot
2 T. reduced sodium soy sauce
1 tsp. sesame or vegetable oil
½ c. chicken broth (fat-free,
  reduced-sodium)

3 c. packaged fresh stir fry
  vegetables (found in produce
  section)
1 tsp. cornstarch
4 c. hot cooked rice

Mix shrimp, gingerroot, soy sauce, and oil in shallow non-metal dish, cover and refrigerate for 45 minutes. Heat ¼ cup of broth in wok or skillet for 10 minutes. Add stir fry vegetables, and stir fry until liquid evaporates. Add shrimp mixture, stir fry 3 to 5 minutes or until shrimp are pink and firm. Mix cornstarch and remaining ¼ cup broth, stir into shrimp mixture. Cook 1 minute, or until sauce is thickened, stirring constantly. Serve over rice.

Note: Low fat dish. Three grams of fat; 1 gram saturated. It's worth buying the sesame oil, as it brings out the flavor of Asia.

Mary Jane Sassin
Park Hills, Kentucky

Matthew 11:28 -- Come unto me, all ye that labour and are heavy laden, and I will give you rest.

50191-03

MICROWAVE SHRIMP & SCALLOP SCAMPI

2 lbs. sea scallops
2 lbs. jumbo shrimp (16 ct.)
2 T. good extra virgin olive oil
½ c. butter (don't scrimp here, use
  the real stuff)

8 lg. cloves garlic
1 tsp. dried basil
½ tsp. dried oregano
Salt & pepper to taste
1 lb. pasta of your choice

Peel and devein the shrimp. Put the olive oil in the bottom of a microwave-safe, shallow dish and move the dish around to make sure the oil coats the entire bottom. In a bowl combine the scallops and shrimp. Crush (brings out more of the flavor) the cloves of garlic into the bowl and add the remaining dry ingredients. With your hands mix everything together lightly (without breaking the scallops or shrimp). Pour the seafood mixture into the oiled dish and spread evenly throughout the dish. Place all the butter in pats distributed over the top of the seafood mix and cover tightly with plastic wrap (I use two layers). Place in the microwave. Cook on medium (50%) power for about 20 minutes, or until desired doneness (I like mine fully cooked throughout).

Note: My microwave is about 1500 watts and has a rotating tray. If your's doesn't, please adjust time to suit, I use medium power because the microwave applies radiation in a on/off pattern, which keeps the food from cooking too fast and expanding the plastic wrap too much. (It will bubble up but then shrink down again as this process continues.) If your microwave does not have a rotating tray, rotate the tray ¼ turn manually every two minutes. PLEASE BE CAREFUL TAKING OFF THE PLASTIC WRAP AS IT WILL BE VERY HOT AND STEAMING! Serve, juices included, over the pasta of your choice. Serves my family only four servings but we're big eaters and love this dish.

Note: This was one of the few dishes that my son would eat and try to keep down when he was getting chemo. Always a favorite with everyone.

Bruce Paul
Staten Island, New York

STUFFED GROUPER FILLETS

⅓ c. chopped celery
2 T. chopped onion
⅓ c. butter (melted)
1 c. herb-seasoned stuffing mix
  (crushed fine - Pepperidge Farm
  Farmhouse Garden Herb)
1 T. chopped fresh parsley
1 tsp. grated lemon rind
1 T. lemon juice

¼ tsp. salt
¼ tsp. pepper
4 grouper fillets (about 1 lb.)
3 T. butter (melted)
¼ tsp. chopped fresh dill weed or
  ¼ tsp. dried whole dill
Paprika
4 lemon slices
Fresh dill weed

In a medium size skillet, sauté celery and onion in ⅓ cup melted butter, until tender. Remove from heat. Stir in stuffing mix, parsley, lemon rind, lemon juice, salt and pepper. Set aside. Cut each fillet in half. Arrange 4 halves in a lightly greased 9-inch square baking pan. Spoon ¼ of stuffing mixture on each. Top with a fillet half. Combine 3 tablespoons of melted butter and dill weed. Drizzle over stuffed fillets. Sprinkle with paprika. Place a lemon slice on each. Bake at 350° for 25 to 30 minutes or until fish flakes easily when tested with a fork. Garnish with fresh dill weed. Makes 4 servings.

Judy Cleves
Cincinnati, Ohio

SEAFOOD CASSEROLE

1 lb. canned or frozen crab meat
1 lb. cooked shelled shrimp
1 c. mayonnaise
½ c. chopped green pepper
¼ c. finely chopped onion

1½ c. finely chopped celery
½ tsp. salt
1 T. Worcestershire sauce
2 c. coarsely crushed potato chips
Paprika to sprinkle

Combine crab meat and shrimp. Add mayonnaise, green pepper, onion, celery salt, Worcestershire sauce. Butter a 2½-quart casserole dish. Pour into baking dish. Top with crushed potato chips, sprinkle with paprika. Bake at 400° for 20 to 25 minutes.

Louise Hickman
Morehead, Kentucky

50191-03

TUNA RICE CASSEROLE

1 c. milk
1 c. evaporated milk
⅓ c. cooking wine
1 (10.5-oz.) can cream of
  mushroom soup
1⅓ c. Minute rice
3 (6-oz.) cans tuna (drained)

1 (3-oz.) jar chopped mushrooms
2 T. parsley flakes
¼ tsp. minced garlic
2 T. toasted almonds
2 T. margarine
Sprinkle of paprika

Stir together milk, canned milk, wine and soup. Add Minute rice, tuna, mushrooms, parsley flakes, and garlic. Grease a 2-quart casserole. Pour mixture into pan. Top with almonds, margarine and paprika. Bake at 325° for 50 minutes.

Note: To toast almonds, sprinkle almond slices in ungreased heavy skillet. Cook over medium heat 5 to 7 minutes, stirring frequently until nuts begins to brown, then stirring constantly until golden brown.

Louise Hickman
Morehead, Kentucky

TUNA CASSEROLE

1 (10.5-oz.) can cream of
  mushroom soup
1 (6-oz.) can tuna in water
  (drained)

2 c. uncooked macaroni
1 c. cheese, opt. (any)
1 c. bread crumbs (opt.)

Boil macaroni according to directions and drain. In a 9 x 13-inch baking dish add macaroni, soup and tuna. (**Optional:** Top with cheese or bread crumbs.) Heat in 350° oven for approximately 25 minutes, or until thoroughly warmed.

Joan Scott
Batavia, Ohio

"Happiness Cake: Two heaping cups of patience, one heartful of love, dash of laughter, one handful of understading. Sprinkle generously with kindness. Add plenty of faith and mix well. Spread over a lifetime. Serve everyone you meet."

Unknown

CASHEW CHICKEN STIR-FRY

2 c. chicken broth, divided
¼ c. cornstarch
1 lb. boneless, skinless chicken
  breasts, cut in ½-in. strips
2 garlic cloves

1 (16-oz.) bag stir-fry vegetables
3 T. soy sauce
½ tsp. ground ginger
1½ c. cashews
Hot cooked rice, opt.

In a skillet, heat 3 tablespoons of broth. Meanwhile, combine the cornstarch, soy sauce, ginger and remaining broth until smooth; set aside. Add chicken to skillet; stir-fry over medium heat until no longer pink about 3 to 5 minutes. Remove and keep warm. Add garlic and stir-fry veggies and stir-fry till crisp tender, 4 to 5 minutes. Stir broth mixture; add to the skillet with chicken. Cook and stir for 2 minutes. Stir in cashews. Serve over rice if desired. Yields 4 servings.

Margie Bruns
Coldwater, Ohio

EASY CHICKEN & TOMATOES (PROSTATE FRIENDLY)

1 T. oil
1 T. butter
1 med. onion (coarsely chopped)
6-8 frozen boneless, skinless
  chicken tenderloins
Marjoram (generous to taste)

Salt & pepper to taste
1 (15-oz.) can Hunt's tomato
  sauce
1 (14.5-oz.) can Hunt's diced
  tomatoes (undrained)

Melt oil and butter. Place frozen tenderloins in non-stick skillet. Toss in onions. Sprinkle with salt, pepper or marjoram. Cook over medium heat until juices of chicken no longer run pink and onions are tender. Add tomato sauce and diced tomatoes (undrained). Serve over rice or pasta.

Note: Great quick dish! Can be doubled, tripled, etc. with ease. Never again worry about unexpected dinner guests with these easy to stock ingredients! Prostate friendly.

Mary Jo Karch
Cincinnati, Ohio

50191-03

CAJUN CHICKEN PASTA ALFREDO

5-6 boneless, skinless chicken
  breasts
Cajun seasoning of choice
12-oz. box rigatoni
2 T. olive oil
1 lg. red onion
1 red pepper

1 med. zucchini
8 oz. sliced button mushrooms
1 bunch fresh basil
16-oz. jar prepared Alfredo sauce
Fresh grated Parmesan cheese
Fresh grated pepper

Sprinkle Cajun seasoning over both sides of each chicken breast to lightly cover. Grill until cooked through (not pink in center). Cut chicken into strips and set aside. Slice onion, pepper, and zucchini into strips, then in skillet, sauté with olive oil, mushrooms and basil until just soft. Do not overcook! As the vegetables are cooking, cook rigatoni in water per package directions. Drain. Drain vegetables of excess olive oil. In large bowl, or serving platter, layer drained pasta, drained vegetables, strips of chicken. Cover generously with Alfredo sauce and toss until mixed and coated with sauce. Sprinkle with fresh Parmesan cheese, fresh grated pepper to taste. Serve immediately while still warm.

Note: Great restaurant quality dinner to serve to guests! Goes great with a fresh salad and bread.

Kelly Lynch
Middletown, Ohio

"Say a prayer just for today, and ask God's help along the way."
Bonnie Eddy, from the poem "Hello."

CHICKEN TETRAZZINI FOR 12 OR MORE

10 chicken breasts
16-oz. pkg. spaghetti
16 oz. fresh mushrooms
4 (10.5-oz.) cans cream of chicken
  soup
3 c. sour cream
1 (4-oz.) jar chopped pimento
  (drained)

½ c. butter
1 c. bread crumbs
Parmesan cheese to sprinkle
Approx. 4 c. chicken broth
Approx. 2 T. butter

Simmer 10 chicken breasts, in enough broth to cover, until cooked through. Remove skin and bones. Cut into large bite-size pieces. Break entire package of spaghetti into one-inch pieces. Cook and drain. Sauté mushrooms with 2 tablespoons butter. Mix together soup and sour cream. Mix together chicken, spaghetti, mushrooms, soup/sour cream and pimentos. Divide into two, buttered 9 x 13-inch baking dishes. Pour ¼ cup butter over each casserole. Sprinkle each with ½ cup bread crumbs and Parmesan cheese to taste. Bake at 300° for 40 minutes, or until bubbly. Can freeze, but thaw before baking. Serves at least 12 people.

Barb White
Eatonton, Georgia

CHICKEN AND SWISS CHEESE CASSEROLE

6 skinless, boneless chicken breast
  halves
6 slices Swiss cheese
1 (10.5-oz.) can condensed cream
  of chicken soup

¼ c. milk
1 (8-oz.) pkg. dry bread stuffing
  mix
½ c. melted butter

Preheat your oven to 350° (175° C). Lightly grease a 9 x 13-inch baking dish. Arrange chicken breasts in the baking dish. Place one slice of Swiss cheese on top of each chicken breast. Combine cream of chicken soup and milk in a medium bowl, and pour over chicken breasts. Sprinkle with stuffing mix. Pour melted butter over top, and cover with foil. Bake for 50 minutes, or until chicken is no longer pink and juices run clear.

Note: A tasty dish to try on the family!

Amanda Smith
AML Leukemia Survivor
Ocala, Florida

50191-03

EASY BAKED CHICKEN

4 boneless, skinless chicken
  breasts
1 (6-oz.) box Stove Top stuffing
1 (10½-oz.) can cream of chicken
  soup

4 slices Swiss cheese
1 (10½-oz.) soup can of water or
  opt. wine
2 T. butter

Preheat oven to 350°. Spray a large baking dish with Pam. Spread stuffing in dish. Lay chicken on top of stuffing. Combine water (or optional wine) and soup. Pour over chicken and stuffing. Dot with butter. Top with cheese. Cover with foil. Bake at 350° for 60 minutes.

Note: Great for working moms!

Kandy Collins
Proctorville, Ohio

CHICKEN & STUFFING CASSEROLE

3- to 4-lb. chicken, skinned,
  cooked & deboned
1 (10.5-oz.) can cream of
  mushroom, celery or chicken
  soup (any of 3 is good)
¾ c. milk

½ c. butter or margarine
1 c. chicken broth
1 (8-oz.) pkg. Pepperidge Farm
  seasoned stuffing mix, crumb-
  style

Preheat oven to 350°. Spray or grease a 9 x 13-inch baking pan. Spread chicken, cut into bite-size pieces, in a 9 x 13-inch baking dish. Mix soup and milk together and pour over chicken. Melt butter or margarine, mix together with broth and stuffing mix, crumble over the top of the coated chicken. Bake uncovered, at 350°, approximately 20 minutes, or until hot and bubbly. Serves 4 to 6.

Note: In loving memory of my Uncle Bob Case.

Pat Bruce
Batavia, Ohio

CHICKEN CASSEROLE

6-8 boneless, skinless chicken
  breasts (can precook in
  microwave)
4 T. butter or margarine
4 T. flour
4 c. milk

1 tsp. salt
1/4 tsp. pepper
2 1/2 c. shredded cheddar cheese
  (divided)
1 lg. (6-oz.) can Durkee onions
  (divided)

Cheese mixture: Melt butter or margarine in pan. Add flour and stir. Add milk and stir until thickens. Add salt, pepper, 2 cups of the cheese and 1/2 of the can of onions. Stir together. Place chicken in 9 x 13-inch casserole dish. Pour cheese mixture over top, bake 50 minutes at 350°. Turn oven off and sprinkle the rest of the onions and 1/2 cup of cheese on top of casserole. Place dish in oven for 10 more minutes. Remove and serve.

Anonymous
Cincinnati, Ohio

CHICKEN SOUFFLÉ

8 slices day old bread
2 c. cooked chicken
1 c. mayonnaise
1 c. diced celery
1 c. onion (finely chopped)
1 c. green pepper (finely chopped)

Salt & pepper to taste
4 eggs (beaten)
3 c. milk
1 (10 1/2-oz.) can cream of
  mushroom soup
1 c. grated cheddar cheese

Cut 4 slices of the bread into cubes. Remove crusts from the other 4 slices. Line bottom of baking dish with bread cubes. Combine chicken, mayonnaise, celery, onion and green pepper, season to taste with salt and pepper. Spread this mixture over bread cubes. Cover with reserved 4 bread slices. Combine beaten eggs and milk and pour over bread slices. Cover and place in refrigerator overnight. One hour before serving, bake soufflé in 350° oven for 15 minutes. Remove and pour undiluted cream of mushroom soup over mixture and continue to bake for 30 more minutes. Sprinkle top with grated cheese and return to oven for an additional 15 minutes. Yield: 10 to 12 servings.

Note: From Kitchen Memories, written by Lynn.

Lynn Ellinghausen
Brent, Alabama

50191-03

CHICKEN AND RICE CASSEROLE

1½ c. Uncle Ben's rice
2½ c. water
1 pkg. Lipton onion soup mix
1 or 2 (10.5-oz.) cans cream of
  mushroom soup

4 chicken breasts
Dried parsley
Paprika

Spread rice evenly in a 9 x 13-inch casserole dish. Pour in water. Sprinkle onion sop mix over rice and water. Place chicken breasts in dish. Pour 1 or 2 cans of cream of mushroom soup over chicken. Sprinkle parsley and paprika on top. Cover with foil. Bake for 2 hours at 350°. Remove foil during the last 20 minutes of cooking.

Paula Kidney
Ft. Thomas, Kentucky

CHICKEN AND ALMONDS

2 c. diced cooked chicken
1 (10.5-oz.) can cream of chicken
  soup
¾ c. mayonnaise
1 c. diced celery
1 c. uncooked rice
1 T. lemon juice

1 T. grated onion
½ tsp. salt
1 (3- or 4-oz.) can mushrooms
2 T. butter
1 c. cornflakes
½ c. almonds

Mix chicken, soup, mayonnaise, celery, rice, lemon juice, onion, salt and mushrooms gently. Spoon into 2-quart casserole. Melt 1 to 2 tablespoons butter in small frying pan and combine with 1 cup cornflakes and ½ cup almonds for topping. Pour topping onto mixture in the casserole dish. Bake at 375° for 30 minutes.

Jack Herring
Fort Walton Beach, Florida

"The world of achievement has always belonged to the optimists."
J. Harold Wilkins

"NIGHT BEFORE" ALMOND CHICKEN CASSEROLE

2 heaping c. cooked, cubed chicken
1 c. cooked rice
1 (10.5-oz.) can cream of chicken
  soup

2 T. minced onions
2 T. lemon juice
³/₄ c. mayonnaise (not Miracle
  Whip)

Topping:

½ c. sliced almonds
½ c. cornflakes

½ c. Special K cereal
¼ c. melted butter

Combine chicken, rice, cream of chicken soup, onions, lemon juice and mayonnaise and place in buttered casserole dish overnight. The next day, combine almonds, cornflakes, Special K, melted butter and spread on top of chicken mixture. Bake at 350° for 45 minutes.

Sister Mary Florence, SND
Covington, Kentucky

RIDICULOUSLY EASY OVEN FRIED CHICKEN

3 c. cornflake crumbs
1 cut up chicken

¼ c. butter or margarine (melted)
Salt & pepper to taste

Rinse the chicken, dry with paper towels, then brush skin with melted butter or margarine. Roll in cornflake crumbs. Sprinkle with salt and pepper to taste. To make clean up really easy, line a large, shallow baking pan with aluminum foil. Arrange chicken, skin side up, in the pan. Don't let the chicken pieces touch each other. They need room to get crispy on all sides. Bake in a 375° oven for 50 minutes or until chicken is done.

Hint: If you don't have cornflake crumbs, use ½ cup of bread crumbs instead.

Note: I am a cancer survivor, a volunteer with the Thyroid Cancer Survivors' Association, www.thyca.org, and the author of several songs which lend humor to a difficult time, www.thyroidcancersongs.com.

Megan Stendebach
San Antonio, Texas

50191-03

CHICKEN AND STRIP DUMPLINGS

4 T. Crisco (melted)	1 c. milk (boiling hot)
3 c. plain flour (divided)	2 eggs
1 tsp. baking powder	½ tsp. sugar
1 tsp. baking soda	1 whole chicken fryer (cut up)

Fill a large heavy pot with water and boil chicken. When tender, remove from pot and set aside. Keep water (now broth) boiling. In a separate bowl, add 2½ cups flour, Crisco, salt, baking powder, sugar, eggs and 1 cup of the warm broth from the still boiling pot. Cover pot and turn off heat. Set pot/broth aside for later use. Combine flour mixture well until stiff dough is formed. Divide dough into 2 equal parts and refrigerate until cold. When cold, roll out each half thin, on well floured (use approximately ½ cup flour) board or flat surface, into a square. Start at one end and roll dough up like a long jellyroll. You will now have two "jellyrolls" of dough. Meanwhile, return your chicken broth to a boil. Begin cutting ½-inch slices from each "jellyroll", dropping each piece into the boiling broth. Pour hot milk over dumplings as they boil in broth. Cook with lid on until cooked through. Do not stir. Add chicken or serve separately.

Note: I'd like to dedicate this recipe to my mother Clara Allen. This recipe has been in the family for more than 50 years. I remember my mother making these when I was a little girl.

Evelyn Adams
Barboursville, West Virginia

CREAMY MUSHROOM CHICKEN

3 chicken breasts (cut in ½ to make 6 pieces)	1 c. (½ pt.) sour cream
1 (10.5-oz.) can mushroom soup	8 oz. noodles
	Salt, pepper to taste

Salt and pepper chicken. Mix soup and sour cream together. Spread half of the mixture in a shallow baking pan or dish. Arrange chicken on top of mixture. Cook 1 hour at 375°. Cook noodles according to package and stir in remaining soup and sour cream mixture. Put noodles on top of chicken and return to oven to heat through.

Note: Great for a family of four and easy to make.

Pat Purdy
Marion, Indiana

$\mathcal{E}$DWINA BURKE'S CHICKEN BROCCOLI CASSEROLE

1 lb. broccoli (if frozen 16-oz. pkg.)
5-6 skinless chicken breasts
1 (10.5-oz.) can cream of chicken soup
¼ c. heavy whipping cream
Salt & pepper (to taste)
½ c. grated Parmesan cheese
1 T. butter
Paprika

Cook broccoli until tender. Cook chicken breasts (boil approximately 40 minutes). Place broccoli in greased casserole dish with chicken. Chicken can be either whole or bite-size pieces. In saucepan, mix soup, whipping cream, seasoning and ¼ cup of cheese. Heat until well blended. Pour over chicken and broccoli. Sprinkle on remaining cheese, dot with butter. Sprinkle with paprika. Bake at 450° for 15 minutes; if in refrigerator, bake 25 minutes.

Note: Great for dinner parties. When serving as leftovers, double the sauce.

Gail Arnold
Cincinnati, Ohio

$\mathcal{C}$RUNCHY CHICKEN CASSEROLE

3-3½ c. diced cooked chicken
1 (4-oz.) can mushrooms (drained)
2 (8½-oz.) cans cut asparagus (drained)
1 (8½-oz.) can sliced water chestnuts (drained)
1 (10½-oz.) can cream of chicken soup
1 (10½-oz.) can cream of mushroom soup
½ c. mayonnaise
¼ c. chopped green olives
1½ c. cracker crumbs or dry Pepperidge Farms stuffing

Combine cream of chicken soup and cream of mushroom soup. Gently add chicken, mushrooms, asparagus, water chestnuts, mayonnaise and olives. Spoon into a 2-quart casserole dish. Top with 1½ cups cracker crumbs or dry Pepperidge Farm stuffing mix. Bake at 350° for about 30 minutes until topping slightly browns. Serves 8 people.

Note: Freezes beautifully!

Jack Herring
Fort Walton Beach, Florida

50191-03

TEXAS CHICKEN FOR TWO

2 lg. pieces heavy-duty Reynold's Wrap
2 boneless, skinless chicken breasts
1 (11-oz.) sm. jar salsa (any type)
1 (15.25-oz.) can white or yellow corn (well drained)
1 (15-oz.) can black beans (well drained)
Cheddar cheese as desired
Tortilla chips
Sour cream

Preheat oven to 450°. Place each chicken breast on a piece of foil. Divide each can (beans, corn, salsa) in half and place on top of the chicken. Fold up foil to create a tight packet. Place on a baking pan and bake for 35 minutes. Remove from oven and lay packets in the sink. Using a knife or fork, gently poke holes in the bottom of packet, to allow excess liquid to run out. Open packets and sprinkle with cheese, then spoon onto a bed of tortilla chips. Serve with sour cream.

Note: Very quick to prepare, and very yummy!

Lisa Millikin
Corpus Christi, Texas

"What the mind conceives the body believes."

Yvonne Cole

Sour Cream Enchilada Casserole

2 whole chicken breasts
2 (10½-oz.) cans cream of chicken soup
1 pt. (2 c.) sour cream
1 (4-oz.) can chopped green chilies (save some for garnish)
1 doz. flour tortillas (8 in.)
¼ c. chopped onion
3 c. grated cheddar or Monterey Jack cheese (or a combination of both)
Ripe black olives

Boil chicken breasts in enough water to cover, 20 to 25 minutes. Remove meat from bone and chop. Mix chicken meat, soup, sour cream, and the chilies together. Spread a thin layer of creamed mixture over the bottom of a 9 x 13-inch pan. Spread equal amounts of creamed mixture down the middle of each tortilla (reserve some creamed mixture for top). Roll up tortilla and place seam side down in prepared pan. Pour remaining mixture over the top of the rolled tortillas and sprinkle with remaining cheese. Bake 25 to 30 minutes at 350°. Garnish with black olives and additional chilies.

Note: Can be prepared ahead of time and refrigerated before baking. Serves 6 to 8.

Note: This was a favorite of mine during my recovery of cancer.

Marci A. Breinholt
Salt Lake City, Utah

"I am a slow walker, but I never walk backwards."
Abraham Lincoln

50191-03

CHICKEN ENCHILADAS

1 onion (chopped)
½ c. butter
4-oz. can diced green chilies
2 (10-oz.) cans chicken broth
5 chicken breasts (cooked &
  cubed)

6 T. flour
2 tsp. cumin
¼ tsp. ground pepper
12 (8-in.) flour tortillas
2 c. Monterey Jack cheese

Brown onion in 2 tablespoons butter; add chilies and mix in chicken. Set aside. Melt remaining butter and add flour, pepper and cumin. Gradually add broth and cook until thickened. Add ½ cup butter sauce and ½ cup cheese to chicken mixture. Pour ½ of the remaining butter sauce in bottom of 9 x 13-inch pan. Fill tortillas with chicken mixture, roll up, lay in pan and cover with rest of the sauce and cheese. Bake uncovered for 30 minutes at 350°.

Note: Everyone will love this dish!

Chris Soranno
Flower Mound, Texas

CHICKEN POT PIE

3 c. cooked chicken (cubed)
½ lb. lean pork sausage
  (sautéed & drained well)
¼ c. butter
⅓ c. flour
1 garlic clove (minced)

1 (10½-oz.) can chicken broth
⅔ c. milk
Salt & pepper to taste
1 (10-oz.) pkg. frozen peas &
  carrots (thawed & drained)

Topping:

Favorite crust, such as phyllo
  dough, pie crust or canned
  biscuit

Melt butter over medium heat. Stir in flour and cook for 1 or 2 minutes until flour loses its starchy taste and the resulting roux is lightly colored. Don't let brown. Add garlic, broth, and milk. Cook, stirring constantly, until thickened. Add sausage and chicken. Blend well. Add peas and carrots, salt and pepper. Spread mixture in a sprayed casserole dish and top with your favorite crust. Bake at 375° until mixture is bubbly and dough has browned (approximately 20 or 25 minutes).

Carol A. Mullen
Ft. Wright, Kentucky

*M*OM'S TURKEY BURGERS

1 lb. ground turkey
2 slices of onion (chopped)
1 arm of celery (chopped)
1 T. Wesson oil or butter
1 egg (beaten)

1 slice white bread
1 c. cornflakes
Salt & pepper to taste
¼ c. Wesson oil (for frying
  patties)

Place onion, celery and oil in pan. Sauté until soft. Set aside. In a separate bowl, beat egg. Break bread into small cubes and add to egg until bread is moist. Add dash of salt and pepper. Work in cornflakes until moist. Add onions and celery. Add ground turkey. Make turkey into patties and fry in Wesson oil (add to pan 1 tablespoon at a time, as needed to prevent sticking). Add a bit of water to pan to help keep pan moist.

Note: I am a survivor of Hodgkin's disease stage IIIB! This recipe given to me by Barbara Nowak.

Donna Nowak
Brooklyn, New York

*I*MPOSSIBLE TURKEY PIE

2 c. cut-up cooked turkey
1 (4½-oz.) jar sliced mushrooms
  (drained)
½ c. sliced green onions
½ tsp. salt

1 c. shredded natural Swiss cheese
1½ c. milk
3 eggs (beaten)
¼ c. Bisquick baking mix

Filling: Lightly mix turkey, mushrooms, green onions, salt and Swiss cheese. Grease 10-inch pie plate. Place mixture in pie plate. Combine milk, eggs and Bisquick in blender and mix for 15 seconds on high (may beat 1 minute by hand mixer). Pour over other ingredients in pie plate. Bake at 400° until knife inserted in center, and around edges, comes out clean (30 to 35 minutes). Cool 5 minutes before serving.

Louise Hickman
Morehead, Kentucky

50191-03

KENTUCKY HOT BROWN

Sauce:

2 T. butter
¼ c. flour
2 c. milk
¼ tsp. salt

1 tsp. Worcestershire sauce
¾ c. grated sharp cheddar cheese
¼ c. Parmesan cheese

Hot brown:

8 slices bread (toasted)
16 thin slices turkey (divided)
16 thin slices ham (divided)
16 slices tomato, lightly salted &
  peppered (divided)

12 slices bacon
4 c. (16 oz.) Parmesan cheese
  (divided)
4 ovenproof baking dishes

Sauce: Melt butter in saucepan. Add flour and stir well. Add milk, cheddar cheese, Parmesan cheese, salt, and Worcestershire sauce. Cook while constantly stirring. **To make individual hot browns:** Cut crust from 8 slices of toasted bread. Cut into half diagonally. Place 4 triangles of bread on bottom of each ovenproof serving container. Layer 4 slices of turkey and 4 slices of ham on top of toast. Cover with the hot cheese sauce. Top with 4 lightly salted and peppered tomato slices and 3 partially cooked bacon slices. Sprinkle 1 cup grated Parmesan cheese. Bake at 425° until bubbly. Makes 4 servings.

Note: Originated at the Brown Hotel, Louisville, Kentucky, late 1920's.

Sr. Jeanne Francis Cleves, SND
Morehead, Kentucky

"There is no such thing in anyone's life as an unimportant day."
Alex Woollcott

KENTUCKY HOT BROWN #2

Sauce:

¼ c. margarine
¼ c. all-purpose flour

2 c. milk
2 chicken bouillon cubes

Hot brown:

6 toasted bread slices
6 slices ham
6 slices turkey
6 sliced cheddar cheese

6 slices tomato
6 slices fried bacon
Approx. 1 c. mushrooms, opt.

White sauce: Melt margarine over low heat. Add flour, stirring until smooth. Cook 1 minute, stirring constantly. Gradually add milk and bouillon cubes and cook over medium heat, stirring until thick and bubbly. Set aside. **Hot brown:** Place 6 slices of toast in a buttered 9 x 13-inch baking dish. Top each slice of bread with turkey and ham slices. Spoon white sauce over meat slices. Place slice of cheddar cheese over sauce, top with a tomato slice and crumbled bacon. **Optional:** Top with mushrooms as well. Bake at 350° for 20 to 25 minutes.

Sr. Jeanne Frances Cleves, SND
Morehead, Kentucky

Genesis 15:1   Fear not Abram, I am thy shield, and thy exceeding great reward.

50191-03

QUICHE LORRAINE

9-in. (1-crust) pie crust
12 slices bacon, crisply fried &
  crumbled
1 c. Swiss cheese, shredded
1/3 c. onion, chopped finely

4 eggs
2 c. (1 pt.) half-and-half
3/4 tsp. salt
1/4 tsp. pepper
1/8 tsp. red pepper

Prepare pastry, or use premade pastry crust. Sprinkle bacon, cheese and onion in pastry shell. Beat eggs slightly and add half-and-half, salt, pepper and red pepper. Pour egg mixture over pastry shell. Bake uncovered in 425° oven for 15 minutes. Reduce oven temperature to 300°. Cook uncovered until a knife inserted halfway between center and edge comes out clean, about 30 minutes. Let stand 10 minutes before cutting. **Make ahead tip:** After sprinkling pastry shell with bacon, cheese and onion, cover and refrigerate. Beat remaining ingredients, cover and refrigerate. Store no longer than 24 hours. Stir egg mixture before pouring into pastry shell. Continue as directed but increase second cooking time to about 45 minutes. **Chicken quiche:** Substitute 1 cup chicken, cooked and chopped in place of bacon, 1½ teaspoons dried thyme in place of the red pepper. **Crab quiche:** Substitute 1 (7½-ounce) can crab meat, drained with the cartilage removed in place of the bacon. Pat crab meat dry with paper towels. Increase salt to 1 teaspoon.

Note: I make this a lot. It is quick and easy and even more so with premade pie shells I keep on hand.

Esther Albritton
Tukwila, Washington

"Our greatest glory is not in never failing but in rising up every time we fail."

Ralph Waldo Emerson

ꟅPAM SPREAD

12-oz. can Spam luncheon meat	1 sm. jar pimento olives
8 oz. shredded cheddar cheese	3 T. mayonnaise
2 hard-cooked eggs (chopped)	½ c. chili sauce
⅓ c. onion (chopped)	12 hot dog buns or loaf of bread

Chop or grate the Spam luncheon meat, cheddar cheese, boiled eggs, and onion. Mix together. Slice the olives and add to the mixture. Blend in the mayonnaise and chili sauce. You can serve this cold on bread or buns, or you can put in 12 hot dog rolls and wrap in foil and bake at 400° for 15 minutes. Can be frozen.

Note: Great to have on hand for lunches!

Diane & Terry O'Keefe
Erie, Pennsylvania

"We are what we repeatedly do; therefore, excellence is not an act, but a habit."

Aristotle

50191-03

GLAZED HAM BALLS

2 eggs
½ c. pineapple juice
½ c. fine cornflakes*
¼ c. chopped onion

2 T. chopped parsley (I use parsley
  flakes, 4 tsp.)
1 lb. ground ham
1 lb. ground lean pork

Beat eggs lightly. Add pineapple juice, cornflakes, onion and parsley. Mix well. Add ground ham and ground pork, mix gently. Shape into balls allowing a rounded tablespoon for each. Arrange ham balls in single layer in shallow baking pan. Bake 30 minutes at 350°. *Put cornflakes in plastic bag and crush with rolling pin.

Sauce/Glaze:

½ c. brown sugar
1 c. pineapple juice
1 T. cornstarch
½ tsp. dry mustard

¼ tsp. cloves
¼ c. light corn syrup
2 T. vinegar (white/clear vinegar)

Combine brown sugar, cornstarch, mustard and cloves in saucepan. Gradually stir in pineapple juice, corn syrup and vinegar. Cook and stir until thickened. Remove ham balls from oven and drain off any excess fat. Pour thickened sauce/glaze over ham balls and return to oven to bake about 15 minutes at 350°. Makes 8 servings.

Note: I'm a 2 year soft tissue sarcoma survivor, 36 year old wife and mother of two boys. I'm grateful to all 4 of my wonderful doctors, to my loving, supporting husband, his family, and all my great friends who were there during the down moments.

Donna Mulinski
Elsie, Michigan

"Nothing will ever be attempted if all possible objections must first be overcome."

Samuel Johnson

SWEET AND SOUR PORK

1 T. cooking oil
2 lbs. stew pork meat (cubed)
1 bulb of garlic (crushed with
  skin)
2 sm. Thai chilies or jalapeño,
  opt. to taste (chopped or whole)
1 med. onion (cubed)
2 leeks (chopped)

2 med. tomatoes (cubed)
¼ c. vinegar
3 T. sugar
2 T. fish sauce/soy sauce
2 T. rice wine/cooking wine (opt.)
Salt & pepper to taste
½ c. water

Sear the pork meat with oil until brown with crushed garlic and chili peppers. Add onion, leeks, tomatoes, vinegar, sugar, fish sauce/soy sauce, wine, salt, pepper and just enough water to cover the meat. Cook under medium heat until meat is tender, approximately 2 hours. Best served the next day. Flavor can be adjusted according to personal taste. Serve over a bed of steamed rice with steamed or stir fried vegetables.

Note: My wife is Chinese and she knows how to serve and eat pork.

Paul and Jennie Leverett
Houston, Texas

"If God brings you to it, He will bring you through it."

Unknown

50191-03

NASI GORENG

4 eggs
1⅓ T. Japanese or Chinese soy
  sauce
3 T. vegetable oil (or palm oil, if
  available)
2 T. peanut butter
2 sm. onions (minced)
½ sm. bay leaf
½ clove garlic (minced)
½ tsp. ground cumin seed
⅓ c. pork (minced)
⅓ c. shrimp (cooked & shelled)

1 tsp. ground coriander
Pinch of mace
⅓ c. lump crabmeat
Salt & pepper to taste
¼ c. celery (chopped fine)
1⅓ c. hot red peppers (sliced thin)
  more or less to taste
⅓ c. fried crisp onion flakes
1⅓ c. cold cooked rice
Strips of Smithfield ham as
  desired

Beat eggs. Heat skillet and grease with a few drops of oil. Make 4 thin omelets by putting 2 tablespoons of the beaten egg at a time into the skillet, tipping to spread over the bottom of the pan thinly. Cook over moderate heat until light brown underneath. Roll each omelet and cut into ⅛-inch strips. Reserve for garnish. Add 1 tablespoon of oil to skillet and heat. Pour in remaining beaten eggs and make 1 thicker omelet. Cut into ½-inch squares. Fry onions and garlic in 1 tablespoon of oil for 2 minutes. Add pork and cook until done, stirring constantly. Add shrimp, omelet squares, soy sauce blended with peanut butter, salt, pepper, ½ bay leaf, cumin, coriander and mace. Stir until mixed, then add rice. Continue cooking on low heat for 10 minutes longer. Garnish with sliced omelets, red peppers, strips of ham, crabmeat, celery and onion flakes. Serve with side dishes of chilled, thinly sliced cucumbers, sliced bananas, and unripe fruit chutney.

Note: Delicious! Time consuming but well worth the effort. Once you learn to make this dish, it is not hard if you follow directions. This recipe is from the Hotpoint Storybook Kitchen Cookbook and is taken from the Indonesian Restaurant at the New York World's Fair.

Shirley Satterfield
Daisy, Oklahoma

ℬAKED PORK CHOPS

6 (1-in.) pork chops
1 T. flour

1½ env. dry onion soup mix
2½ c. boiling water

Brown chops lightly in frying pan. Remove to a 9 x 13-inch baking pan. Add flour and soup mix to frying pan. Blend in boiling water. Stir until flour and soup mix is dissolved. Pour over pork chops. Cover with foil and bake at 350° for 35 minutes. Uncover and bake another 35 minutes.

Note: A warm and comforting meal that's easy to prepare.

Robin Govenitto
Hamburg, New York

𝒮AUCY PORK CHOPS

6 (½-in. thick) pork chops
1 T. vegetable oil
1½ c. applesauce

¼ c. soy sauce
1 T. instant onion flakes
⅛ tsp. cinnamon

Brown pork chops slowly in oil and set aside. In mixing bowl, combine applesauce, soy sauce, onion flakes, and cinnamon. In a shallow baking pan, arrange pork chops in a single layer. Spoon applesauce mixture evenly over pork chops. Cover pan with foil. Bake for 45 minutes at 350°. Remove foil, turn pork chops over. Recover pork chops with applesauce mixture in pan. Return to oven and bake, uncovered, for 15 minutes.

Connie Roenker
Cincinnati, Ohio

"If we did all the things we are capable of doing, we would literally astound ourselves."

Thomas Edison

50191-03

NORTH CAROLINA BARBECUED PORK

2 onions (quartered)
2 T. brown sugar
1 T. paprika
2 tsp. salt

½ tsp. ground black pepper
1 (4- to 6-lb.) boneless pork butt
   or shoulder roast

Sauce:

4 tsp. Worcestershire sauce
1½ tsp. crushed red pepper flakes
1½ tsp. sugar
½ tsp. dry mustard

½ tsp. garlic salt
¼ tsp. cayenne
¾ c. cider vinegar

Place onions in crockpot or in large pan. Combine brown sugar, paprika, salt and pepper. Rub over roast. Place roast on top of onions in pan. Combine ingredients for sauce and stir to mix well. Drizzle about ⅓ of mixture over roast. Cover and refrigerate remaining mixture. Cover pan/crockpot and cook on low for 8 to 10 hours (high 4 to 6 hours) or until pork falls off of bone. Drizzle about ⅓ of reserved sauce over roast during last ½ hour of cooking. Remove meat and onions. Shred pork using two forks and chop onions. Serve with buns and remaining sauce.

Andrea Hounshell
Raleigh, North Carolina

TANGY BARBECUE SANDWICHES

1 c. onion (chopped)
1 c. ketchup
1 c. barbecue sauce
1 c. water
2 T. vinegar
2 T. Worcestershire sauce
2 T. brown sugar

1 tsp. chili powder
1 tsp. salt
½ tsp. pepper
½ tsp. garlic powder
1 (3- to 4-lb.) trimmed, boneless
   chuck roast
14-18 hamburger buns

In a slow cooker, combine onion, ketchup, barbecue sauce, water, vinegar, Worcestershire sauce, brown sugar, chili powder, salt, pepper and garlic powder. Mix well. Add roast. Cover and cook for 6 to 7 hours on low. Remove roast and cool. Shred meat and return to sauce in slow cooker. Heat through. Serve on buns.

Jana Cleves
Brookfield, Wisconsin

$\mathcal{E}$ASY BEEF BARBEQUE

2-lb. chuck roast (cut into 1-in. cubes)
1 (24-oz.) bottle ketchup
24 oz. water

2 lg. onions (sliced)
4 arms celery (chopped)
2 bay leaves

Brown the cubed meat in a heavy roaster. When brown, add the onions, celery and bay leaves. Add the ketchup. Fill empty ketchup bottle completely with water, pour over meat. Roast in a 325° oven with the lid on for 5 to 6 hours. Check frequently, making sure the liquid always just covers the beef. If needed, add more water or ketchup to keep beef covered. When very tender, remove the bay leaves. Mash the cubed meat with a heavy potato masher. This is the basic recipe. It will serve 10 people. Serve on buns. The flavor is mild. If you want more of a "bite", add a large tablespoon of chili powder or teaspoon of hot sauce.

Note: A long time family favorite. It is easily halved or doubled. Pork may be substituted for the beef.

Marlene Dickman
Park Hills, Kentucky

$\mathcal{C}$HILI DOGS FOR THE GANG

3 (15-oz.) cans chicken chili
3 (15-oz.) cans pork & beans
1/2 c. chopped onion
1 c. grater cheddar cheese
21 Hebrew National hot dogs

Sesame seed buns
1 bottle ketchup
1 bottle mustard
1 bottle relish

Mix chili with pork and beans in large saucepan. Bring to a boil and simmer for about 5 minutes. Put hot dogs in a pot of boiling water and boil for about 5 minutes. Place cheese and onion in separate bowls. Let everyone put their own hot dogs together. For a finishing touch, you can microwave the chili dogs for 30 seconds to melt the cheese and heat the bun. Make ketchup, mustard and relish available to those who do not care for chili. Serves 10 to 12 people.

Note: Simple, hot and yummy! Great for guests on a Sunday afternoon after church. Serve with chips or fresh fruit.

Lonna Williams
Lake Arrowhead, California

50191-03

ROASTED HOT DOGS

1 (8-ct.) pkg. hot dogs	*Ketchup, mustard or relish,*
8 hot dog buns	*possible garnish*

Build a campfire. Skewer the dogs on some kind of roasting implement (coat hanger, long handled fork, etc.). Insert the dogs into the flames or against the glowing embers, and let 'em cook till they're done the way you like 'em. I like mine charred. Stick 'em in a bun and garnish to taste. I don't worry about hot dogs being bad for you. After all, you're dealing with cancer, so what's a hot dog compared to that??!!

Note: Four days after my surgery, my son, Brian, our friend Jay and I, went camping. We had a splendid hot dog roast and enjoyed our food in that crisp mountain air. All while being treated to a magnificent view of the principal peaks in the Cascades. Man, that's living!

Burt Keeble
Beaverton, Oregon

TEXAS BURGERS

1 lb. ground round or ground turkey	½ c. bell pepper
1 egg	½ tsp. seasoned salt
½ c. hickory barbecue sauce	½ tsp. garlic powder
½ sm. onion	1 c. crackers, crushed

Mix meat, egg, barbecue sauce, crackers, onion, pepper, garlic, seasoned salt in a large bowl. If mix is too moist, add more crackers. Make patties like hamburgers. Cook on low so not to burn. I grill them on my barbecue grill. Be sure to add foil. You can also bake them for 30 minutes at 300°.

Kandy Collins
Proctorville, Ohio

LI'L CHEDDAR MEAT LOAF

1 egg
¾ c. milk
1 c. (4 oz.) shredded cheddar
  cheese
½ c. quick-cooking oats
½ c. chopped onion

1 tsp. salt
1 lb. ground beef
⅔ c. ketchup
½ c. packed brown sugar
1½ tsp. prepared mustard

In a bowl, beat the egg and milk. Stir in cheese, oats, onion and salt. Add beef and mix well. Shape into 8 loaves; place in greased 13 x 9 x 2-inch baking dish. Combine ketchup, brown sugar and mustard; spoon over loaves. Bake uncovered at 350° for 45 minutes or until the meat is no longer pink and a meat thermometer reads 160°. Remove from oven and serve on individual plates.

Note: Easy to make. Leftovers are good too.

Jerry E. Jones
Beaver Dam Lake, Indiana

GOETTA MEAT LOAF

½ lb. Glier's goetta
1 lb. ground beef
½ c. catsup or tomato sauce

1 egg
1 c. cracker crumbs
1 sm. onion

Combine goetta, ground beef, egg, cracker crumbs, onion, salt and pepper. Mix well and mold into a loaf. Bake in a loaf pan at 350° for 55 minutes. Pour catsup or tomato sauce over the meat loaf for the last 10 minutes of baking.

Note: Goetta (a Cincinnati/Northern Kentucky tradition) is a wonderful combination of ground pork/beef mixed with pinhead (or steel cut) oats and seasonings. You can make your own, buy it in the grocery store or find it on www.goetta.com. Also great fried for breakfast!

Sister Mary Justa, SND
Covington, Kentucky

50191-03

GRANNY'S SPAGHETTI AND MEATBALLS

Meatballs:

1¼ lbs. ground chuck
2 cloves finely grated garlic
2-3 T. Parmesan cheese
2 slices toasted bread
1 finely grated onion

½ tsp. salt
½ tsp. pepper
2 eggs
2 T. parsley flakes

Sauce:

1 can diced tomatoes
2 (6-oz.) cans tomato paste
¼ tsp. oregano
2 cloves grated garlic

2 T. Parmesan cheese
⅓ c. finely chopped onion
½ tsp. basil

Prepare sauce first. Blend together in large Dutch oven: 1 can tomatoes, 2 cans tomato paste, ⅓ cup onion, ¼ teaspoon oregano, ½ teaspoon basil, 2 cloves grated garlic, and 2 tablespoons Parmesan cheese. Simmer at least two hours, adding just a little water when sauce gets too thick. Once sauce is simmering immediately prepare meatballs. Mix together ground chuck, 2 cloves grated garlic, 3 tablespoons Parmesan, 2 slices toasted bread (crumbled), 1 grated onion, salt, pepper, 2 eggs and parsley flakes. Form into meatballs and brown slightly in skillet. Add to sauce for duration of cook time so that meatballs are cooked through.

Note: A favorite in our family.

Sherry C. Dickson
Ft. Wright, Kentucky

"We never know how high we are till we are called to rise."
Emily Dickinson

MEATBALLS IN ONION SAUCE

1 lb. ground beef
3/4 c. rolled oats (quick or reg.)
1 egg
1/2 c. milk
1 tsp. salt
1/8 tsp. pepper
1/2 tsp. nutmeg
Dash of crumbled sweet basil
1/3 c. flour
1 env. dry onion soup mix
2 c. hot water

Combine beef, oats, egg, milk, salt, pepper, nutmeg, and basil. Shape into 25 balls. Roll in flour and brown in skillet. Combine onion soup mix and water. Pour over meatballs and cook over low heat (covered) for 25 minutes. Serve over cooked noodles. Serves 5 to 6 people.

Note: My mother's recipe (1926 - 1998). Cancer took her from us. Among the many things she taught me was how to be strong and dignified at the end of life.

Linda Robinson
St. Clair Shores, Michigan

SPAGHETTI PIE

6 oz. spaghetti
2 T. margarine
1/3 c. Parmesan cheese
2 well beaten eggs
1 c. cottage cheese
1 lb. ground beef
1/2 c. chopped onion
1/4 c. chopped green pepper
8-oz. can tomatoes (cut up)
6-oz. can tomato paste
1 tsp. sugar
1 tsp. dried oregano
1/2 tsp. garlic salt
1/2 c. shredded mozzarella cheese

Cook spaghetti according to package directions, drain (about 3 cups). Stir margarine into hot spaghetti. Stir in Parmesan cheese and eggs. Form spaghetti mixture into a "crust" in a buttered 10-inch pie plate. Spread cottage cheese evenly on spaghetti crust. In skillet, cook beef, onion, and green peppers until vegetables are tender and meat is browned. Drain fat. Stir in undrained tomatoes, tomato paste, sugar, oregano, and garlic salt. Heat through. Pour meat mixture into spaghetti crust. Bake uncovered for 20 minutes at 350°. Sprinkle with mozzarella. Bake for 5 minutes longer or until cheese melts. Makes 6 servings.

Note: Given to me by my mother-in-law, Virginia Ann Langguth, who died of breast cancer in 1999.

Debbie Langguth
Ft. Mitchell, Kentucky

50191-03

ℒEE'S LASAGNA

1 tsp. olive oil
2 cloves garlic (minced)
1 med. onion (chopped)
1 lb. ground chuck
½ lb. Italian sausage
1 (28-oz.) can spaghetti sauce

1 c. chicken broth
1 T. Italian seasoning
9 uncooked lasagna noodles
15-oz. container cottage cheese
2 c. shredded mozzarella cheese

Over medium heat, heat in Dutch oven. Add garlic, onion, ground chuck and sausage. Cook until meat is no longer pink. Add spaghetti sauce, broth and seasoning. Heat and stir for about 10 minutes. Spray lasagna pan with non-stick cooking spray. Put a scant amount of sauce in the bottom of the pan. Place three uncooked lasagna noodles on top of the sauce. Spread a third of the cottage cheese, then a third of the mozzarella cheese and a third of the sauce on top of the noodles. Repeat, making three layers and ending in sauce. Be sure to serve with garden salad and garlic bread. Bake uncovered at 375° for 20 to 30 minutes (or until bubbling but not burnt). Remove from oven and allow to stand 10 or 15 minutes before serving.

Note: I made this for my husband on our third date. This was one of the first meals he wanted this summer after being released from the hospital. He now has a clean bill of health after having undergone lung cancer surgery.

Lee Ann Smith Ward
Huntington, West Virginia

"Whatever name you call God or even if you don't acknowledge Him. . .He acknowledges you. . .'bidden or unbidden, God is present.' "
- Yvonne Cole

No-FUSS LASAGNA

1 lb. lean ground beef
½ tsp. salt
¼ tsp. cayenne pepper (opt.)
1 (28-oz.) jar spaghetti sauce
1 (14½-oz.) can stewed tomatoes
  (chopped, undrained)
1 (10-oz.) pkg. frozen spinach
  (thawed & well drained)

1 (15-oz.) ctn. ricotta cheese
¼ c. grated Parmesan cheese
1 egg (beaten)
10 uncooked lasagna noodles
1½ c. (6 oz.) shredded mozzarella
  cheese

Preheat oven to 375°. In a large skillet, brown ground beef over medium heat until browned (8 to 10 minutes); drain. Add salt, pepper, spaghetti sauce, stewed tomatoes. Stir until well blended. Set aside. In medium bowl, combine spinach, ricotta cheese, Parmesan cheese and egg. Mix well. Coat a 9 x 13-inch pan with cooking spray (Pam). Spread 2 cups of the sauce mix over bottom of dish. Place 4 uncooked noodles lengthwise over the sauce and 1 noodle crosswise over the end of the baking dish, completely covering the sauce mix layer. Press noodles down in sauce layer. Spread ricotta mixture evenly over noodles, sprinkle with 1 cup mozzarella cheese. Cover cheese layer evenly with 1½ cups sauce mix. Arrange remaining noodles over sauce, pressing lightly into sauce. Spread remaining sauce over top. Bake for 45 minutes, until noodles are tender. Remove from oven, sprinkle with remaining ½ cup mozzarella cheese. Cover with aluminum foil, let sit at room temperature for 15 minutes before cutting.

Gayle Cogan
Cincinnati, Ohio

"It's not the size of the dog in the fight, it's the size of the fight in the dog."
Mark Twain

126

FETTUCCINE

2 T. butter
3 garlic cloves (minced)
½ c. chicken broth
2 tsp. salt
½ c. diced carrots
½ c. chopped broccoli
½ c. chopped mushrooms

¾ c. heavy cream
1 c. Parmesan cheese
5 qt. water
2 T. olive oil
2 tsp. salt
1 lb. fettuccine

Bring water to a boil, adding olive oil and salt. In a separate large saucepan or Dutch oven, melt butter on low heat. Add garlic and warm. Add chicken broth, salt, carrots, broccoli and mushrooms and simmer. Add fettuccine to boiling water and cook according to package directions stirring often. Add cream to vegetable mixture. Drain pasta and add to vegetable mixture. Toss pasta well and add ½ cup Parmesan cheese. Meal is ready to serve. Garnish with remainder of cheese.

Note: Great quick vegetarian dish.

Kristy Seither
Ludlow, Kentucky

"The best way to predict the future is to create it."

Peter Drucker

"MAULTASCHENSUPPE" FROM THE AREA OF THE BLACK FOREST

Dough:

3 c. flour   *Dash salt*
3 eggs (beaten)

Filling:

8.5 oz. minced pork meat   ½ c. dried & milled bread
1 onion   Parsley to taste
2.5 oz. smoked bacon   Salt & pepper to taste
2 eggs   Nutmeg to taste
1 c. steamed spinach

   Sift together flour and salt. Mound flour mixture and make a deep well in the center. Place eggs in the well. Gradually add flour to the well, kneading gently until the mass of dough comes together. Knead dough until it is smooth and resilient. If dough is sticky, knead more flour into it. Cover with plastic wrap and allow to sit for 30 minutes. Cut bacon and onions in fine, small cubes and steam them. Add the pork, 2 eggs, spinach, bread crumbs, parsley, salt, pepper and nutmeg. Mix well into a mass that is easy to spread. Set aside. Roll out dough and cut out into 3-inch squares. Spread filling on half of the squares and cover with the remaining dough squares. Press the edge to seal. Put them in weak cooking salt water for 12 minutes. Serve in a beef stock.

Volker Geuting
Duesseldorf, Germany

"How do you climb Mount Everest? One step at a time."

Unknown

50191-03

PECOS PASTA

1 lb. elbow macaroni
1 onion, chopped
1 green pepper, chopped
3 T. oil
1 c. TVP (textured vegetable
  protein) or ground turkey
¾ c. water with 2 T. soy sauce
  added

1 (12-oz.) can crushed tomatoes
1 c. salsa
1 T. chili powder
2 c. red kidney beans, cooked
Salt to taste
Grated cheese (garnish)

Cook macaroni, drain and set aside. Sauté onion and pepper in oil until cooked. Add TVP or ground turkey and sauté until cooked. Add water, tomatoes, salsa, and chili powder and simmer on low heat for 5 minutes. Add beans and heat through. Serve over elbow macaroni and top with grated cheese. May put the macaroni into the rest of ingredients and make it a casserole type dish.

Note: From the "Heart of the Harvest Cafe" cookbook. Great vegetarian dish!

Yvonne Cole
Santa Rosa Beach, Florida

"Each day is a gift, untie the ribbons."

Unknown

ITALIAN BROCCOLI ROLL

2 (1-lb.) loaves Bridgford white
  bread (frozen)
10-oz. box chopped frozen broccoli
1½ lbs. Italian sausage (I prefer
  hot, but sweet or mild can be
  substituted)

1 sm. onion (chopped)
3-4 c. shredded mozzarella cheese
2 T. butter or margarine
2-4 T. grated Parmesan cheese
26-oz. jar Prego spaghetti sauce

Allow bread loaves to defrost several hours at room temperature. With rolling pin, roll loaves into an approximate size of 13 x 6 inches on floured surface. Cook broccoli according to instructions, drain and set aside. In large frying pan, cook sausage thoroughly with chopped onion; drain well and add cooked broccoli, mixing well. Divide meat mixture and spread over bread loaves, leaving approximately ½ inch on sides and ends. Smother each with mozzarella cheese. Carefully begin to roll up, starting from the wider end and shape into a crescent roll shape, pinching the ends. Bake at 350° on a lightly greased cookie sheet for approximately 30 to 45 minutes, until bread dough is golden brown. Leave several inches between loaves, allowing room as the bread expands and rises. After removing from oven take a stick of margarine and rub across the bread; sprinkle Parmesan cheese onto the melted margarine over each loaf. Slice approximately 1½ inches apart and spoon heated spaghetti sauce over the top. Enjoy!

Note: This is a great way to get the kids to eat broccoli - among the top most requested meals by my teenagers!

Roxanne del Rosario
Santee, California

"*I have been driven many times upon my knees by the overwhelming conviction that I had nowhere else to go.*"

Abraham Lincoln

ITALIAN BEEF STEW

1 lb. stew beef meat
¼ c. flour
1 (8-oz.) pkg. fresh mushrooms
  (rinsed & drained)
1 (32-oz.) jar Italian basil,
  garlic & oregano tomato sauce
  (or use diced tomatoes & purée)

4 potatoes (cubed)
1 onion (chopped)
1 c. baby carrots
Other vegetables may be used as
  well, whatever your preference

In crockpot, combine stew beef and flour. Mix until meat is covered with flour. Add mushrooms, sauce, potatoes, onions and carrots. Cook on low 5 to 6 hours. Stirring occasionally.

Note: Great main dish for a cold winter night.

Susan Beth Thomas
Highland Heights, Kentucky

BURRITO BAKE

1 c. Bisquick
¼ c. water
1 (16-oz.) can refried beans
1 lb. ground beef (cooked &
  drained)

1 avocado (sliced, if desired)
1 c. thick taco salsa
1½ c. shredded cheddar cheese

Grease 10-inch pie plate. Mix Bisquick, water and beans. Spread in pie plate. Layer ground beef, avocado, salsa and cheddar cheese on top of bean mixture. Bake for 30 minutes at 375°. Serve with sour cream if desired.

Note: In honor of my wife, Nancy. This was one of her favorite recipes.

Bill Grinonneau
Perrysburg, Ohio

BEV'S EASY TACO SUPPER

2 lbs. ground beef
1 med. onion
2 env. taco seasoning mix
1 (10-oz.) can Ro-Tel chopped
  Mexican tomatoes
1 (10½-oz.) can cheddar cheese
  soup

½ (15-oz.) jar salsa con queso
1 c. shredded mozzarella cheese
1 (15-oz.) bag nacho cheese
  tortilla chips

Garnish:

Lettuce
Tomato
Cheddar cheese

Onion
Salsa

Cook meat and onion, drain off grease. Add taco seasoning and cook as directed. Break up chips and spread in bottom of 9 x 13-inch pan. Layer meat mixture on top of chips. In separate bowl, combine salsa con queso, cheddar cheese and tomatoes in bowl. Pour on top of meat mixture. Bake at 350° for 20 minutes or thoroughly heated. Remove from oven and sprinkle with mozzarella. Return to oven until cheese has melted. Garnish with lettuce, tomato, cheddar cheese, onions and salsa.

Note: This will be your favorite taco dish ever!

Bev Clay
Coal Grove, Ohio

"You must be the change you wish to see in the world."

Gandhi

50191-03

HOPPIN' JOHN

½ lb. pork sausage
1 T. vegetable oil
1 sm. onion (coarsely chopped)
½ green pepper (coarsely chopped)
½ red pepper (coarsely chopped)
1 clove finely chopped garlic
¼ tsp. paprika
1 tsp. chili powder
1 (16-oz.) can black-eyed peas
1 (3.5-oz.) bag Success rice, cooked
1 T. lemon juice

Heat oil in large, heavy skillet. Crumble sausage into skillet and cook briskly until browned. Add onion, peppers, and garlic to skillet with sausage. Sprinkle with paprika and chili powder and cook until vegetables are transparent. Pour off grease. Add peas, cooked rice and lemon juice, mixing well in skillet. Reduce heat and simmer for about 10 minutes. (Dish should be moist.) Serves 4.

Note: I do not care much for black-eyed peas, but this dish is very good. I cook it every New Year's Day for good luck. I also use hot red pepper to taste instead of the red bell pepper, or both.

Shirley Satterfield
Daisy, Oklahoma

BEEFY TATER TOT CASSEROLE

1 (32-oz.) bag Tater Tots
1 lb. ground beef (cooked &
   drained)
1 (10.5-oz.) can 98% fat-free cream
   of mushroom soup
1 (10.5-oz.) can 98% fat-free cream
   of chicken soup
1 (16-oz.) bag (4 c.) shredded
   cheddar cheese (divided)

In a large bowl, combine cream of mushroom soup, cream of chicken soup. Add cooked hamburger, 3½ cups cheese and Tater Tots. Mix well. Place in a greased 9 x 13-inch pan. Spread evenly and sprinkle ½ cup cheese on top. Bake at 350° for 40 minutes.

Note: I am a fallopian tube cancer survivor! In memory of my mother, Joyce Kennedy and father-in-law, Allen Coats.

Linda West
Marion, Indiana

CHINESE HAMBURGER AND RICE

1 lb. ground beef
1 bell pepper (diced)
1 med. onion (diced)
3 stalks celery (diced)
1 c. uncooked rice (not instant)

2 (10.5-oz.) cans beef consommé
1 tsp. Kitchen Bouquet
2 tsp. low sodium soy sauce
2 T. butter

Sauté bell pepper, onion, celery in butter. Add ground beef and brown. Add rice, consommé, Kitchen Bouquet, soy sauce. Simmer 20 minutes until rice is tender.

Judy Kulhank
San Jose, Califonia

WORLD'S EASIEST CROCKPOT BEEF STROGANOFF

1 lb. stew beef
1 (10.5-oz.) can cream of
  mushroom soup
1 (10.5-oz.) can cream of celery
  soup

1 pkg. dry onion soup mix
1 (8-oz.) pkg. fresh mushrooms
  (sliced), opt.

In a crockpot combine stew beef, cream of mushroom soup, cream of celery soup, dry onion soup mix and (optional) mushrooms. Cook on high for 5 hours or on low for 8 hours, until meat easily falls apart. Stir every 2 to 3 hours. Serve over rice or noodles.

Note: Easier than any Stroganoff recipe you can find! Guests will love this! Easily doubled or tripled.

Nowim Dunn
Batavia, Ohio

50191-03

SKILLET MACARONI AND BEEF

1 lb. ground beef	1 (15-oz.) can tomato sauce
1 green bell pepper (chopped)	1 (15-oz.) can water
1 sm. onion (chopped)	1 T. Worcestershire sauce
1½ c. raw macaroni	

In a large skillet, brown hamburger with raw macaroni, bell pepper, and onion. Mix in tomato sauce, water and Worcestershire sauce. Simmer for 30 minutes.

Note: This recipe came from my mother, Geneva Cedonna McCoy. She was diagnosed with lung cancer in 1988 and passed in 1989, at the age of 74.

Barbara J. Cochran
New Vienna, Ohio

ROUND STEAK AND GREEN BEANS, PLUS!

2 lbs. fresh green beans (string removed & snapped into thirds)	Water to cover
5-6 lg. red potatoes (peeled)	1-lb. round steak (cut into 4- to 5-in. pieces)
1 lg. Granny Smith apple (peeled, cored & cubed)	Sm. onion (diced)

Cut potatoes into 2-inch cubes, cover with cold water. Cook until potatoes are just tender. Add string beans, apples, and onions. Cook over medium heat with lid on until beans are tender. Meanwhile, in a large heavy skillet, brown round steak in small amount of oil (approximately 1 to 2 tablespoons), then cook on low until tender. When steak is done, remove steak from skillet and set aside. Add broth from the bean mixture to skillet and stir. Be sure to scrape the bottom of the skillet so all brown bits left by the meat blend in with the broth. Serve the broth with round steak, poured on top or on the side. Serve with potatoes, beans, apples and onions.

Marlene Dickman
Park Hills, Kentucky

CRAB STUFFED NEW YORK STRIP

1 c. crabmeat
3 T. fresh bread crumbs
2 T. chopped fresh parsley
1 T. mayonnaise
2 T. prepared horseradish sauce

4 beef New York Strip steaks, cut
  1-in. thick
Milk (as needed for creaminess)
Salt & pepper to taste

Preheat grill to medium. Combine crabmeat, bread crumbs, parsley, mayonnaise and horseradish. Cut a pocket in the side of each steak. Spoon crab mixture into the pockets. Season steaks with salt and pepper. Grill steaks for 8 to 12 minutes for medium-rare. Turn once, halfway through grilling. Serves 4.

Note: Tastes like you're eating in a fancy restaurant!

Cathy Scheffter
Owensville, Ohio

BEST STEAK EVER

1 choice cut steak, such as Shell
  or Delmonico (1-1½ in. thick)
5 tsp. cracked black pepper
5 tsp. garlic powder (do not use
  garlic salt)

5 tsp. onion powder (do not use
  onion salt)
⅓ c. red wine vinegar
⅓ c. beer

Heat outdoor grill on high, or set oven to broil. Place meat in large glass or plastic rectangular casserole dish. Mix together pepper, garlic powder and onion powder with fork in cereal bowl until blended. Coat meat well with mixture and lightly rub mixture into meat. Pour red wine vinegar into dish, do not pour over meat, pour into corners of dish. After 10 minutes turn meat over and pour beef into dish. Let set another 10 minutes. **Grill instructions:** Grill 1 to 2 minutes each side on high; then turn grill to medium and continue cooking 7 to 10 minutes, depending on how well done you want your steak (7 minutes will be medium-rare) turning once or twice. **Oven instructions:** Place steak in broiler-safe pan and cook 3 to 5 minutes each side. Season with salt and enjoy. Serving size dependent upon size of steak. Add 2 additional teaspoons of each dry ingredients and ⅛ cup of each wet ingredient for each additional steak.

Note: Easiest and best tasting marinade I've ever tried!

Jeannie M. Bilodeau
Union Beach, New Jersey

50191-03

BEEF TENDERLOIN

1½-lb. beef tenderloin or sirloin
 tips, cut into ½-in. strips
2 T. butter
8 oz. fresh mushrooms (capped &
 sliced)
1 med. onion (chopped)
1 (10½-oz.) can beef broth

2 T. ketchup
1 sm. garlic clove
1 tsp. salt
3 T. flour
1 c. (½ pt.) sour cream
4 servings cooked wide egg
 noodles

Melt butter in skillet and add mushrooms and onion. Cook and stir until onions and mushrooms are tender. Pour into bowl and set aside. Use same skillet to brown meat. Reserve ⅓ cup of beef broth. Use remainder of can of beef broth, ketchup, garlic and salt and add to meat. Cover and simmer for 20 minutes. Add the reserved beef broth and flour to the meat mixture and stir. Add the mushrooms and onions and heat until boiling, stirring constantly. Reduce heat and simmer until the meat is tender. Add sour cream after meat is tender, close to serving time. Serve over wide egg noodles. Makes four servings.

Joyce Bricking
Florence, Kentucky

BEEF CREOLE (BOEUF CREOLE)

2 c. coarsely chopped cooked beef
2 T. lard or drippings
½ sm. green pepper (chopped)
1 sm. onion (minced)
3 T. flour
1 c. or 8-oz. can drained Trappey's
 okra (opt.)
1 c. diced celery

2 c. canned tomatoes
½ tsp. chili powder
½ tsp. salt
1 T. Trappey's Worcestershire
 sauce
Chef Magic kitchen seasoning to
 taste

Heat lard in a heavy skillet. Slowly sauté meat, green pepper, onion and celery for 10 minutes. Sprinkle with flour and blend it in. Add okra, chili powder, salt, Worcestershire sauce, Chef Magic and tomatoes. Cook slowly for 20 minutes, or until done, stirring frequently. Serves 4. Use Mexi-Pep for pepper seasoning.

Note: This is good served with rice or potatoes. Taken from The Secret of Creole Cooking from Trappey's Sons.

Shirley Satterfield
Daisy, Oklahoma

*S*WEET SAUERBRATEN

3-lb. chuck roast
2 T. vegetable oil
⅔ c. grape jelly
3 lg. onions (sliced)
6 whole black cloves or ½ tsp.
  ground cloves
2 bay leaves
2 tsp. salt

½ tsp. allspice
½ tsp. pepper
⅔ c. white vinegar
½ c. water (may add more if
  needed throughout cooking)
1 tsp. Kitchen Bouquet or
  Worcestershire sauce
Approx. ¼ c. flour

Brown meat in a little fat or oil. Add grape jelly, onions, cloves, bay leaves, salt, allspice, pepper, white vinegar, water, and Kitchen Bouquet or Worcestershire sauce. Cover and simmer for several hours. Add additional water as needed to prevent sticking. Thicken juices with flour. Serve with potato pancakes or noodles.

Note: Tried and true recipe that has pleased our family and many guests.

Veronica Mitchell
Park Hills, Kentucky

*F*LEMISH BEEF STEAK

4 T. butter
3 onions, sliced
4 lbs. beef (12, 1-in. thick pieces,
  5.3-oz. each)
2 T. flour
3 c. water
2 c. beer

2 T. vinegar
2 tsp. salt
½ tsp. pepper
1 tsp. sugar
3 T. chopped parsley
2 bay leaves
½ tsp. thyme

Melt butter in large heavy saucepan. Add the onions and sauté until brown, stirring frequently. Remove the onions and set aside. Brown the beef on both sides and remove. Sprinkle the flour on the pan juices and mix until smooth. Add the water, stirring constantly. Return the onions and beef to the pan. Add beer, vinegar, salt, pepper, sugar, parsley, bay leaves, thyme. Cover and cook on low heat 2 hours. Serve with boiled potatoes.

Note: Excellent family dish.

Donna L. Anderson
Indiana

138

_S_WEET AND SOUR ELK OR VENISON

1 env. dry onion soup mix	1 T. cider vinegar
¼ c. water	1½-lb. elk or venison steak (cut
1 (12-oz.) jar apricot preserves	into ½-in. wide, bite-size strips)
½ c. Russian or Catalina salad	1 tsp. salt
dressing	¼ tsp. pepper
¼ c. brown sugar (packed)	Hot cooked rice

In a bowl, combine soup mix and water; let stand for 15 minutes. Add preserves, salad dressing, brown sugar, and vinegar; mix well. Place elk/venison in a greased 9 x 13 x 2-inch baking dish. Sprinkle with salt and pepper. Pour apricot mixture over meat. Cover and bake at 350° for 45 minutes. Uncover and bake 30 to 40 minutes longer or until meat is fork tender. Serve over rice. Yield: 4 to 6 servings.

Note: This is really tasty!

Gert Cleves
Ft. Thomas, Kentucky

_L_IVER "BERLINER ART" OR THE BERLIN WAY OF LIVER

10 slices of calf liver (approx. 1½	10 thin slices of apple
lbs. total, 2.5 oz. per slice)	Scant c. beef stock
Salt & pepper to taste	5 c. sliced onions
Flour to coat liver slices	Paprika to taste
⅔ c. butter	Oil for frying

Powder onion slices with flour and paprika. Fry them in very hot oil until golden. Remove and place onto paper towels. Fry the slices of apple in butter until tender. When finished, warm them in the oven at 200°. Heat some butter in a pan. Spice the slices of liver with salt, pepper and turn them in flour. After that, fry the slices in heated butter. After frying, put the slices on plates. Arrange the onions and slices of apple side by side. To this dish you can serve stamped (mashed) potatoes.

Volker Geuting
Duesseldorf, Germany

CORNED BEEF STEW

⅓ c. oil
2 basting spoons plain flour
4 onions, chopped
5 lbs. potatoes, cut in ½

Salt, to taste
Pepper to taste
2 (15-oz.) cans corned beef

In large pot, pour in oil and heat on high temperature. Combine flour and chopped onions; stirring until a thick consistency to create a roux. Add potatoes, cut in half and fill pot with water (enough to cover potatoes). Stir until well mixed; salt and pepper to taste. Cook on low heat until potatoes are "almost" to desired doneness (about ¾ way cooked), then add 2 cans of corned beef. Cover; simmer for 30 to 45 minutes on low heat, stirring occasionally. Serve over white rice.

Note: A family favorite and tradition. In honor of our mother, Barbara Dixon.

Barbara Ann Dixon
Hattiesburg, Mississippi

Recipe Favorites

50191-03

Desserts

Terry Healey - California

Patricia Mohr - Indiana

Janet Scheuneman (2nd from left) and friends - Minnesota

50191-eb-6

My Story: At Face Value

At 20 years old, life was great. Attending college, I was confident, athletic and even the president of my fraternity. Some even considered me handsome.

Suddenly, I noticed a bump pushing against my nostril that wouldn't go away. I made a doctor's appointment. He suggested a biopsy. I had a tumor, a rare fibrosarcoma, but only a minor procedure was needed to remove it.

Six months later, another lump appeared and my cheek began tingling. My previous, supposedly unthreatening tumor had procreated a life threatening malignancy. This time the surgery was major. Half of my nose was removed, along with half of my upper lip, muscle and bone from my right cheek, the shelf of my eye, six teeth and part of my hard palate. My doctor promised to make me "streetable" before I left the hospital. It was his way of preparing me for a life of disfigurement.

After I left the hospital, people would stare, point and sometimes laugh. My self-esteem sank. Five years and 20 reconstructive surgeries later, I was still plagued with insecurity. My mental and emotional scars had become far more disfiguring than my physical ones ever had. I began using prayer and support from loved ones to boost my spirit and self-esteem. I volunteered at The Wellness Community (a cancer support organization). There I found my greatest form of therapy - offering inspiration and hope to those coping with cancer.

Everyone has insecurities. Today I am thankful for who I am - a much stronger and wiser person than the old Terry. Cancer free for 17 years, I have published a book about my experiences, and am now an inspirational speaker traveling the country. If there is only one message I ask people to remember, it's this: Refrain from making judgements at face value.

Terry Healey
Alamo, California
Author, At Face Value

For further information see: www.at-face-value.com

Desserts

*K*EY LIME PIE

1 premade graham cracker pie
  crust (deep)
2 (8-oz.) pkgs. cream cheese
  (softened)
³/₄ c. fresh lime juice
1 (14-oz.) can sweetened
  condensed milk

1 tsp. finely grated lime zest
¹/₄ c. powdered sugar
2 c. (1 pt.) heavy cream
2 T. buttermilk
8 lime slices, garnish

Thirty six hours in advance: Combine 2 cups heavy cream and 2 tablespoons buttermilk in medium bowl. Cover with plastic wrap and let stand at room temperature for 24 to 36 hours. Cream (called creme fraiche) should thicken and take on a nutty-tart flavor. Store tightly covered. May be kept for up to 2 weeks. Once creme fraiche is ready, you are ready to begin making pie. **Note:** Creme fraiche may sometimes be found, already prepared, in some grocery stores.

In a food processor, blend cream cheese, lime juice and condensed milk until smooth. Add lime zest and pulse blender until just combined. Pour filling into pie crust. In a bowl with an electric mixer, beat 1 cup creme fraiche with powdered sugar until it forms peaks. Spread evenly over pie filling and arrange lime slices on top for garnish. Chill in refrigerator loosely covered for at least 12 to 24 hours before serving.

Kim Andersen
Flower Mound, Texas

"The shortest way to do many things is to do only one thing at a time."
Cecil

ANG PIE

8 oz. cream cheese (softened)
8 oz. Cool Whip (thawed)
1 (14-oz.) can Eagle Brand
  sweetened condensed milk

½ c. Tang
1 graham cracker crust

Mix cream cheese, Cool Whip, Eagle Brand milk and Tang together and pour into graham cracker crust. Chill 4 hours and serve.

Note: My kids love this easy to throw together pie. Its very creamy, kinda like an orange Dreamsicle.

Brenda Adams
Barboursville, West Virginia

PERFECT PASTRY CRUST

6¼ c. flour
1 T. salt

1 lb. (2¼ c.) shortening

Mix the flour and salt. For tenderness, cut in about ⅔ cup of the shortening (1½ cups) until as fine as meal. **For flakiness:** Cut in remaining shortening (about ¾ cup) until the size of large peas. Do not over mix. **To make a single crust:** Combine 1½ cups of the mixture and two tablespoons of ice water. Avoid using hands when mixing. Body warmth toughens dough. This mixture can be stored in an airtight container in the refrigerator indefinitely. Makes approximately six crusts.

Note: This recipe is tried and true!

Veronica Mitchell
Park Hills, Kentucky

"What does not kill me makes me stronger."

Friedrich Nietzsche

50191-03

AUNT CELESTE'S NO FAIL PIE CRUST

4 c. all-purpose flour
1 T. sugar
2 tsp. salt
1¾ c. Crisco (no substitutes)

½ c. water
1 T. white vinegar
1 lg. egg

Blend with a fork, flour, sugar and salt. Add Crisco and continue blending with fork until crumbly. In a small bowl, beat egg, water and vinegar. Add flour mixture and combine until mixture is moist. Divide dough into 3 portions (3 portions if using for regular pie pans, 2 balls if using for deep dish pies), forming each into a ball. Wrap each ball in waxed paper and chill for 30 minutes. When ready to use, lightly flour a flat surface (counter top is fine) and roll out one of the dough balls to pie pan size. Place in pie pan and fill with any pie calling for an unbaked crust. If pie requires a baked crust, bake crust in a pie pan at 375° for about 10 minutes, until golden brown (watch carefully). **To freeze a dough ball for later use:** Keep dough wrapped in waxed paper and place in plastic bags. May be kept in the freezer for 2 months. **To use a frozen dough ball:** Allow it to thaw in the refrigerator, starting the night before you need to use it.

Note: This pie crust came from my Aunt Celeste, in Columbus, Ohio. You cannot fail with this recipe!

Bev Clay
Coal Grove, Ohio

"Do not go where the path may lead, go instead where there is no path and leave a trail."

Ralph W. Emerson

Coconut Cream Pie with Meringue

Filling:

2 c. milk
½ c. white sugar
1 c. fresh shredded coconut
½ tsp. salt
4 egg yolks

3 T. cornstarch
3 T. water
1 T. butter
1 tsp. vanilla extract

Meringue topping:

4 egg whites
1 tsp. vanilla
½ tsp. cream of tartar

½ c. white sugar
Prebaked pie shell

Filling: In a bowl, combine milk, ½ cup sugar and salt. Add 1 cup of coconut and cook in medium saucepan until bubbly. In a separate bowl, beat egg yolks and blend in cornstarch with water. Add to milk mixture, continue to cook and stir one minute. Add butter and 1 teaspoon vanilla. Pour filling into pastry shell of your choice. **Meringue topping:** Combine egg whites, 1 teaspoon vanilla, cream of tartar and ½ cup white sugar. Beat about 5 minutes until stiff, glossy peaks form. Spread on top of pie evenly. Cook pie at 400° until meringue turns light brown.

Gail Gorrell
Haines City, Florida

Two Pumpkin Pies

1 (28-oz.) can pumpkin
2 (12-oz.) cans evaporated milk
1 c. white sugar
¾ c. brown sugar
¼ tsp. salt

4 eggs (beaten)
1 tsp. cinnamon
¼ tsp. nutmeg
2 unbaked pie shells

Combine pumpkin, milk, sugar, brown sugar, eggs, cinnamon, nutmeg in bowl and blend thoroughly. Pour half of the mixture into each unbaked pie shell and bake at 400° for 45 minutes or until set. Remove and cool. Makes two pies.

Note: In memory of my mother, Audry Stewart. This was her recipe and it's wonderful, especially with Aunt Celeste's pie crust!

Bev Clay
Coal Grove, Ohio

50191-03

CHESS PIE

1 (7½-in.) unbaked pastry shell	3 eggs (beaten)
½ c. butter	1 T. white vinegar
1½ c. sugar	1 tsp. vanilla

Chill pastry shell. Heat butter and sugar until butter is melted (do not boil). Cool slightly. Add vinegar, vanilla and eggs to butter/sugar mixture. Mix well. Pour mixture into unbaked shell. Bake on lower shelf at 375° for about 45 minutes or until center is almost set but still soft. Cool. Serve with whipped cream, small slices.

Ellen Bell
Cincinnati, Ohio

EGG CUSTARD PIE

9-in. pastry shell	¼ tsp. nutmeg
4 eggs (slightly beaten)	¼ tsp. salt
⅔ c. sugar	2 c. milk
1 tsp. vanilla	Additional nutmeg for garnish

Bake shell 5 minutes at 400°. Let cool. Combine sugar, salt, nutmeg. Slightly beat eggs and add to sugar mixture. Beat well. Stir in milk and mix well. Add vanilla. Pour into shell. Sprinkle with nutmeg. Bake at 400° for 15 minutes reduce heat to 325° and bake for 35 minutes or until knife inserted in center comes out clean. Cool to room temperature before serving.

Note: In honor of my grandfather, Earl Lucas, Sr. This was one of his favorite pies to make and share with his family.

Brenda Adams
Barboursville, West Virginia

"Never, never, never give up."

Winston Churchill

HELEN'S PEANUT BUTTER PIE

1 c. brown sugar
½ c. granulated sugar
½ c. peanut butter
2 eggs (beaten)
2 T. flour

1½ c. milk
½ tsp. vanilla extract
1 graham cracker crust or baked
  pie shell

Mix brown sugar, granulated sugar, peanut butter, eggs and flour. Gradually stir in milk. Cook over medium heat, stirring until thick (do not boil). Remove from heat and stir in vanilla. Pour into graham cracker crust or a baked pie shell. Chill until set. Keep refrigerated until ready to serve.

Helen Montgomery
Morehead, Kentucky

CHOCOLATE ECLAIR PIE

2 (3.4-oz.) pkgs. instant vanilla
  pudding
3 c. milk
8 oz. Cool Whip
1 box graham crackers (approx. 60
  squares)

2 (1-oz.) sq. semi-sweet chocolate
1 c. powdered sugar
2 tsp. vanilla extract
3 T. milk

Mix instant pudding with 3 cups milk. Fold in Cool Whip. Line the bottom of a 9 x 12-inch pan with whole graham crackers. Spread half the pudding mixture on top. Repeat. Top with a third layer of graham crackers. Melt chocolate in the top of a double boiler. Add powdered sugar, vanilla extract and 3 tablespoons milk. Stir until smooth. Spread over top layer. Refrigerate at least 24 hours. Serve cold.

Barb Benkert
Cincinnati, Ohio

"You gain strength, courage and confidence by every experience in which you really stop to look fear in the face. . .You must do the thing which you think you cannot do."

Eleanor Roosevelt

50191-03

ANDY BAR PIE

1 (8½-oz.) Hershey's almond bar   1 (9-in.) graham cracker crust
8 fl. oz. (½ pt.) whipping cream   Sliced almonds (garnish)
1 tsp. vanilla

Melt candy bar in double boiler or microwave. Slightly cool chocolate mixture. Whip cream and add vanilla. Fold cream into chocolate. Spoon into graham cracker crust and chill for at least 1 hour. Garnish with sliced almonds.

Note: This is the easiest pie to make and people love it!

Ann Adams
Highlands Ranch, Colorado

THE ULTIMATE CARAMEL CHOCOLATE PECAN PIE

Crust:

2 c. finely chopped pecans   ¼ c. margarine (melted)
¼ c. sugar

Filling:

1 pkg. or 48 caramels   ⅓ c. milk
¼ c. milk   ¼ c. powdered sugar
1 c. chopped pecans   ½ tsp. vanilla
1 pkg. semi-sweet chocolate (8
  squares)

Crust: Heat oven to 350°. Mix pecans, sugar and margarine. Press onto bottom and sides of 9-inch pie plate. Bake 12 to 15 minutes or until lightly browned. Cool. **Filling:** Melt caramels with ¼ cup milk in heavy saucepan over low heat, stirring frequently until smooth. Pour over crust; sprinkle with pecans. Stir chocolate, ⅓ cup milk, powdered sugar and vanilla in heavy saucepan over very low heat just until melted. Pour over caramel pecan filling, spreading to desired edges of pie. Refrigerate. Can serve with whipped cream if desired.

Jane Gorton
Reading, Ohio

ECAN PIE

1 unbaked pie shell	1 tsp. vanilla
3 eggs (well beaten)	1/4 tsp. salt
3/4 c. white sugar	2 T. butter (melted)
1 c. dark Karo syrup	1 c. chopped pecans

Mix eggs, sugar, syrup, vanilla, salt, butter and pecans well and pour into unbaked pie shell at 350° for 1 hour. Top with whipped cream or ice cream if desired.

Note: Secret recipe for years, until now!

Irene Long
Lantana, Florida

CANADIAN BUTTER TARTS

1 c. brown sugar	1/4 c. raisins
1/4 c. butter	1/4 c. walnut pieces
1 egg (well beaten)	4 T. corn syrup
1/2 tsp. vinegar	12 tart shells

Mix together brown sugar, butter, egg, vinegar, raisins, and walnut pieces. Set aside. Pour 1 teaspoon corn syrup into each tart shell, then fill each shell with brown sugar mixture. Bake at 350° for about one hour, until shells are barely brown. Makes 12 tarts.

Note: Most requested recipe every Christmas!

Irene Long
Lantana, Florida

"More things are wrought by prayer than this world dreams of."
Alfred Lord Tennyson

50191-03

CREAM CHEESE PIE

Crust:

1¹/₃ c. graham crackers (crushed)   ¹/₄ c. butter (melted)

Filling:

8 oz. cream cheese (room temp.)   2 c. (1 pt.) sour cream
2 eggs (room temp. & beaten)   ¹/₈ tsp. cinnamon
¹/₂ c. sugar   5 T. additional sugar
1 tsp. pure vanilla extract

Crust: Combine the graham cracker crumbs and butter. Form crust in 9-inch pie pan. Bake 5 minutes at 350°. **Filling:** Beat cream cheese well and add ¹/₂ cup sugar, blend in eggs and ¹/₂ teaspoon vanilla. Beat well. Pour into crust and bake at 325° for 20 minutes. Let cool and set for 20 to 30 minutes (at least). **Topping:** Mix sour cream, ¹/₂ teaspoon vanilla, 5 tablespoons sugar and cinnamon. Blend well. Pour over filling. Bake at 325° for 5 minutes. Refrigerate for 2 hours. Serve and enjoy.

Note: In honor of John C. Frede, Lorraine E. Kohl and deceased members of the Meyers family.

Paula S. Meyers
Cincinnati, Ohio

"Faith is a refusal to panic."

D. Martyn Lloyd-Jones

CHOCOLATE CHEESECAKE

Crust:

25 chocolate wafers (crushed)
6 T. butter (melted)

¹/₄-¹/₂ tsp. cinnamon

Filling:

3 (8 oz.) pkgs. cream cheese
  (softened)
1 c. sugar
3 eggs
8 oz. semi-sweet chocolate
  (melted & cooled)

2 tsp. cocoa
1 tsp. vanilla extract
2 c. (1 pt.) sour cream

For the crust: Mix chocolate wafers, butter and cinnamon thoroughly and press into a well buttered 10-inch springform pan. Chill. Preheat oven to 350°. In a large bowl, beat cream cheese until fluffy and smooth. Add sugar and beat in eggs one at a time. Stir in chocolate, cocoa and vanilla, beating well after each addition. Add sour cream and continue beating until very smooth and well blended. Pour into crust. Bake for one hour and 10 minutes. Cake may appear to be too liquid, but it will become firm when chilled. Cool to room temperature, then chill for at least 5 hours.

Note: One of my mother's best. I could eat this all those times I was on soft diets, which was way too many times. Serves 12.

Terry Healey
Alamo, California

NO-BAKE CHEESECAKE

1 (6-oz.) Keebler ready crust
  graham cracker pie crust
1 (8-oz.) pkg. cream cheese
  (softened)
¹/₃ c. sugar

1 c. (¹/₂ pt.) sour cream
2 tsp. vanilla
1 (8-oz.) ctn. Cool Whip (thawed)
Fresh strawberries for garnish

Beat cream cheese until smooth, gradually beat in sugar. Blend in sour cream and vanilla. Fold in whipped topping, blending well. Spoon into crust. Chill until set, at least 4 hours. Garnish with fresh strawberries if desired. Preparation time: 15 minutes.

Sister Mary Florence, SND
Covington, Kentucky

50191-03

RASPBERRY SOUR CREAM TART

Crust:

8 whole graham crackers (16 sq.),
  coarsely broken

¼ c. (packed) light brown sugar
¼ c. unsalted butter (melted)

Filling & topping:

6 oz. cream cheese (room temp.)
⅓ c. sugar
½ c. sour cream
2 tsp. fresh lemon juice

½ tsp. vanilla extract
2 (½-pt.) baskets raspberries (I
  usually get 3 just in case)
¼ c. seedless raspberry jam

Crust: Preheat oven to 375°. Grind crackers and sugar in processor until coarse crumbs form. Add butter and process until crumbs are evenly moistened. Press crumb mixture firmly onto bottom and up sides of 9-inch diameter tart pan with removable bottom. Bake until crust is firm to touch, about 8 minutes. Cool crust on rack. **Filling and topping:** Using electric mixer, beat cream cheese and sugar in medium bowl until smooth. Beat in sour cream, lemon juice and vanilla. Spread filling in cooled crust. Chill until firm, at least four hours. (Can be made one day ahead. Cover and keep chilled.) Arrange berries in a circular pattern over filling. Whisk jam in small bowl to a loose consistency. Drizzle over berries. Serve immediately or chill up to 3 hours.

Note: This has got to be my all time favorite dessert! Not only does it taste absolutely amazing, but it looks like you purchased it from some hoity toity Patisserie! It's so easy to make and yet so impressive.

Karin Deti
Des Moines, Washington

"The greatest mistake you can make in life is to be continually fearing that you will make one."

Ellen Hubbard

MOUSSE AU CHOCOLATE AMER

(Chocolate Mousse)

*8½ oz. good quality dark, bitter
  chocolate, cut into pieces*
¼ c. butter (do not substitute)

5 very fresh eggs (separated)
⅛ tsp. (or pinch) cream of tartar
2 T. granulated sugar

Melt the chocolate and the butter together in a double boiler, or in a heavy saucepan over low heat, stirring constantly with a wooden spoon to prevent burning. Remove the pan from heat. With a hand mixer, beat the egg whites along with the cream of tartar, until stiff peaks form. In a separate bowl on low speed with a hand mixer, or by hand with a wire whisk, beat the egg yolks and the sugar together until thickened and paled. This can take about 5 minutes. The eggs should be lighter in color and take on the consistency of a heavy cream. Carefully fold the yolks and chocolate together until just combined. Next, fold in about one-fourth of the egg whites, carefully folding until just combined. Finally, fold in the remaining egg whites very delicately, until just combined. Some white streaks may still appear, but it is important not to mix the mousse too much or it will thin. Refrigerate the mousse at least 3 hours. Serve in individual parfaits, garnished with chocolate curls and real, fresh, whipped cream. Bon Appetit!

Note: This is a perfect ending to a small dinner party. The mousse will be especially delicious if you splurge on the best quality chocolate.

*Amy Guisinger
Paris, France*

"The sea is dangerous and its storms terrible, but these obstacles have never been sufficient reason to remain ashore."

Ferdinand Magellan

50191-03

TIRAMISU ANACAPRI

1 c. cold water
1 (14-oz.) can fat-free sweetened condensed milk
1 (1.4-oz.) pkg. sugar free vanilla instant pudding mix
1 (8-oz.) pkg. 1/3 less fat cream cheese (softened)
1 (8-oz.) tub frozen reduced-calorie whipped topping (thawed)

1 c. hot water
1/2 c. Kahlua (coffee liqueur)
1 T. instant espresso or 2 T. instant coffee granules
24 ladyfingers, 2 (3-oz.) pkgs.
3 T. unsweetened cocoa (divided)

In a large bowl, combine 1 cup cold water, condensed milk and pudding mix. Stir well with whisk. Cover surface with plastic wrap and chill 30 minutes or until firm. Remove plastic wrap and add cream cheese. Beat mixture on medium speed until well blended. Gently fold in whipped topping. In a separate bowl, combine 1 cup hot water, Kahlua, and espresso. Split ladyfingers in half, lengthwise. Arrange 16 ladyfinger halves, flat side down, in a trifle bowl or a large glass bowl. Drizzle with 1/2 cup Kahlua mixture. Spread 1/3 of pudding mixture evenly over ladyfingers. Sprinkle with 1 tablespoon of cocoa. Repeat layers, ending with cocoa. Cover and chill at least 8 hours. Yields 12 servings (1/2 cup each).

Karrie Langer
Cleveland, Ohio

"If you can dream it, you can do it."

Walt Disney

SWEDISH RICE PUDDING

½ c. uncooked white rice
1 med. cinnamon stick
4 c. whole or 2% milk (divided)
3 eggs (beaten)
½ c. sugar

¼ tsp. salt
1 tsp. vanilla extract
1 tsp. almond extract
1 c. raisins (opt.)

Rinse rice. Place rice, cinnamon stick, and 2 cups milk in double boiler. Heat over medium heat until most of the milk soaked up by rice (20 to 30 minutes). Stir often. Remove from heat and add eggs and 2 cups milk, sugar, salt, vanilla extract and almond extract. Mix well. Butter medium size dish and pour in rice mixture. Place entire medium dish in a larger pan. Fill larger pan with 1 inch of water so water is surrounding medium pan. Bake in 325° oven. After 30 to 40 minutes stir mixture and sprinkle with sugar and cinnamon. Do not cover dish. Bake until knife inserted in center comes out almost dry.

Note: In memory of my parents, Eric and Helga Edlund, Swedish immigrants, who both died of cancer.

Janet Scheuneman
St. Paul, Minnesota

"Obstacles are those frightful things you see when you take your eyes off your goal."

Henry Ford

50191-03

*B*READ AND BUTTER PUDDING

Scant 2¼ c. milk
Scant 2¼ c. double (heavy) cream
Pinch of salt
1 tsp. vanilla extract
Approx. 4 T. butter
6 lg. eggs

1⅛ c. sugar
6 slices good quality white bread
(enough to cover base of your
dish)
2 T. sultanas (i.e. Sun-Maid
golden raisins)

Preheat a moderate oven to 160° C / 325° F. Grease a medium baking dish with some of the butter. In a saucepan, bring the milk, cream, salt and vanilla extract to a boil and remove from heat. Beat the eggs together until pale, then gradually add the milk mixture, stirring as you do. Butter the slices of bread and arrange in the bottom of the pie dish. Pour the milk mixture over them and sprinkle the sultanas evenly over everything. The bread will float to the top. Put the dish inside a bigger baking dish and fill the larger dish with hot water to a level halfway up the sides of your smaller dish inside (classic bain marie technique!) Cook for 45 to 50 minutes. When the pudding is ready it will still be a bit wobbly in the middle. Remove from the oven and cool a little. Dust with powdered sugar. Serve while still warm. A friend of mine adds a bit of bourbon for some holiday flavor!

Note: Given to me by my fourth year cookery teacher, Mrs. Mansell.

Sue Saier
London, England

"We are, each of us angels with only one wing, and we can only fly by embracing one another."

Luciano de Crescenzo

$\mathcal{B}$READ PUDDING

Bread pudding:

1 loaf French bread	2 T. vanilla extract
1 qt. milk	1 c. raisins
3 eggs	3 T. butter (melted)
2 c. sugar	

Sauce:

½ c. butter	1 egg (well beaten)
1 c. sugar	Bourbon to taste

Break bread into small chunks and soak in milk. Crush with hands until well mixed. Add eggs, sugar, vanilla and raisins and stir well. Put melted butter in bottom of 9 x 13-inch pan. Pour bread mixture on top of butter and bake at 350° for approximately 1 hour (watch closely so does not burn). Bake until very firm. Remove from oven when finished and allow to cool to desired serving temperature (may serve hot, warm or cool). **Whiskey Sauce:** Cook sugar and butter in double boiler (or heavy saucepan) until very hot and well dissolved. Then add well beaten egg and whip real fast so egg doesn't curdle. Let cool off and add whiskey to taste. Not too strong - not too weak. To serve, you may pour whiskey sauce over bread pudding and heat dish under broiler to warm or serve whiskey sauce in a dish on the side. Serves 6 to 8 people.

Note: Enjoy! This is easy and dee-licious! We always triple the sauce to have plenty - yum!

Mary Jo Karch
Cincinnati, Ohio

"God had one Son on earth without sin, but never one without suffering."
St. Augustine

50191-03

GRANDMOM'S CORNSTARCH PUDDING

3 T. sugar
2 c. milk
2 T. cornstarch

1 egg (beaten)
1 T. vanilla

Dissolve sugar in 1½ cups of milk. Combine cornstarch with remaining (½ cup) milk, then combine with sugar and milk mixture. Add beaten egg. Cook slowly, stirring constantly until thick. Add vanilla. When well mixed, remove from heat and cool. Chill in refrigerator until ready to serve.

Note: Very simple recipe. I am a survivor of Hodgkin's Disease stage IIIB. This was given to me by Maude Campbell.

Donna Nowak
Brooklyn, New York

LEMON FLUFF

1 (12-oz.) can evaporated milk
1 (3-oz.) pkg. lemon gelatin
1¾ scant c. boiling water
⅓ c. lemon juice (use real lemons for the juice)

1 c. sugar
2½ c. vanilla wafer crumbs (divided)
10-oz. jar maraschino cherries (garnish)

Chill unopened can of evaporated milk for 3 to 4 hours. Stir Jello into boiling water. Chill until partially set (approximately 90 minutes). Whip until light and fluffy. Add lemon juice and sugar. Mix thoroughly. Whip evaporated milk until thick. Fold into Jello mixture. Coat bottom of pan with portion of vanilla wafer crumbs. Pour Jello mix on top. Sprinkle remaining vanilla wafer crumbs on top. Chill until ready to serve. Cut into squares. Garnish with maraschino cherries. Serves 12 to 16.

Note: This fluff is always nice and light and men seem to like it really well.

Kathy Flynn
Pensacola, Florida

$\mathcal{S}$T. PATRICK'S DELIGHT

½ c. butter (softened)
1 c. flour
2 T. sugar
1 (8-oz.) pkg. cream cheese
  (softened)
1 c. sugar

2 T. milk
2 (3.4-oz.) boxes instant pistachio
  pudding
3 c. milk
2 (8-oz.) ctns. frozen whipped
  topping (thawed)

Combine butter, flour and 2 tablespoons sugar. Pat mixture into a 9 x 13-inch pan. Bake 12 to 15 minutes until lightly browned. Cool. In mixing bowl, beat cream cheese, 1 cup sugar, 2 tablespoons milk. Fold in 1 container whipped topping. Spread in 9 x 13-inch pan over cooled crust. Combine 2 boxes pudding, with 3 cups milk. Beat slowly for 2 minutes, then spread evenly over cream cheese mixture. Refrigerate 15 minutes. Spread 1 container of whipped topping over pudding. Refrigerate until ready to serve. Makes 20 servings.

Note: In honor of my daughter, Patti Rottenbiller, a 13 year breast cancer survivor!

Emily Rausch
Napoleon, Ohio

$\mathcal{B}$LUEBERRY DELIGHT

2 (3-oz.) pkgs. grape Jello
2 c. boiling water
1 (20-oz.) can crushed pineapple
  (undrained)

1 (21-oz.) can blueberry pie filling

Topping:

8 oz. cream cheese (softened)
½ c. sour cream
⅓ c. sugar

1 tsp. vanilla extract
½ c. chopped nuts

Dissolve Jello in water. Chill until the consistency of syrup. Add pineapple and pie filling. Pour into an 8 x 12-inch dish. Chill until set. **Topping:** Beat cream cheese, sour cream, sugar, vanilla, until smooth and creamy. Spread over blueberry mixture. Sprinkle with nuts.

Margaret Cooper
Morehead, Kentucky

50191-03

*B*LUEBERRY COBBLER

2 c. fresh or frozen blueberries
1³/₄ c. sugar (divided)
3 T. butter (softened)
1 tsp. baking powder

¹/₄ tsp. salt
¹/₂ c. milk
1 c. all-purpose flour
1 T. cornstarch

Preheat oven to 375°. Cover the bottom of a 8-inch square pan. (I prefer to use a glass Pyrex pan) with the blueberries. In a separate mixing bowl, mix ³/₄ cup of sugar, butter, baking powder, salt, milk and flour together until combined; pour this mixture over the blueberries. In another bowl mix remaining 1 cup sugar and cornstarch; sprinkle this mixture over the flour mixture. Pour ²/₃ cup of boiling water over the top of the cobbler. Bake at 375° for 45 minutes. Makes 9 servings.

Note: This recipe won a baking contest. It is also requested by a lot of my friends that have tasted it. It is pretty easy to make on top of it.

Lesley Kilgore
Batavia, Ohio

*B*LUEBERRY WHIP

1¹/₂ c. frozen blueberries
¹/₂ c. unsweetened soy, rice or
  almond milk

1 T. vanilla-flavored protein
  powder

Place blueberries, milk and protein powder in food processor and turn it on. Add or delete milk to get desired whipped-looking consistency. Serve like you would ice cream.

Note: My girls are on a sugar-free, dairy-free diet at present, and this recipe makes them feel like they're not missing out. The children at school want their moms to make it for their lunches, too.

Dorene Campbell
Vancouver, Washington

$\mathcal{D}$IABETIC APPLE CRISP

1½ lbs. apples, sliced (5 med.
  apples)
2 T. lemon juice
¼ tsp. cinnamon
⅔ c. all-purpose flour

½ c. uncooked oatmeal
⅓ c. margarine
3 packets granulated sugar
  substitute

Toss apples in lemon juice and cinnamon. Spread apples in lightly oiled, two-quart casserole. In a separate bowl, combine flour, oatmeal and sugar substitute. Cut in margarine with a fork or pastry blender until mixture is crumbly. Spread over fruit. Bake in 375° oven for 40 minutes or until apples are tender. Makes 8 servings.

Note: In honor of my daughter, Linda L. Pense, RD, MS, CD.

Paul R. Anderson
Indiana

$\mathcal{F}$AVORITE FRUIT COBBLER

½ c. butter or margarine
1 c. all-purpose flour
1 c. sugar
2 tsp. baking powder

1 c. milk
4 c. fresh blueberries, blackberries
  or peeled peaches

Melt butter and pour in 9 x 13 x 2-inch baking pan. Set aside. In a separate bowl, combine flour, sugar, baking powder and milk. Whisk together and pour over melted butter in the 9 x 13-inch pan. Spread fruit evenly on top of mixture. Bake at 350° for 45 minutes.

Note: In memory of John, Donna and Michael Owen Pierce.

Dianne Pierce
Farmerville, Louisiana

50191-03

LEMON BARS

Crust:

1 c. butter (softened)   ½ c. sugar
2 c. flour

Filling:

4 eggs   1 tsp. baking powder
2 c. sugar   Pinch salt
6 T. lemon juice   Powdered sugar to sprinkle
4 T. flour

Mix butter, 2 cups flour, ½ cup sugar. Spread in 9 x 13-inch pan. Bake at 325° for 20 minutes. Meanwhile, in separate bowl, mix together eggs, 2 cups sugar, lemon juice, 4 tablespoons flour, baking powder and salt. When crust is ready, spread lemon mixture on across crust and bake for 20 additional minutes. Sprinkle with powdered sugar.

Note: My friend Pam leaves these on my front porch as a "surprise" every Christmas and I love 'em. They're the best you've ever tasted!

Bev Clay
Coal Grove, Ohio

"To give anything less than your best is to sacrifice the gift."
Steve Prefontaine

BAKLAWA

1 lb. fillo dough (approx.)	2 c. unsalted butter (melted)

Filling:

1 lb. chopped walnuts	1 T. vanilla
2 c. sugar	

Syrup

2 c. sugar	2 T. lemon juice
1 c. water	½ tsp. orange blossom water

Mix walnuts, 2 cups sugar, vanilla and set aside. Melt butter. Butter the baking pan (9 x 13-inches). Separate dough in half making sure the sheets are kept moist by keeping under plastic wrap. You must work fast to keep the fillo sheets from drying out. Each time you put a sheet of dough into the pan, you must brush it with melted butter. Put half the sheets in the pan this way and spread the nut filling on top. Then put the rest of the sheets on top brushing between layers. Depending on the size of sheets, you might have to fold each sheet in half with butter in between. Pour extra butter on top and let stand for 20 minutes. Cut into diamond shapes. (Cut parallel lines lengthwise about 1½ inches apart. Then cut diagonal lines 1½ inches apart.) Bake at 350° for 15 minutes then turn down to 325° for 25 minutes or until golden brown. Mix 2 cups sugar and 1 cup water. Bring to a boil and cook 7 minutes. Remove from heat and add 2 tablespoons lemon juice and ½ teaspoon orange blossom water. Let cool. Pour over warm baklawa.

Note: A traditional favorite. This wonderful dessert is made by my grandmother, who is a colon cancer survivor!

Sadie Karam
Canton, Ohio

"Wheresoever you go, go with all your heart."

Confucius

50191-03

APPLE PIE SQUARES

Crust:

Approx. ½ c. milk
2½ c. flour
1 T. sugar

1 tsp. salt
1 c. lard
2 eggs

Filling:

1 tsp. cinnamon
1½ c. sugar
6 med. McIntosh apples (peeled &
sliced)

2 c. cornflake crumbs

Glaze:

½ c. 10X powdered sugar

3-4 T. milk

Crumb flour, sugar, salt and lard. Set aside. Put 2 egg yolks (reserve whites) in measuring cup and add enough milk to make ⅔ cup. Add to flour mixture and blend. Divide into 2 balls and chill at least 2 hours. Roll out one ball of pie crust to fit into 9 x 13-inch pan. Grease and flour pan, press in the crust, cover crust with cornflake crumbs, apples, 1½ cups sugar and cinnamon. Roll second ball of pie crust, cover and slit. Brush with lightly beaten egg whites, bake at 350° for 1 hour. Cool for 15 minutes. **Optional glaze:** One half cup powdered sugar, add milk slowly to a consistency of fudge syrup. This varies with humidity and altitude, about 3 to 4 tablespoons. Drizzle on top crust after baking. Cut into squares and serve.

Note: This pie crust is fool-proof. I use it for making pies too. Just make sure the dough is cold when you roll it out, and you will have a nice, light golden brown crust every time. I am a cervical cancer survivor and my mother is a cervical and colon cancer survivor!

Margaret Hubbard
Byron, Michigan

ſPICY PECAN SQUARES

1 c. soft butter	2 c. flour
1 c. brown sugar (packed)	½ tsp. salt
1 tsp. vanilla	1 tsp. cinnamon
1 egg (separated)	1 c. chopped pecans

Cream butter and sugar, vanilla and egg yolk. Beat until light. Add sifted dry ingredients and ½ cup nuts. Mix well. Press into greased 15 x 10 x 1-inch pan. Lightly beat egg white and brush top. Sprinkle nuts on top. Bake at 350° for 25 minutes or until light brown. Let cool, cut into squares. Makes 3 dozen.

Note: My mother, Ann Brubaker made these cookies every year at Christmastime. These were my favorite, easy to make and delicious.

Kate Lawson
Bloomfield Hills, Michigan

"We are always on the anvil; by trials God is shaping us for higher things."
Henry Ward Beecher

50191-03

PUMPKIN PECAN TASSIES

Base:

½ c. butter (softened, no substitute)	1 c. all-purpose flour
1 (3-oz.) pkg. cream cheese (softened)	

Filling:

¾ c. brown sugar (packed & divided)	1 T. half-and-half cream
¼ c. cooked or canned pumpkin	1 tsp. vanilla extract
4 tsp. plus 1 T. butter (melted & divided)	¼ tsp. rum extract
1 egg yolk	⅛ tsp. ground cinnamon
	⅛ tsp. ground nutmeg
	½ c. pecans (chopped)

In a small mixing bowl, cream butter and cream cheese. Beat in flour. Shape into 24 balls. Press onto the bottom and up the sides of greased miniature muffin cups. Bake at 325° for 8 to 10 minutes or until edges are slightly brown. Meanwhile, in a bowl, combine ½ cup brown sugar, pumpkin, 4 teaspoons butter, egg yolk, cream, vanilla extract, rum extract, cinnamon and nutmeg. Spoon into warm cups. Combine the pecans and ¼ cup brown sugar and 1 tablespoon butter. Sprinkle over filling. Bake 23 to 27 minutes longer or until set and edges are golden brown. Cool for 10 minutes before removing from pans to wire racks. Yield: 2 dozen.

Rosemary Huntsman
Morehead, Kentucky

"Where there is great love there are always miracles."

Willa Cather

$\mathcal{B}$EV'S PUMPKIN CRUNCH

1 (18.25-oz.) pkg. yellow cake mix
1 (15-oz.) can solid pack pumpkin
1 (12-oz.) can evaporated milk
3 lg. eggs
1½ c. sugar
1 tsp. cinnamon

1 tsp. pumpkin pie spice
½ tsp. salt
½ c. chopped nuts (pecans)
1 c. butter
Whipped topping, garnish

Preheat oven to 350° and grease the bottom of a 9 x 13-inch pan. Combine pumpkin, milk, eggs, sugar, cinnamon, pumpkin pie spice and salt in a large bowl. Pour into pan. Sprinkle dry cake mix evenly over pumpkin mixture. Top with pecans. Drizzle melted butter over pecans. Bake for 50 to 55 minutes, or until golden brown. Cool. Serve chilled with whipped topping.

Note: This is great as a take along dish.

Bev Clay
Coal Grove, Ohio

"It is during our darkest moments that we must focus to see the light."
Taylor Benson

50191-03

Pumpkin roll:

3 eggs
1 c. sugar
²/₃ c. pumpkin
1 tsp. lemon juice
¾ c. all-purpose flour

1 tsp. baking powder
2 tsp. cinnamon
1 tsp. ginger
½ tsp. nutmeg
½ tsp. salt

Filling:

1 (8-oz.) pkg. cream cheese
  (softened)
4 T. butter or margarine

1 c. powdered sugar
½ tsp. vanilla extract
Pumpkin pie spice to taste

Pumpkin roll: In a large bowl combine eggs and sugar, beating well. Add pumpkin and lemon juice, mixing well until blended. In a separate bowl, combine flour, baking powder, cinnamon, ginger, nutmeg and salt. Add dry mixture to egg mixture, mixing well. Spread batter into a greased and wax paper-lined 10 x 15-inch jelly-roll pan (cookie sheet). Bake at 375° for 15 minutes. Remove from oven. Cool for 15 minutes. Gently peel off wax paper. Place cake on a clean tea towel (sprinkle some powdered sugar on towel). Cool 10 minutes longer. From 10-inch side, roll cake up in a towel. Set aside. **To prepare filling:** In large bowl, beat cream cheese and butter. Stir in 1 cup of powdered sugar and the vanilla extract. Blend all until smooth. Add pumpkin spice to taste. Unroll cake. Evenly spread filling over cake. Roll up cake, removing towel as you roll. Wrap in plastic wrap, cover and chill at least 60 minutes. Decorate as you like.

Note: Great for Thanksgiving dessert. In honor of my daughter Maria Scott.

Marie Owen
Keene, New Hampshire

RAINBOW BLONDIES

1 c. butter or margarine (softened)
1½ c. firmly packed brown sugar
1 lg. egg
1 tsp. vanilla extract
2 c. flour

½ tsp. baking powder
1 (12-oz.) pkg. M & M's mini
   baking bits
1 c. chopped walnuts or pecans
   (opt.)

Preheat oven to 350° (325° for glass pan). Cream butter and sugar until light and fluffy. Add egg and vanilla extract. Combine flour and baking soda. Add to creamed mixture just until combined. DOUGH WILL BE STIFF. Stir in M & M's and nuts. Spread dough into a greased 9 x 13-inch baking pan. Bake 30 to 35 minutes or until wooden pick inserted in center comes out slightly moist with crumbs. Cool completely before cutting.

Debbie Langguth
Ft. Mitchell, Kentucky

APPLESAUCE BROWNIES

Brownies:

½ c. cocoa
1 c. butter (softened)
1 c. sugar
4 eggs
1 c. applesauce

2 tsp. vanilla
2 c. flour
1 tsp. baking powder
½ tsp. baking soda
½ tsp. salt

Icing:

½ c. butter (softened)
1 tsp. vanilla extract
⅓ c. evaporated milk

¼ c. cocoa
Approx. 1-2 c. powdered sugar

Mix cocoa, butter, sugar, eggs, applesauce and vanilla together. Set aside. Mix flour, baking soda, baking powder, and salt together. Add to butter mixture. Grease and flour a 9 x 13-inch dish. Spread batter in pan evenly and bake at 325° for 25 to 30 minutes. **Icing:** Combine butter, vanilla extract, evaporated milk, cocoa. Gradually add powdered sugar until slightly thickened. Once brownies have finished baking, remove from oven. Pour icing over brownies while they are still hot.

Note: Recipe handed down by my grandmother, Buelah Kinman.

Melissa Howard
Crescent Springs, Kentucky

50191-03

*E*LVA MAE'S BROWNIES

Brownies:

1 c. water
6 T. cocoa
1 c. oleo or butter
2 c. sugar
2 c. flour

½ c. buttermilk
2 eggs
1 tsp. vanilla extract
1 tsp. baking soda

Frosting:

6 T. buttermilk
4 T. cocoa
½ c. oleo or butter (softened)

1 lb. powdered sugar (approx. 4 c.)
1 c. chopped nuts

Brownies: Bring water, cocoa and 1 cup oleo or butter to a boil. Remove from heat and add sugar and flour. Mix well and add buttermilk, eggs, vanilla and baking soda. Bake in a 10 x 15-inch pan at 400° for 20 minutes. **Frosting:** Bring buttermilk, cocoa and ½ cup oleo (or butter) to a boil. Remove from heat and add powdered sugar and chopped nuts. Spread evenly on brownies and allow to cool before cutting.

Note: Elva Mae Hanson was a sweetheart and often brought these brownies to functions at our church.

Ann Adams
Highlands Ranch, Colorado

"You haven't failed until you quit trying."

Unknown

JUNIOR MINT BROWNIES

Cooking spray
1/4 c. butter
2 full size peppermint patties
1 c. all-purpose flour
1/4 tsp. baking soda

1/8 tsp. salt
2/3 c. sugar
1/3 c. unsweetened cocoa
1 lg. egg
1 lg. egg white

Preheat oven to 350°. Coat bottom of 8-inch square pan with cooking spray. Combine butter and mints in microwave-safe dish. Microwave 30 seconds and stir until smooth. Set aside. Lightly spoon flour into a dry measuring cup. Add soda and salt. Set aside. In a large bowl, combine sugar, cocoa, 1 egg and 1 egg white. Blend well. Add flour mixture and beat at low speed until blended well. Add butter/mint mixture and blend well. Pour into pan. Bake for 20 minutes or until wooden pick comes out clean. Cool completely on wire rack.

Note: This is an excellent reduced-fat recipe when you are really craving something chocolate.

Brenda Adams
Barboursville, West Virginia

BROWNIE MELTAWAYS

1 (21.5-oz.) pkg. brownie mix
3 c. powdered sugar
1/3 c. margarine plus 2 tsp.
  margarine
2 T. milk (may need slightly more
  desired consistency)

1 1/2 tsp. vanilla
2 sq. (1-oz. each) unsweetened
  chocolate

Heat oven to 350°. Prepare brownies as directed on package. Bake as directed, cool. Mix powdered sugar, 1/3 cup softened margarine and vanilla, stir in milk (1 teaspoon at a time, until spreading consistency). Spread over brownies. Refrigerate until firm (about 30 minutes). Heat chocolate and 2 teaspoons margarine until melted. Drizzle across top of firm mixture, spread evenly. Refrigerate until chocolate is firm, about 15 minutes. Store in refrigerator.

Mardi Owczarzak
St. Joseph, Missouri

50191-03

MEXICAN BROWNIES

2 c. flour
2 c. sugar
1 c. butter or oleo
¼ c. cocoa
1 c. hot water
½ c. buttermilk (if buttermilk is
not available, mix ½ tsp. white
vinegar with ½ c. homogenized
milk)

2 eggs
1 tsp. baking soda
1 tsp. vanilla
½ tsp. salt
1 T. cinnamon

Mix flour and sugar together and set aside. Bring to a gentle boil; butter or oleo, cocoa, hot water. Pour over flour and sugar mixture and mix well. Add buttermilk, eggs, baking soda, vanilla, salt, cinnamon and mix well one minute. Pour into pre-floured (or spray with Pam) 9 x 13-inch baking dish and bake at 400° for 20 minutes. Wait until completely cooled to frost.

Note: Sensational brownies with a new twist! I sometimes sprinkle nuts over the top once it is frosted.

Frosting:

½ c. butter or oleo
¼ c. cocoa
½ c. homogenized milk

1-lb. box (4 c.) powdered sugar
1 T. cinnamon
1 tsp. vanilla

Bring to a gentle boil butter or oleo, cocoa, milk. Pour mixture over powdered sugar, cinnamon, vanilla. Mix well and pour over cooled brownie cake.

Barbara Bagley
San Antonio, Texas

"In all things it is better to hope than to despair."
Johann Wolfgang von Goethe

$\mathcal{E}$ASY CHOCOLATE CARAMEL BROWNIES

2 T. skim milk
27 sm. soft caramel candies (about
    8 oz.)
$\frac{1}{2}$ c. fat-free sweetened condensed
    milk (not evaporated skim milk)
1 (18.25-oz.) pkg. devil's food cake
    mix (with pudding in the mix)

$\frac{1}{2}$ c. applesauce
1 lg. egg white (lightly beaten)
Cooking spray
Flour (to lightly coat pan)
1 tsp. all-purpose flour
$\frac{1}{4}$ c. semi-sweet baking chips

Preheat oven to 350°. Combine skim milk and caramels in a bowl. Microwave on high 1½ to 2 minutes (stop to stir with a whisk every minute) or until caramels melt and mixture is smooth. Set aside. Combine sweetened condensed milk, cake mix, applesauce and egg white in a bowl; stir well (mixture will be very stiff). Coat bottom only of 9 x 13-inch baking pan with cooking spray. Dust lightly with flour. Evenly press ⅔ of batter into prepared pan using floured hands (layer with be thin). Bake at 350° for 10 minutes. Remove from oven. Sprinkle with chocolate chips. Drizzle caramel mixture over chips. Carefully drop remaining batter by spoonfuls over caramel layer. Bake at 350° for 30 minutes. Let cool completely in pan on a wire rack. Makes about 30 squares.

Note: Bake contest winner!

Rea Jean Hix
Grove City, Ohio

"The value of persistent prayer is not that He will hear us...but that we will hear Him."

William McGill

50191-03

*D*EATH BY CHOCOLATE

1 (18.25-oz.) pkg. dark chocolate
   cake mix
1 (4-serving size) pkg. chocolate
   mousse dessert mix (prepared)
2 c. whipping (35%) cream

2 T. liquor (such as amaretto or
   Kahlua)
4 (1.4-oz.) crisp toffee chocolate
   bars (such as Skor or Heath
   bars), crushed

Prepare cake according to package directions to make two (8- or 9-inch) round layers. Cool two minutes in pans on a wire rack, then remove layers and cool completely. Reserve 1 layer for another use and cut other layer into 1-inch cubes. Prepare mousse mix according to package directions. In a separate bowl, beat whipping cream to stiff peaks. Put half the cake cubes in trifle bowl. Drizzle half the liqueur on top. Sprinkle half the mousse, then half the whipped cream on top. Sprinkle half the chocolate bars over cream. Repeat layering with remaining ingredients. Cover bowl with plastic wrap and chill for at least 4 hours before serving. Store leftover dessert in refrigerator.

Tips: Prepare the cake ahead and freeze, cut into cubes while still semi-frozen. **To crush chocolate bars:** Chill them first, then pound them right in the package using an unbreakable utensil such as the back of a wooden spoon, a rolling pin or a hammer. Use any liqueur that you like that goes well with chocolate such as amaretto, Kahlua, Tia Maria or creme de cacao. **For a cakey dessert:** Use both cake layers.

Judy Gucciardo
Toledo, Ohio

Matthew 7:7-8 Ask, and it shall be given you; seek, and ye shall find; knock, and it shall be opened unto you.

DEATH BY CHOCOLATE TORTE

1 (15.5 oz.) brownie mix
2 T. coffee liqueur
1 (9.2-oz.) chocolate mousse mix
  (Jello Brand chocolate silk pie or
  Nestle)

1 (8 oz.) Cool Whip
2 Heath candy bars

Make an 8 x 8-inch pan of brownies according to package directions. When cool, brush with coffee liqueur. Cut cooled brownies into 16 pieces. Make chocolate mousse according to package directions but reserve the included chocolate crumbs for a later use. Layer in trifle bowl: 8 brownies, then half of the mousse, then half of the chocolate crumbs, then half of an 8 ounce Cool Whip, then 1 pulverized Heath bar. Repeat layers. Refrigerate.

Barb White
Eatonton, Georgia

"People need your love the most when they appear to deserve it the least."
John Harrigan

50191-03

CHOCOLATE CANDY BAR CAKE

1 (18-oz.) box German chocolate
  cake
2 (4-oz.) pkgs. instant chocolate
  pudding
1 (8-oz.) ctn. frozen whipped
  topping (thawed)

3 c. cold milk
12 oz. jar hot fudge sauce
12.25-oz. jar caramel sauce
5 toffee candy bars, chopped

Equipment needed:

2 (8- or 9-in.) cake pans
1 (8- or 9-in.) glass bowl with
  high straight sides

Prepare cake mix according to package directions. Pour half the mixture into each of the cake pans. When cakes are done, remove to rack and let cool completely, then remove from cake pans. Meanwhile, prepare the puddings according to package directions (except, use 1-1½ cups milk per box, instead of 2); set aside. In the clear bowl with high sides, place one of the cakes. Then cover with one half of the pudding mixture, then a layer of half the whipped topping, then drizzle with half the fudge sauce, then half the caramel sauce and then sprinkle one half of the chopped candy bars. Repeat this with the second cake, the rest of the pudding, the rest of the whipped topping, then the fudge sauce, the caramel sauce and ending with the rest of the chopped candy bars. Refrigerate ½ hour and then serve.

Note: It may be a little rich, but if you like chocolate dessert, you'll love this one.

Jerry E. Jones
Beaver Dam Lake, Indiana

GERMAN CHOCOLATE CAKE

Cake:

1 (4-oz.) bar German chocolate
½ c. boiling water
1 c. butter (softened)
2 c. sugar
4 eggs (separated)

1 tsp. vanilla
2½ c. sifted flour
½ tsp. salt
1 tsp. baking soda
1 c. buttermilk

Frosting:

2 c. evaporated milk
2 c. sugar
6 egg yolks
1 c. butter

2 tsp. vanilla
2⅔ c. coconut
2 c. chopped pecans

Cake: Melt chocolate in the boiling water and cool. Cream butter and sugar until fluffy. Add egg yolks one at a time and mix after each addition. Add melted chocolate and vanilla and mix well. Sift together flour, salt and soda. Add, alternating with milk, to chocolate mixture and beat until smooth. Fold in stiffly beaten egg whites. Pour into three greased and floured cake pans. Bake at 350° for 30 to 40 minutes. Cool before icing. **Frosting:** Combine evaporated milk, sugar, egg yolks, butter and vanilla. Cook over medium heat until thickened, about 12 minutes. Add coconut and pecans. Stir until thick enough to spread. Pour over each layer. Enjoy.

Note: For over 35 years, Mom has been making this cake for my father's birthday. It is now my husband and brother-in-law's favorite birthday cake too! In honor of my mother, Jeannie Roberts, breast cancer survivor, and in memory of my grandmother, Marie Griffith.

Jennifer Giovingo
Lake Village, Arkansas

50191-03

$\mathcal{T}$URTLE CAKE

1 (18.5-oz.) pkg. German chocolate
   cake mix
¾ c. butter (softened)
1 (14-oz.) pkg. Kraft caramels
⅓ c. evaporated milk
1 c. chocolate chips
1 c. pecans

Prepare cake mix according to package directions. Add ¾ cup butter to mixture. Set aside. Grease and flour a 9 x 13-inch pan. In a saucepan, melt caramels and evaporated milk. Pour ½ of the cake mix in 9 x 13-inch prepared pan and bake for 15 to 20 minutes in a 350° oven. Pour melted caramels on top of half cooked cake. Sprinkle on chocolate chips and pecans and then pour the rest of the cake mix on top and spread to edges. Bake until done. When cool, sprinkle with powdered sugar.

Lois Vallandingham
Villa Hills, Kentucky

$\mathcal{B}$LACK FOREST CAKE

1 (18.25-oz.) pkg. devil's food cake
   mix
1 (21-oz.) can cherry pie filling
2 eggs
1 tsp. almond extract
1 c. sugar
⅓ c. milk
5 T. margarine
1 c. chocolate chip morsels

Place the cake mix, cherry pie filling, eggs and almond extract in a large bowl. Beat with electric mixer till smooth. Bake at 350° in a greased 9 x 13-inch pan for 35 minutes or until a toothpick comes out of the middle clean. In a medium-size saucepan, combine the margarine, milk and sugar. Bring to a boil for 1½ minutes. Lower heat to medium and slowly add chocolate chips. Stir constantly as you add chocolate until smooth. Dump frosting over hot cake, it will harden as it cools.

Note: Everyone wants this recipe!

Robin Govenitto
Hamburg, New York

TEXAS SHEET CAKE

1½ c. margarine (divided)
1 c. water
8 T. cocoa (divided)
2 c. flour
2 c. sugar
½ tsp. salt
2 eggs

½ c. sour cream
1 tsp. baking soda
6 T. milk
1-lb. box powdered sugar (approx. 4 c.)
1 tsp. vanilla

In a large bowl combine flour, sugar and salt. Set aside. Bring to a boil 2 sticks of margarine, 1 cup water and 4 tablespoons cocoa. Add to dry ingredients in large bowl and mix well. Beta in eggs, sour cream and baking soda. Pour in greased cookie sheet with raised sides (15½ x 10½ x 1 inches). Bake for 20 minutes at 350°. **Icing:** Bring to boil 1 stick margarine, 4 tablespoons cocoa and milk. Add powdered sugar and vanilla. Spread icing on hot cake.

Jean McCarter
Edgewood, Kentucky

KILLER CHOCOLATE CAKE

1 (18.25 oz.) devil's food cake mix
1 (3.4-oz.) pkg. instant fudge pudding mix
2 eggs
½ c. strongly brewed coffee
½ c. vegetable oil
½ c. rum
8 oz. sour cream (½ pt.)

8 oz. chocolate chips (1⅓ c.)
1 (16-oz.) tub chocolate fudge icing
2 T. milk
Margarine & flour to grease baking dish
Bundt pan

Mix cake mix, pudding mix, eggs, coffee, vegetable oil, rum, sour cream, and chocolate chips. Grease and flour bundt pan. Pour batter into pan. Bake at 350° for 50 to 55 minutes. Let cool for 30 minutes before unmolding. Heat icing in microwave to make runny. Blend with milk until smooth. Drizzle over cake.

Note: Many calories, but worth it - especially for chocoholics!

Christy Henry
Cincinnati, Ohio

50191-03

2 c. flour
2 tsp. baking powder
2 tsp. baking soda
½ c. Crisco
2 c. sugar
2 eggs

1 c. milk
¾ c. cocoa
1 c. warm black coffee (fairly
  strong)
1½ tsp. vanilla extract

Icing:

3 c. powdered sugar
6 T. margarine or butter (melted)
Dash of salt (¼ tsp. ok)

4 T. milk (¼ c.)
1 tsp. vanilla extract

Sift together flour, baking powder, and baking soda. Set aside. In a large bowl, blend with mixer, Crisco, sugar, eggs, milk and cocoa. When thoroughly blended, alternately add the flour mixture and coffee to the Crisco mixture. Mix until the batter is smooth and glossy. Add vanilla extract. Blend some more, then pour batter into a greased 9 x 13-inch cake pan. Bake at 350° (300° if using the convection bake feature) for 40 to 45 minutes. Leave in pan to cool and ice. **Icing:** Combine powdered sugar, butter, salt, milk and vanilla in bowl and mix. This makes enough for a generous coating.

Note: Even non-chocolate fans will like this! Years ago, I baked this to split with my friend Hugo. When it was done, I decided to sample, one thing led to another, and soon Hugo's portion was gone! I've made it many times, still Hugo has not received his fair share!

Frenchy Corbeille
Castle Rock, Washington

"When you get to the end of your rope - tie a knot and hang on."
Franklin D. Roosevelt

ℬLACK RUSSIAN CAKE

1 (18.25 oz.) yellow cake mix
1 sm. (3.4-oz.) pkg. instant
  chocolate pudding mix
1/4 c. Kahlua
1/4 c. vodka

4 eggs
1 c. oil
3/4 c. water
1/4 c. chopped pecans

Mix cake mix, pudding mix, Kahlua, vodka, eggs, oil and water. Spray the bundt pan really well with non-stick spray. Sprinkle pecans on the bottom of the pan and pour cake mixture over pecans. Bake at 350° for 50 minutes. Take out of the pan immediately.

Janine Ervin
Highlands Ranch, Colorado

"The really happy person is the one who can enjoy the scenery even when they have to take a detour."

Sir James Jeans

50191-03

$\mathcal{G}$REAT AUNT ROSA'S SPONGE CAKE

Cake:

1 c. sifted flour	1 c. sifted sugar
Juice of ½ lemon	6 egg yolks
1 tsp. baking powder	6 egg whites

Cream filling:

1 qt. milk	6 oz. bittersweet chocolate
1 c. sugar	(shaved)
4 egg yolks	Cinnamon (to sprinkle on top)
½ c. cornstarch	16 oz. whipping cream (vanilla
1 tsp. vanilla	flavor)
Dash of salt	

Cake: Beat 6 egg yolks with beater until thick and lemon color. Add sugar gradually, beating well after each addition. Add lemon juice and mix well. In separate bowl, beat 6 egg whites until stiff peaks form, but not dry. Fold into egg yolk mixture. Gradually fold in flour a bit at a time. Divide batter between 2 (9-inch) round (ungreased) pans. Bake at 350° for 18 to 20 minutes. Remove from oven and invert pans on rack for about 1 hour until cake is cool before removing from the pans. **Cream filling:** Sift together sugar, cornstarch and salt. Set aside. Scald milk on top of double boiler over boiling water. Meanwhile, in separate bowl, beat 4 egg yolks until light and lemon color. Add sugar mixture to egg yolks a little at a time and mix well after each addition. Add ½ cup scalded milk and stir well. Pour entire mixture into scalded milk in the double boiler, stirring constantly until thickened (about 5 to 8 minutes). Add vanilla. Cool. Split cakes in half. Spread each layer with cream filling and sprinkle with cinnamon and shaved bittersweet chocolate. Frost with whipped cream flavored with vanilla.

Note: In memory of my niece, Katherine Ann Gioia, who died of cancer at age five. She inspired her mother, Anne, and me to start the Rosewell Park Alliance. We're a volunteer organization that raises funds/awareness for the Rosewell Park Cancer Institute in Buffalo, New York.

Donna M. Gioia
Buffalo, New York

ED VELVET CAKE

Cake:

½ c. butter (slightly softened)	1 tsp. salt
1½ c. sugar	1 tsp. vanilla
2½ c. cake flour	1 T. white vinegar
3 eggs	1 tsp. baking soda
1 oz. red food color	1¼ c. buttermilk
2 tsp. cocoa	

Icing:

1 c. whole vitamin D milk	1 c. butter (slightly softened)
5 T. reg. flour	1 tsp. vanilla extract
1 c. milk	

Cake: First, cream together butter and sugar, with hands, in large mixing bowl. Add eggs to butter/sugar mixture. In separate bowl, sift cake flour together with cocoa, salt and baking soda. Add flour mixture to butter mixture, folding in small portions until completely mixed. Add red food color, vanilla extract, vinegar and buttermilk. Mix thoroughly, noting mix may not be 100% smooth due to butter. Coat two (9-inch) round cake pans with margarine and dust with regular flour. Pour mix into pans and bake at 350° for approximately 25 minutes. Check with toothpick at about 23 minutes. Remove cakes when toothpick comes out clean. A little moist is better than a little dry. Remove cakes and allow to cool completely before icing. **Icing:** This requires slow and patient cooking. Sift together sugar and flour into a medium saucepan. Then, slowly add a little milk until sugar/flour is completely damp. Then add additional milk slowly, stirring and making sure mix is smooth. Heat on medium heat, stirring constantly. Remove from heat when mix is thick, paste like, but flowable mix. Immerse pan in cold icy water, enough to surround pan but not let it float. Mix must be thoroughly cooled before proceeding or icing will fail. Once mix is thoroughly cooled, add butter and vanilla and whip with beater. Mix until creamy smooth. Add icing to completely cooled cake. Stick cake in freezer for several minutes to stiffen icing. Then cover cake with plastic bag, seal and freeze. Allow to sit 4 hours before serving. Return any leftovers to refrigerator. Also can be made up as cupcakes with a batch yielding about 20.

(continued)

Note: Very rich. A great cold weather dessert! In memory of my grandma, Hazel Huelsman, of Louisville, Kentucky. She bought this cake every year for special occasions, finally received this recipe, and passed it on!

Walter Dunlevy
Louisville, Kentucky

PEANUT BUTTER CRUNCH CAKE

1 (18.25-oz.) pkg. yellow cake mix
1 c. peanut butter
½ c. light brown sugar (packed)
1 c. water
3 eggs
¼ c. vegetable oil

1 (11-oz.) bag Nestle peanut
butter & milk chocolate morsels
(divided)
½ c. honey roasted peanuts
(chopped)

In a mixing bowl, beat cake mix, peanut butter, and brown sugar on low speed until crumbly. Set aside ½ cup of this mixture for later use. Add water, eggs, and oil to remaining crumb mixture; blend on low until moist then beat on high for two minutes. Stir in ½ the bag of morsels. Pour into a greased 13 x 9 x 2-inch pan. Combine chopped nuts, reserved ½ cup of crumb mixture, and remaining morsels. Sprinkle over batter. Bake at 350° for 40 to 45 minutes or until knife comes out clean. Serves 12 to 16.

LuAnn Miltenis
Flower Mound, Texas

"Yesterday is not ours to recover but tomorrow is ours to win or lose."
Lyndon B. Johnson

WINKIE CAKE

1 (18.25-oz.) box yellow cake mix	5 T. flour
1 c. milk	1 c. sugar
½ tsp. salt	½ c. vegetable oil
½ c. butter (softened)	1 T. vanilla

Prepare cake mix as directed on the package and bake in a 9 x 13-inch pan. Cool. Remove from pan and cut in half lengthwise. **To prepare filling:** Place milk in a saucepan on medium heat. Stir in flour slowly and bring to a boil, stirring constantly until thick. Cool. Combine sugar, salt, vegetables oil, butter and vanilla in a bowl and beat until fluffy. Add milk mixture and beat again until fluffy. Spread the filling on one half of the cake and place the other half on top. Cover cake and store in refrigerator for 24 hours to develop flavor.

Note: Both children and adults will enjoy this dessert.

Jerry E. Jones
Beaver Dam Lake, Indiana

GOOEY BUTTER CAKE

1 (18.5-oz.) pkg. yellow butter cake mix	2 c. sugar
4 eggs (divided)	2 T. cornstarch
1 c. butter (slightly melted)	1 (8-oz.) pkg. cream cheese (softened)

Preheat oven to 350°. Butter a 9 x 13-inch pan. Mix butter, 2 eggs, and dry cake mix (be sure to use a yellow BUTTER cake mix). Press batter into prepared pan. In a medium-sized bowl, mix together sugar and cornstarch. Mix the remaining 2 eggs with the cream cheese, and add to sugar mixture. Pour evenly over the cake batter mixture in the pan. DO NOT STIR. Bake at 350° for 35 to 45 minutes, until brown on the edges, slightly wiggly in the middle.

Note: If you like a cheesecake Danish, you will love this cake! Dedicated to my friend, Chris, who lives in Pierce Township.

Janet Schlaak
Amelia, Ohio

50191-03

COCONUT BLACK WALNUT POUND CAKE

2 c. sugar
4 eggs (beaten)
½ tsp. salt
½ tsp. baking powder
1 c. chopped nuts (black walnuts)
1 c. salad oil

3 c. all-purpose flour
½ tsp. baking soda
1 c. buttermilk
1 c. flaked coconut
2 tsp. coconut extract

Syrup:

1 c. sugar
2 T. butter

½ c. water
1 T. coconut extract

Combine sugar, salad oil and eggs. Beat well. Combine salt, baking powder, flour, and baking soda. Add to sugar mixture, alternating with buttermilk, beating well after each addition. Stir in nuts, coconut, and coconut extract. Pour batter into a well greased and floured 10-inch tube pan. Bake at 325° for 1 hour and 5 minutes, or until cake tester comes out clean. **To make syrup:** Combine 1 cup sugar, 2 tablespoons butter, ½ cup water in saucepan. Bring to boil. Boil for 5 minutes. Remove from heat and stir in flavoring. When cake is done and still in the pan, pour hot coconut syrup over the hot cake. Allow cake to remain in the pan for 4 hours to absorb syrup. Remove from pan and wrap well. Cake will be very moist.

Note: This cake sold for over $200.00 at a local auction! Very good!

Sr. Jeanne Francis Cleves, SND
Morehead, Kentucky

"To the world you may be one person, but to one person you may be the world."

Unknown

COCONUT POUND CAKE

1 c. margarine (softened)	½ tsp. baking powder
1 c. Crisco	¼ tsp. salt
5 eggs	1 tsp. vanilla
1½ c. whole vitamin D milk	¼ tsp. lemon juice
3 c. plain flour	1 c. Angel Flake coconut

Cream margarine and Crisco and 3 cups of sugar. Add eggs one at a time. Mix well. Sift flour, baking powder and salt and add to the margarine mixture alternating with milk. Mix well and add 1 teaspoon vanilla, ¼ teaspoon lemon juice. Fold in 1 cup Angel Flake coconut. Pour into floured and greased tube cake pan. Start in cold oven at 350° for about 1½ hours. Leave in pan until cool on rack.

Note: This recipe has been in the family over 50 years. I have made so many, they are good for showers and to send to the sick. They always go over well. In honor of Carolyn Hensley.

Evelyn Adams
Barboursville, West Virginia

APPLE CAKE WITH NUTS AND CINNAMON

4 eggs	1 c. chopped nuts (pecans), divided
1¾ c. sugar	4 T. melted butter (divided)
2¼ c. flour	Cinnamon sugar, to sprinkle to
4 tsp. baking powder	taste
¾-1 c. cream	2 (9 x 9-in.) pans
7-12 apples (cored, peeled & sliced), divided	

Place apples (sliced into wedges, not rings) in cold water. Whip eggs with sugar into a thick, white foam. Set aside. Mix together flour and baking powder. Alternate adding egg mixture and cream to flour mixture. Mix gently. Grease two 9 x 9-inch baking pans. Pour half of the dough into each pan. Cover each pan of dough with rows of apple slices. Drizzle 2 tablespoons of butter over the apples in each pan. Sprinkle each pan with cinnamon sugar to taste. Top each pan with ½ cup of nuts. Bake at 400° for approximately 35 minutes or until golden (watch carefully).

Note: This is easy and fast to bake for many people.

Peter Randlov
Vaerlose, Denmark

50191-03

FRESH APPLE POUND CAKE

Cake:

3 c. unsifted flour	1 tsp. baking soda
1 tsp. salt	1½ c. corn oil
2 c. sugar	3 eggs
2 tsp. vanilla extract	2 c. apples (peeled & finely
1 c. pecans (chopped)	chopped)

Topping:

½ c. butter	2 tsp. milk
½ c. brown sugar (firmly packed)	

Grease and flour 10 x 4-inch bundt pan. Thoroughly stir together flour, baking soda, and salt. Set aside. In a large bowl, beat together oil, sugar, eggs and vanilla, at medium speed, until combined. Gradually beat in flour mixture until smooth. Fold in apples and pecans. Pour into bundt pan and bake at 325° for about 1 hour and 10 minutes, or until a cake tester, inserted in the center comes out clean. Allow cake to cool in pan. When cake is still slightly warm, prepare topping. In a small saucepan, stirring constantly, bring butter, brown sugar, and milk to a boil. Boil for 2 minutes. Turn cake out of pan. Spoon topping over while cake is still warm. Cool completely. Can be stored for a couple of days at room temperature. Refrigerate for longer storage. Better if it sets a few days. If using self-rising flour, omit salt and baking soda.

Rosemary Huntsman
Morehead, Kentucky

FRESH APPLE CAKE

2 c. sugar	1 tsp. vanilla extract
3 c. self-rising flour	3 c. diced apples
3 eggs (beaten)	1 c. chopped pecans
1¼ c. cooking oil	

Combine sugar and flour. Add eggs and oil. Beat well. Add vanilla extract and blend well. Add diced apples and chopped pecans. Grease and flour a tube (bundt) pan and pour in batter. Bake at 350° for about 1 hour.

Julia Kautz
Morehead, Kentucky

DANISH APPLE CAKE

⅔ c. butter
1⅓ c. sugar
2 eggs
2¼ c. flour
2 level tsp. baking powder
1 level tsp. baking soda
1 scant tsp. salt

1 level tsp. cloves
2½ level tsp. cinnamon
1 level tsp. nutmeg
2 tsp. vanilla powder or extract
7 apples or more to taste (peeled,
  cored & coarsely chopped)
Bread crumbs, to sprinkle

Combine butter, sugar and eggs and whip to foam. Add cloves, cinnamon and nutmeg. Mix well. Add baking powder, baking soda, salt, vanilla powder or extract and apples. Stir dough and pour into a well greased baking dish. Bake at 350° for approximately 40 minutes. Remove carefully from pan after a short cooling down.

Note: Tastes even better the next day! If your figure allows, try it with a little vanilla ice cream.

Peter Randlov
Vaerlose, Denmark

"*People see God every day, they just don't recognize Him.*"
Pearl Bailey

50191-03

APPLESAUCE STACK CAKE

Dough:

1 c. butter
1/4 c. Crisco
3 eggs
1 tsp. vanilla extract
4 c. flour
1 1/2 c. sugar

1 tsp. salt
3 1/2 tsp. baking powder
1/2 tsp. nutmeg
1/4 c. milk
Cinnamon to sprinkle

Filling:

40-oz. jar applesauce
1/2 c. sugar

2 1/2 tsp. cinnamon
1 tsp. nutmeg

Preheat oven to 400°. Combine butter, Crisco, eggs and vanilla extract in large mixing bowl and mix well. Set aside. Sift together flour, sugar, salt, baking powder and nutmeg. Gradually add to butter mixture alternating with milk. Dough will be soft. Separate into 10 equal portions. Turn a cake pan upside down and spray the OUTSIDE flat surface with nonstick cooking spray. Spread a portion of dough into a flat circle across the sprayed surface. Prick dough with fork and sprinkle with a little cinnamon. Bake approximately 7 minutes. Carefully remove to wax paper. Repeat process for 9 remaining portions (respray pan each time). **Filling:** Heat applesauce, sugar, cinnamon and nutmeg in saucepan. Spread about 1/2 cup of filling on first layer. Add a layer of cake, then another layer of filling. Repeat for all layers ending with the last of the applesauce mixture on top. Chill until ready to eat. Best after sitting in refrigerator for a few days.

Note: Delicious! Easy to make, just takes a little extra time.

Carole Cleves
Crestview Hills, Kentucky

APPLE BUNDT CAKE

3 c. unsifted flour
1 tsp. baking soda
1 tsp. cinnamon
1 tsp. salt
¼ tsp. nutmeg
2 c. sugar

3 eggs
1 c. vegetable oil
2 tsp. vanilla extract
3 c. tart apples (peeled & diced)
½ c. raisins

Combine flour, baking soda, cinnamon, salt and nutmeg in medium bowl. Set aside. In large mixing bowl, beat sugar, eggs, oil and vanilla. Gradually beat in flour mixture. Fold in apples and raisins. Batter will be very stiff. Spray bundt pan with cooking spray. Bake at 325° for 1 hour and 10 to 15 minutes. Cool 10 minutes before removing from pan.

Jane Scheuneman
St. Paul, Minnesota

APRICOT NECTAR CAKE

Cake:

1 (18.25-oz.) box yellow cake mix
1 (3.4-oz.) box vanilla instant
 pudding mix
½ c. apricot nectar
½ c. Wesson oil

½ c. water
4 eggs
¼ c. chopped nuts (pecans,
 walnuts, etc.)

Sauce:

1 c. sugar
½ c. margarine

¼ c. apricot nectar

Combine cake mix, pudding mix, apricot nectar, oil, water. Add one egg at a time and mix well. Grease bundt pan and sprinkle with nuts. Add batter and bake at 325° for hour. While cake is cooking, prepare sauce. In a saucepan, combine 1 cup sugar, ½ cup margarine and ¼ cup apricot nectar. Bring to a boil. Keep sauce warm. When cake is finished, loosen from pan and turn out on a large plate. While cake is still warm, poke holes in cake using a meat fork. Pour warm sauce over cake.

Note: This is a REAL good cake!

Margaret Cooper
Morehead, Kentucky

50191-03

PEACHES N' CREAM CAKE

1 (18.25-oz.) box cake mix	1 egg
¼ c. butter (softened)	¼-½ c. sugar
2 (15-oz.) cans sliced peaches	Cinnamon
8 oz. (½ pt.) sour cream	

Mix cake mix and butter until crumbly. Pour into a greased and floured 9 x 13-inch pan. Bake at 350° for 10 to 15 minutes to form crust. Spread peaches over crust in a single layer. In separate bowl, mix egg and sour cream, then pour over peaches. Sprinkle sugar and cinnamon over all. Bake at 350° for an additional 25 minutes. Serve warm.

Note: This is delightful!

Andrea Wiederhold
Amelia, Ohio

"I am not discouraged because every wrong attempt discarded is another step forward."

Thomas Edison

"REAL" STRAWBERRY CAKE WITH STRAWBERRY CREAM CHEESE ICING

1 (10-oz.) pkg. frozen strawberries in syrup (thawed)	½ c. water
1 (3-oz.) pkg. strawberry gelatin	1 c. unsalted butter (softened)
1 (18.25-oz.) box white cake mix	4 oz. cream cheese (softened)
1 c. oil	1 tsp. vanilla
4 eggs	1-lb. box powdered sugar (approx. 4 c.)
3 T. flour	3 (8½- or 9-in.) round cake pans

Preheat oven to 325°. Grease and flour 3 round cake pans. Purée strawberries, divide in half and set aside. In a mixing bowl, soften dry gelatin in half of the purée. Add dry cake mix, oil, eggs, flour and ½ cup water. Beat on low speed until blended, then beat on medium speed 3 minutes. Divide batter among the 3 pans. Bake 25 to 30 minutes until toothpick inserted in center comes out clean. Let cool in pans 15 minutes. Unmold and cool completely. **Frosting:** Let butter and cream cheese soften naturally on the counter, do not heat (microwave, etc.) to soften or your frosting will be too runny. When softened, beat together butter, cream cheese, and vanilla. Add other half of strawberry purée. Gradually beat in powdered sugar. If necessary, refrigerate icing until thick enough to spread. Icing lovers will like any extra icing on the side! Serves 10 to 12.

Note: So rich and good! The strawberry purée makes this cake like no other - a family favorite! In honor of my dad and husband, who always request this cake for their birthdays.

Nowim Dunn
Batavia, Ohio

"Take the first step in faith. You don't have to see the whole staircase, just take the first step."

Dr. Martin Luther King, Jr.

50191-03

$\mathscr{B}$ETSY'S ULTRA LEMON CAKE

1 (18.25-oz.) box lemon cake mix
1 sm. (3-oz.) box lemon gelatin
1 c. water
²/₃-1 c. cooking oil
4 eggs

Glaze:

1¹/₂-2 c. powdered sugar
Juice of 3 lemons (may use
  comparable amount of bottled
  lemon)

Preheat oven to 350°. Mix together 1 box lemon cake mix, 1 box lemon gelatin, water, cooking oil, and eggs. Beat for 4 minutes. Bake in greased, but NOT floured, bundt pan for 40 minutes. While cake is baking, prepare glaze. Combine powdered sugar and lemon juice, mix well. As soon as cake is removed from oven, poke holes using chop sticks and pour glaze on cake. Allow cake to cool in pan and remove from pan after 1 hour.

Note: This is even better the second day.

Sherry Dickson
Ft. Wright, Kentucky

$\mathscr{B}$ANANA SPLIT CAKE

2 c. graham cracker crumbs
1¹/₂ c. margarine
1 (20-oz.) can crushed pineapple
5-6 bananas (¹/₂-in. thin slices)
2 c. powdered sugar
1 egg
1 (12 oz.) Cool Whip
¹/₂ c. chopped pecans
¹/₂ c. chopped maraschino cherries

Melt ¹/₂ cup margarine and mix with graham cracker crumbs. Spread evenly in a 9 x 13-inch baking pan. Beat together powdered sugar, egg and 1 cup melted margarine. Pour over graham cracker crumb layer in dish. Place banana slices over sugar/egg/margarine mixture. Drain pineapple and spread over bananas. Spread Cool Whip and sprinkle top with nuts and cherries. Place in refrigerator until ready to serve. Makes approximately 15 servings.

Note: In honor of my friend Diane Coholich.

Sherry Dickson
Ft. Wright, Kentucky

$\mathcal{P}$INEAPPLE ANGEL FOOD CAKE

1 (18.25-oz.) pkg. angel food cake   1 (20-oz.) can crushed pineapple
  mix

Mix dry cake mix with undrained pineapple in a large bowl. Pour into a greased 9 x 13-inch pan. Bake at temperature stated on cake mix box for 20 to 30 minutes, or until a pick comes out clean.

Recipe Note: A low-fat dessert.

Lois Vallandingham
Villa Hills, Kentucky

$\mathcal{H}$UMMINGBIRD CAKE

3 c. flour (sifted)   1½ c. vegetable oil
2 c. white sugar   1 c. chopped pecans
1 tsp. baking soda   2 c. diced bananas
1 tsp. cinnamon   1 (8-oz.) can crushed pineapple
1 tsp. salt   1½ tsp. vanilla
3 eggs

Frosting:

8 oz. cream cheese (softened)   ½ c. butter (softened)
1-lb. box powdered sugar (approx.   1 tsp. vanilla extract
  4 c.)

Sift flour once, then sift flour with sugar, baking soda, cinnamon and salt. In a separate bowl, beat eggs slightly, add vegetable oil and vanilla. Add to flour mixture. Mix lightly, do not beat. Fold in pecans, bananas and pineapple. Bake 1 hour and 15 minutes at 325° in a greased and floured bundt pan. Meanwhile, to prepare frosting, beat cream cheese, sugar, vanilla and butter until fluffy. When cake has cooled, cover cake with frosting.

Note: This recipe is perfect for any occasion. It keeps for a long time and is very moist. Even kids love it.

Gail Gorell
Haines City, Florida

50191-03

DUMP CAKE

1 (20-oz.) can crushed pineapple
1 (21-oz.) can cherry pie filling
1 (18.25-oz.) box yellow cake mix

½ c. butter or margarine
1 c. chopped pecans
1 c. coconut, opt.

Butter a 9 x 13-inch dish. Pour pineapple (undrained) into pan and smooth into corners. Pour cherry pie filling over pineapple. Sprinkle dry yellow cake mix on top of fruit mixture. Spread evenly. Top with nuts, optional coconut and chunks of butter. Bake approximately 1 hour at 350° until cake is firm and top has slightly browned.

Note: Couldn't be easier and everyone loves this! Baking contest, 2nd place winner!

Melissa Howard
Crescent Springs, Kentucky

FRUIT COCKTAIL CAKE

2 c. flour
1½ c. sugar
1 tsp. baking soda

2 eggs
1 (15-oz.) can fruit cocktail
  (undrained)

Icing:

½ c. butter (softened)
1 (5-oz.) can Carnation
  evaporated milk
1 tsp. vanilla extract

1 (7-oz.) can coconut (or flaked
  coconut)
1 c. sugar

Mix flour, sugar, baking soda, eggs, and fruit cocktail well. Bake at 300° for 45 minutes. Prepare icing while cake is baking. Mix butter, milk, vanilla, coconut, sugar. Cook for 2 minutes. When cake has finished baking and is still warm, cover with warm icing.

Note: A moist cake with a buttery, coconut topping.

Rosemary Huntsman
Morehead, Kentucky

JAM CAKE

Cake:

1 c. chopped nuts	*2 c. buttermilk*
1 c. raisins	*2 c. blackberry jam*
4½ c. flour (divided)	*1 tsp. nutmeg*
½ c. shortening	*2 tsp. cinnamon*
2 c. sugar	*1 tsp. ground cloves*
2 eggs (beaten)	*2 tsp. baking soda*

Icing:

1 c. brown sugar	*1 T. butter*
⅓ c. cream	*Approx. ¾ c. powdered sugar*

Dredge chopped nuts, raisins and 1 cup flour. Set aside. Cream shortening and sugar. Add beaten eggs to creamed mixture and mix well. Add buttermilk and blackberry jam. Set aside. In a large bowl, sift together 3½ cups flour, nutmeg, cinnamon, ground cloves, baking soda. Add to creamed mixture and beat again. Add the raisins, nuts and flour mixture which has been set aside. Grease and flour a large tube (bundt) pan and bake at 350° for about 1 hour and 20 minutes. Cool and cover with icing. **Icing:** Bring brown sugar, cream and butter to a boil. Remove from heat and cool for a few minutes. Add enough powdered sugar for a good consistency to spread. If too stiff, add a little more cream.

Julia Kautz
Morehead, Kentucky

"Most people are about as happy as they make up their minds to be."
Abraham Lincoln

50191-03

MOM'S ONE EGG RAISIN CAKE

¾ c. sugar
¼ c. shortening
1 egg (slightly beaten)
2 c. flour
1 tsp. nutmeg

1 tsp. cinnamon
1 tsp. baking soda
½ tsp. salt
1½ c. raisins
Water to cover

Cream together shortening and sugar. Add slightly beaten egg. Sift together flour, nutmeg, cinnamon, baking soda, and salt. Add to shortening and sugar mixture. In small saucepan cover raisins with water and boil for 10 minutes. Strain and reserve ¾ cup raisins with water. Add raisins to mixture. Stir in raisin water. Pour into lightly greased 8- or 9-inch pan. Bake at 350° for 30 minutes. Let cool in pan for at least 10 minutes.

Note: Whenever my mother served this raisin cake and anyone remarked how good it was, she would always say "And just one egg!" And so it got its name!

Dorothy Little
Ajax, Ontario, Canada

"Faith is daring the soul to go beyond what the eyes can see."
Unknown

$\mathscr{P}$ATTY'S CARROT CAKE

1¾ c. sugar
1¼ c. Wesson oil
4 eggs
2 c. flour
2 tsp. baking soda

2 tsp. baking powder
2 tsp. cinnamon
1 tsp. salt
3 c. grated carrots
1 c. chopped nuts (walnuts)

Icing:

¼ c. butter (softened)
8 oz. cream cheese (softened)
2 tsp. vanilla

4 c. (1 lb.) powdered sugar
1 (8-oz.) can crushed pineapple
  (drained)

Cream together sugar, Wesson oil, and eggs. Set aside. In separate bowl, combine flour, baking soda, baking powder, cinnamon and salt until well mixed. Combine the sugar mixture with flour mixture. Add the carrots and chopped nuts. Grease and flour 3 (8-inch) round cake pans. Preheat oven to 350°. Bake for 30 to 35 minutes. Meanwhile, to prepare icing, combine butter, cream cheese, vanilla and powdered sugar. When cake is done baking, allow to cool. Spread icing on top of one cake layer (reserve some icing to cover other layer and sides of cake). Cover icing with crushed pineapple. Top with second layer of cake. Ice entire outside of cake with remaining icing.

Note: In memory of Pat. A wonderful mother, grandmother and great grandmother. I miss my dear mother. But most of all I miss my best friend.

Patricia Mohr
Indianapolis, Indiana

"How wonderful it is that nobody need wait a single moment before starting to improve the world."

Anne Frank

50191-03

GRANDMA DORIS' CRUMB CAKE

1 c. shortening
2 c. brown sugar
3 c. flour
2 beaten eggs
1½ c. buttermilk (with heaping
  tsp. baking soda dissolved in it)

1 tsp. vanilla
Pinch of salt
Cinnamon to sprinkle on top
Powdered sugar icing to drizzle
  on cake after baking (see recipe
  below)

Mix shortening, brown sugar and flour until crumbly. Take out 1 cup of mixture and set aside. Add eggs, buttermilk, vanilla, and salt to mixture. Grease and flour 9 x 13-inch pan. Pour batter in pan. Sprinkle reserved crumbly mixture on top. Lightly sprinkle cinnamon on whole cake. Bake at 350° for 45 to 60 minutes. After cake cools a few minutes, drizzle with thin powdered sugar icing.

Note: In honor of our grandmother, Doris Drook. This recipe has been in our family for at least 60 years and is absolutely fabulous! We always begged her to make it.

Powdered sugar icing:

⅓ c. butter or margarine
2 c. powdered sugar

1½ tsp. vanilla
2-4 T. hot water

Melt margarine in microwave. Stir in powdered sugar and vanilla. Stir in water, 1 tablespoon at a time, until glaze is thin. Drizzle on top of cake while slightly warm.

Tammy Drummond
Carmel, Indiana

"You will recognize your own path when you come upon it, because you will suddenly have all the energy and imagination you will ever need."
Jerry Gillies

$\mathcal{D}$OUBLE LEMON CURD

1 c. granulated sugar
⅔ c. fresh lemon juice plus zest of lemon

5 eggs (room temp.)
½ c. unsalted butter (melted)

Combine sugar, zest, juice and eggs in blender. Whirl until mixed. On low speed, add butter gradually in thin stream. Put mixture in saucepan and over low heat, stir constantly until mixture is thick enough to coat the back of a spoon and mound slightly, about 8 to 10 minutes. Don't let boil. Cool and store in refrigerator up to 1 week. Use to dollop on tiny phyllo shells, to fill cream puffs or as a refreshing dip for strawberries.

Note: Perfect for tea time! This always reminds me of my mom, who, even when she was terminally ill, always enjoyed her cup of tea.

Rita Heikenfeld
Batavia, Ohio

Recipe Favorites

50191-03

Cookies & Candy

Barbara Schanzle (left) and daughter - Washington

Emma Seelbinder Smith
Mississippi

Bill and Betty McCullough
Missouri

Emma

In 1928, Emma was diagnosed with breast cancer. She was 33 years old. The cancer was in one of her lymph glands, which resulted in a very radical mastectomy. "There was no chemotherapy back then, only the knife," she said. Talking about her cancer did not come easy for her. "Long ago people were ashamed," she said. That's why most people died because they "waited too late." "I can remember when I went into surgery, there were so many young doctors there to watch the operation." The doctors told her she was cut so terribly that she would be hospitalized for six weeks.

There were no follow up treatments, only a few x-rays. "I didn't heal for eight months. I couldn't do anything with my arm. I had it strapped down to my side, but it didn't bother me," Emma said. She wouldn't believe the doctors when they said she would never use her arm again. She began to exercise it herself (this was long before Reach to Recovery volunteers were around, telling us to exercise our arms!) Her husband helped her raise her arm everyday and she eventually regained use of it.

Then, however, another cancer was found in her remaining breast. She had a second mastectomy - experiencing all the fears of cancer again. Some years later, her husband died. She was left to raise their sons alone. Emma did a bit of everything, working in the fields, helping run their dairy farm and finally, teaching fourth grade for over 40 years. Cancer never got in her way.

Emma's story has kept me hopeful year after year, since my own diagnosis, and it will continue to do so for all my days. For what I have saved until now is the best part. Emma lived to be 106 years old! A 73 year survivor! She's truly an Angel of Hope for all breast cancer survivors!

Jane Miller
Memphis, Tennessee

Cookies & Candy

RUSSIAN TEACAKES

1 c. butter (softened)
1 tsp. vanilla
½ c. sifted powdered sugar

2¼ c. flour
¼ tsp. salt
¾ c. finely chopped nuts

Mix butter, powdered sugar, and vanilla thoroughly. Add flour and salt; blend in. Mix in nuts. Chill dough. Heat oven to 400°. Roll dough in 1-inch balls. Place on ungreased baking sheet. Bake 10 to 12 minutes, or until set but not brown. While still warm, roll in powdered sugar. Cool. Roll in powdered sugar again. Makes 4 dozen.

Charlene Seim
Issaquah, Washington

SNICKERDOODLES

1 c. shortening (or ½ c.
  shortening & ½ c. margarine)
1½ c. sugar
2 eggs
2¾ c. sifted flour

2 tsp. cream of tartar
1 tsp. soda
½ tsp. salt
½ tsp. vanilla

Mixture to roll cookies in:

2 tsp. cinnamon

2 tsp. sugar

Cream shortening and 1½ cups sugar. Beat in eggs. Blend in flour, cream of tartar, soda, salt and vanilla. Chill in refrigerator. Roll into walnut-sized balls and roll each in mixture of cinnamon and sugar. Bake on cookie sheet 8 to 10 minutes in 400° oven.

Note: I am a two year breast cancer survivor! These have been a big hit for many years and kids love them.

Shirley Satterfield
Daisy, Oklahoma

SANTA'S WHISKERS

2½ c. all-purpose flour
½ c. pecans (finely chopped)
¾ c. flaked coconut
¾ c. finely chopped red or green
  candied cherries

1 c. butter (softened)
1 c. sugar
2 T. milk
1 tsp. vanilla

In mixing bowl cream butter or margarine and sugar together. Blend in milk and vanilla. Stir in flour, chopped candies and pecans. Form dough into two (8-inch) long rolls. Roll each roll in flaked coconut to coat outside. Wrap in waxed paper and chill thoroughly, about two hours. Cut into ¼-inch slices. Place on an ungreased cookie sheet. Bake at 375° for about 12 minutes or until edges are golden. Makes about 60.

Sherry Dickson
Ft. Wright, Kentucky

ANGEL CRISPS

½ c. brown sugar
½ c. white sugar
½ c. shortening
½ c. margarine
1 egg

1 tsp. vanilla
2 c. flour
1 tsp. cream of tartar
1 tsp. baking soda
½ tsp. salt

In a large mixing bowl combine brown sugar, white sugar, shortening, egg and vanilla until creamy. On a large plate or in another bowl sift together the flour, cream of tartar, baking soda and the salt. Slowly add the flour mixture into the creamed mixture and mix until thoroughly combined. Scoop out teaspoon-size mounds of the dough and shape into balls. Dip top half of the ball into a cup of water and then into some white sugar (you can use a plate or bowl). Place the balls on an ungreased cookie sheet. Bake at 450° for 8 minutes.

Note: I learned how to make this in my home economics class back in the 1980's.

Lesley Kilgore
Batavia, Ohio

50191-03

MONSTER COOKIES

3 eggs
½ c. butter or oleo (softened)
1 c. brown sugar
1 c. white sugar
1 tsp. vanilla extract

1 tsp. corn syrup
2 tsp. baking soda
1½ c. crunchy peanut butter
1 c. raisins
4½ c. quick oatmeal

Optional:

½ c. coconut
⅔ c. chocolate chips

⅔ c. M & M's candies

Beat eggs. Cream with oleo, brown sugar and white sugar. Add vanilla extract, corn syrup, baking soda, crunchy peanut butter, raisins and oatmeal. **Optional:** Also add coconut, chocolate chips or M & M's candies. Mix well. Drop on ungreased cookie sheet with ice cream scoop for giant cookies. Bake at 350° for 12 to 15 minutes. **For small cookies:** Drop with teaspoon and bake 10 to 15 minutes.

Helen Montgomery
Morehead, Kentucky

"Every problem has a gift for you in its hands."

Richard Bach

GRANDMA SAYER'S DATE-FILLED DROP COOKIES

Filling:

2 c. dates (finely chopped)
³/₄ c. sugar

³/₄ c. water

Cookie dough:

1 c. shortening
2 c. brown sugar
2 eggs
¹/₂ c. buttermilk
1 tsp. vanilla

3¹/₂ c. flour
¹/₈ tsp. cinnamon
1 tsp. salt
1 tsp. baking soda

In a small saucepan, mix together the dates, sugar and water. Cook and stir until thickened. Set aside. Heat oven to 400°. Mix together shortening, brown sugar and eggs. Stir in buttermilk and vanilla. In separate bowl, sift together flour, soda, salt and cinnamon. Add to shortening/buttermilk mixture. Mix well. Drop a teaspoonful of dough per cookie onto an ungreased baking sheet. Top that with a half teaspoon of date mixture. Top that with a half teaspoon of dough. Bake 10 to 12 minutes. Yields 5 to 6 dozen.

Note: This is in honor of my grandmother, Amanda Ellen Richardson Sayers, who died in 1985 at age 88 of lymphoma. She loved these delicious cookies, which she made every Christmas. She always made a batch using pineapple instead of dates, too.

Lee Ann Smith Ward
Huntington, West Virginia

"Healing takes courage, and we all have courage, even if we have to dig a little to find it."

Tori Amos

50191-03

AMIE'S COOKIES

Cookies:

2 c. light brown sugar
6 T. Crisco shortening
2 eggs
2 tsp. vanilla
4 oz. unsweetened chocolate
  (melted)

1 c. sour milk (1 c. milk plus 1 T.
  vinegar)
3 c. flour
2 tsp. baking soda
2 tsp. baking powder
1 tsp. salt

Icing:

1 lb. powdered sugar (approx. 4 c.)
½ stick margarine (softened)
1 tsp. vanilla

¼ c. milk
Dash of salt

Mix together brown sugar and Crisco. Add eggs and beat until fluffy. Add vanilla and melted chocolate. Mix well...this will be the original mixture. Mix in a separate bowl: flour, baking soda, baking powder and salt...this will be your dry mixture. Alternately add the dry mixture and sour milk to the original mixture. Once all are mixed well together, drop by teaspoonful onto greased cookie sheet and bake at 375° for 7 to 9 minutes. **Icing:** Mix together powdered sugar, softened margarine, vanilla and milk. If too runny, add more powdered sugar. If too dry, add milk. Refrigerate for 30 minutes and then after it hardens a bit, it is ready to spread on cookies.

Note: It is important that baking soda and baking powder are fresh, and make sure you are using unsweetened chocolate. When cookies are cool, add icing. Yield: 4 to 5 dozen cookies.

Note: I love making these for the holidays and either adding green and red sprinkles or dying the icing. This recipe is from my great grandmother, Mamie.

Eileen Rouse
Melbourne, Florida

GINGERBREAD COOKIES

5-5½ c. all-purpose flour
1 tsp. cloves
1 tsp. baking soda
1 c. shortening
1 tsp. salt
1 c. sugar

2 tsp. ginger
1¼ c. unsulphured molasses
2 tsp. cinnamon
1 tsp. nutmeg
2 eggs (beaten)

Preheat oven to 375°. Thoroughly mix 5 cups flour, soda, salt, cloves, ginger, cinnamon, nutmeg. Set aside. Melt shortening in a large saucepan. Cool slightly. Add sugar, molasses and eggs. Mix well. Add 4 cups of the dry ingredient mixture and blend well. Turn mixture onto a lightly floured surface, knead in remaining dry ingredient mixture by hand. Add a little more flour if necessary to make a firm dough. Roll out on a lightly floured surface to ¼-inch thickness. Cut out shapes. Bake on an ungreased cookie sheet for 6-15 minutes, depending on the size of the cookie cut out. If not going to be used right away, it may be rolled in plastic and kept for one week. Allow 3 hours to soften before baking.

Margaret Cooper
Morehead, Kentucky

MOLASSES COOKIES

1½ c. margarine (soft)
2 c. granulated sugar
2 eggs
½ c. molasses

5 c. plain flour
4 tsp. baking soda
2 tsp. cinnamon
2 tsp. ginger

Cream together margarine and sugar. Add molasses. Mix and add sifted flour, cinnamon, ginger and baking soda. Mix well. Cover and refrigerate. Take dough out the next day and make into balls. Roll in sugar and put in pan. Criss cross with fork. Bake about 10 to 12 minutes at 350°. Cool in pan and store in covered bowl or tin.

Note: I call these cookies my "give away cookies" because they are so easy to make and send to family and neighbors.

Evelyn Adams
Barboursville, West Virginia

50191-03

*S*PICED MOLASSES GINGER COOKIES

2 c. sifted all-purpose flour	¼ c. unsalted butter (room temp.)
2 tsp. baking soda	1 c. firmly packed light brown
2 tsp. ground cinnamon	sugar
1½ tsp. ground ginger	1 egg
1 tsp. ground cloves	¼ c. dark molasses
1 tsp. salt	Ice water
½ c. solid vegetable shortening	Sugar to coat

Preheat oven to 350°. Lightly butter cookie sheets. Sift flour, baking soda, cinnamon, ginger, ground cloves and salt into medium bowl. Using electric mixer, beat shortening, butter and brown sugar in large bowl until fluffy. Add egg and molasses to butter mixture and beat until blended. Mix in dry ingredients. Refrigerate dough one hour. Roll dough into 1¼-inch balls. Dip quickly into ice water, then roll in sugar to coat. Arrange on prepared sheets, spacing 2 inches apart. Bake until cookies are pale golden and cracked on top but still soft to touch, about 10 minutes. Let stand 1 minute. Using metal spatula, transfer to rack and cook completely. Store in airtight container.

Note: I absolutely love molasses cookies and I have to say that I think these are the best I've ever had. Not only are the cookies delicious, they look beautiful as well.

Karin Deti
Des Moines, Washington

"Remember, we all stumble, every one of us. That's why it's a comfort to go hand in hand."

Emily Kimbrough

$\mathcal{E}$MMA SMITH'S REFRIGERATOR COOKIES

1 c. Crisco	1 tsp. salt
½ tsp. vanilla extract	1 tsp. baking soda
2 eggs	1½ c. chopped nuts
2 c. brown sugar	3½ c. flour

Cream Crisco, sugar, vanilla. Dissolve salt and baking soda in a little hot water before adding to mixture. Gradually add flour and nuts. Make into long rolls and chill in the refrigerator overnight. Slice thinly and place apart on a cookie sheet. Bake at 350° for 7 to 10 minutes. Watch closely to make sure they do not burn.

Note: I, as well as MANY others in my family, am a cancer survivor. One cousin was diagnosed at age 16 and is now in her 70's. Emma was diagnosed in 1928, at age 33, and lived to be 106 years old! She is an Angel of Hope for all breast cancer survivors.

Jane Miller
Memphis, Tennessee

$\mathcal{B}$UTTER COOKIES

1 c. margarine (softened)	3 tsp. vanilla
½ c. white sugar	3 c. plain flour
1 egg	½ tsp. baking powder

Cream sugar and margarine. Add egg and vanilla and mix well. Add sifted flour and baking powder. Chill dough overnight. The next morning roll out thin and cut in desired shapes. Place in ungreased pans. Decorate with sugar or ice after they are baked. Bake 5 to 7 minutes at 425°. Makes about 7 dozen.

Note: In honor of my daughter-in-law Bobbie Adams. These cookies are excellent for holidays. Children enjoy helping bake and decorate them also.

Evelyn Adams
Barboursville, West Virginia

50191-03

ℬETTY'S GOOD OLD FASHIONED SUGAR COOKIES

1 c. butter (softened), do not use margarine	2 T. milk
1½ c. sugar	2 T. vanilla extract
2 eggs	2½ tsp. baking powder
	3¾ c. flour

Let butter stand in a mixing bowl until soft. Add sugar, eggs, milk and vanilla, mix well. In a separate bowl, sift baking powder with the flour. Add to butter mixture. Chill well. Roll "thin" on a lightly floured board or counter top. Cut in desired shapes. Place on a greased and flour dusted cookie sheet. Sprinkle with granulated sugar or sprinkles. Bake at 350° for approximately 8 to 10 minutes or until slightly browned on bottom. **Decorating option:** Instead of sprinkling with sugar or sprinkles, bake plain cookies as instructed, cool, and paint with frosting. Makes approximately 2¼ pounds of cookies.

Note: This cookie recipe (in honor of Betty Jane McCullough) has been a family favorite for over 30 years and is fun to do with kids. It is time consuming but well worth the work. Enjoy!

Cindy Ann Lifka
St. Louis, Missouri

"I try to avoid looking forward or backward, and try to keep looking upward."

Charlotte Bronte

MIMI'S SUGAR COOKIES

½ c. margarine or butter
  (softened)
½ c. shortening
1 c. sugar
1 egg (beaten)
1 tsp. vanilla

½ tsp. cream of tartar
½ tsp. baking soda
¼ tsp. salt
2 c. flour
White sugar

Lightly beat one egg. With a wire whisk or electric mixer, mix margarine/butter, shortening, sugar, the beaten egg and vanilla. In a separate bowl, combine all dry ingredients (cream of tartar, baking soda, salt and flour). Combine wet ingredients with dry ingredients and mix well. Fill a small bowl with white sugar, and another with water. Roll dough into teaspoon-sized balls and place on cookie sheet. Dip the bottom of a glass, first in the bowl of water to moisten, then in the bowl of sugar and lightly press each cookie down. Bake at 400° for 6 to 8 minutes or until golden brown. Makes about 2 dozen.

Note: These cookies have long been a family favorite, baked, regularly by my great grandmother, who passed away last spring at the age of 102.

Lindsay J. Brice
St. Paul, Minnesota

PEANUT BUTTER COOKIES

1 c. brown sugar
1 c. granulated sugar
1 c. Jif peanut butter

¾ c. butter
2 c. flour
2 tsp. baking soda

Cream brown sugar, granulated sugar, peanut butter, flour and baking soda. Make into round balls and flatten with table fork. Bake at 375° oven for 8 to 10 minutes.

Note: Recipe in family for over 50 years. In memory of grandmother, Edith Carpenter.

Jacqueline Kamm
Maumee, Ohio

50191-03

RICH CHOCOLATE CHIP OATMEAL COOKIES

2 c. butter (softened)
24 oz. chocolate chips
4 c. flour
2 c. brown sugar
2 tsp. baking soda
1 tsp. salt
2 c. sugar

1 (8-oz.) Hershey's bar (grated)
5 c. oatmeal (blended)
4 eggs
2 tsp. baking powder
2 tsp. vanilla
3 c. chopped nuts (your choice)

Measure oatmeal. Blend in blender to a fine powder. Cream the butter, sugar and brown sugar. Add eggs and vanilla, mix together with flour, powdered oatmeal, salt, baking powder and baking soda. Add chocolate chips, grated Hershey's bar, and nuts. Roll into balls and place two inches apart on a cookie sheet. Bake at 375° for 10 minutes. Makes 112 cookies. Recipe may be cut in half.

Note: Very good!

Roxanne del Rosario
Santee, California

"In the hour of adversity, be not without hope, for crystal rain falls from black clouds."

Persian Poem

GRANOLA SNACKS

1 c. butter
1 c. brown sugar
1 c. white sugar
2 eggs
1 tsp. vanilla
2 c. flour
1 tsp. baking powder
1 tsp. salt

1 tsp. baking soda
1 c. white chocolate chips
1 c. chocolate chips
1 c. raisins
1 c. chopped nuts
1 c. old-fashioned rolled oats
1½ c. any type granola mix

Cream butter, brown sugar and white sugar. Add eggs and vanilla to butter mixture and mix well. In separate bowl, sift flour, baking powder, salt and baking soda. Add to butter and egg mixture. Fold in white chocolate chips, chocolate chips, raisins, nuts, rolled oats and granola mix. When well mixed, roll dough into golf-ball size pieces and bake on ungreased cookie sheet at 375° for 8 to 10 minutes, or until barely golden. Dough keeps well when refrigerated. Bake as needed. Freezes well.

Note: Enjoyed by Zachary and Brandon Pense, Ashley Widmer, Renée, Kristy, Jacob and Maggie Anderson. In honor of their mother and aunt, Linda L. Pense, RD, MS, CD.

Donna Anderson
Indiana

"During your times of trial and suffering, when you see only one set of footprints in the sand, it was then that I carried you."
Poem "Footprints", author unknown

SPECIAL K BARS

1 c. white Karo syrup
1 c. sugar
2 T. butter
6 c. Special K cereal

1½ c. peanut butter
12-oz. pkg. chocolate chips
12-oz. pkg. butterscotch chips

Combine syrup, sugar and butter into medium-sized saucepan and bring to boil over low heat. Pour mixture over Special K and peanut butter in large bowl and mix well until cereal is completely covered. Press mixture into lightly greased 13 x 9-inch pan. Melt chocolate and butterscotch chips over low heat and frost cereal mixture. Refrigerate 1½ hours. Cut into bar-sized pieces and enjoy!

Note: This is a recipe I've used during the holidays to serve when entertaining, going to family/friend gatherings as well as giving to neighbors, coworkers, family and friends! This is very easy for kids to assist in making and is always a winner!

Roxanne del Rosario
Santee, California

"The truth of the matter is that you always know the right thing to do. The hard part is doing it."

Norman Schwarzkopf

℘EANUT BUTTER CHOCOLATE BARS

Crust:

8 med. size butter or chocolate
  chip cookies

¼ c. salted butter

Melted chocolate layer:

15 oz. milk chocolate chips (about
  2½ c.)

Filling:

1½ c. creamy peanut butter
½ c. salted butter (softened)

3 c. powdered sugar
2 tsp. vanilla extract

Preheat oven to 325°. In food processor or blender, process cookies until finely ground. Add ¼ cup butter and mix together completely. Press crumb mixture into the bottom of a 8 x 8-inch baking pan and bake 10 minutes. Cool to room temperature. Melt chocolate in double boiler over slightly simmering water, or microwave the chocolate, stirring every 30 seconds until completely melted. Pour half of the melted chocolate into the pan and smooth evenly over crust. Place pan in refrigerator. Keep remaining chocolate warm. **Prepare the peanut butter filling:** Blend peanut butter and ½ cup butter together until smooth, using the food process or an electric mixer. Slowly beat in powdered sugar and then add vanilla extract. Beat until smooth. Spread peanut butter filling over chilled chocolate layer. Finish by pouring remaining warm chocolate over filling and spread smooth. Chill in the refrigerator 1 hour or until firm. Cut into bars and serve. Yield: 24 to 36 bars.

Note: In memory of my grandmother, Goldie Huffman, who really liked these a lot!

Angela Yvonne Scott
Marion, Indiana

50191-03

*C*HOCOLATE TOPPED CRUNCHY SLICE

3 reg. size (1.76-oz.) Snicker's
  almonds bars (formerly Mars
  bar), chopped

4 T. butter
3 c. rice bubbles (Rice Krispies)

Topping:

1 c. chocolate bits (chocolate
  chips)

1½ T. butter

Grease a 7.5 x 11.5-inch tray. Combine candy bar pieces and butter in large saucepan, stirring constantly over low heat (without boiling) until smooth; stir in rice bubbles. Press mixture evenly into prepared pan, spread with topping. Refrigerate until set before cutting into small squares. **Topping:** Melt chocolate and butter in pan over hot water; stir until smooth. Keeping time is 1 week.

Note: This is just delicious and a real winner! I am a survivor!

Angela Hanslip
Perth, Western Australia

"Nurture your mind with great thoughts, for you will never go any higher than you think."

Benjamin Disraeli

$\mathcal{F}$ATHER'S DAY PRALINE COOKIES

$1^2/_3$ c. all-purpose flour
$1^1/_2$ tsp. baking powder
$1/_2$ tsp. salt
$1/_2$ c. unsalted butter (room temp.)
$2^1/_2$ c. light brown sugar
1 lg. egg

1 tsp. pure vanilla extract
$1/_2$ c. heavy cream
1 c. sifted powdered sugar
1 c. pecan halves (toasted &
   broken into lg. pieces)

Heat oven to 350°. Sift together flour, baking powder and salt in a medium bowl and set aside. In the bowl of an electric mixer, cream butter and 1½ cups light brown sugar on medium speed until light and fluffy, about 3 minutes. Add egg and vanilla, beat until fully combined. Add dry ingredients (from first step), and beat on low speed until combined. Drop batter by rounded teaspoons onto ungreased cookie sheets about 2 inches apart. Bake until firm and barely golden, 10 to 12 minutes. Set pan on a wire rack to cool for about 4 minutes before placing cookies themselves on wire rack. In a small saucepan, combine remaining 1 cup light brown sugar and cream. Bring to a boil over medium heat. Cook, stirring constantly for 2 minutes. Remove from heat. Add powdered sugar and whisk until smooth. (If frosting thickens, thin with cream.) Add pecan pieces. Spoon about ½ teaspoon praline mixture onto each cookie. Let cool, then store in airtight containers. Makes about three dozen.

Michael Toscan
Denver, Colorado

$\mathcal{C}$LARE ANN'S FUDGE

6 c. sugar
1 (12-oz.) can evaporated milk
12-oz. pkg. semi-sweet chocolate
   chips

1 c. margarine (softened)
1 tsp. vanilla

Put sugar and milk in a 4-quart pot. Bring to a boil, stir and boil for 7 minutes. Take off of heat, add chocolate chips and margarine, stir in well. Beat with an electric mixer for 5 minutes, at the 4 minute mark add the vanilla. Pour into a 9 x 13-inch pan. Chill in refrigerator.

Note: This recipe is in its third generation of use. We all love it!

Carla Nielsen
White Bear Lake, Minnesota

50191-03

ℰASY FUDGE

1 whole sq. Baker's unsweetened
   chocolate
1 (12-oz.) pkg. semi-sweet
   chocolate chips
1 (14-oz.) can sweetened
   condensed milk

1 tsp. vanilla extract
½ c. chopped walnuts or almonds
   (opt.)

With spoon, chop Baker's chocolate square in half down the middle where it is sectioned. Put both pieces chocolate square in bottom of medium saucepan. Pour chocolate chips over that, and pour sweetened condensed milk on top. Melt over low heat uncovered, stirring frequently, until completely smooth. Remove from heat. Add vanilla (and nuts, if desired). Stir well. Line 8 x 8-inch square pan with wax paper. Pour mixture into pan and smooth with spatula. Refrigerate until firm, at least 2 hours. After chilled, lift wax paper out of pan by edges, turn upside down, and peel off wax paper. Cut into pieces of desired size. Will keep for quite a while, if kept tightly covered. Does not need to be refrigerated once cut, unless it gets too warm and starts to get soft. Then refrigerate until firm again, or keep refrigerated.

Variations: 1. Plain: Leave out nuts. **2. For an Almond Joy candy bar taste:** Add the walnuts along with about 7 ounces of shredded coconut. **3. For a chocolate covered cherry taste:** Change the vanilla to ¾ teaspoon almond extract, and after removing from heat, add one jar (drained) maraschino cherries. **4. For peanut butter fudge (nuts optional):** After removing from heat, add ½ jar Jif chocolate silk peanut butter. Stir well. If not blending well, can warm slightly over low heat until peanut butter is mixed in. **5. For peppermint fudge:** Change the vanilla to ¾ teaspoon peppermint extract, and after spreading mixture into pan, crumble one large peppermint candy cane over the top before refrigerating. **6. For marshmallow fudge:** After removing from heat, add ½ bag colored mini marshmallows. Stir well until almost completely melted. **7. For vanilla fudge (nuts optional):** Use 1 square Baker's white chocolate instead of unsweetened chocolate, and use a 12-ounce bag of white chocolate chips instead of the regular chocolate chips.

Karen L. Kriz
Indianapolis, Indiana

CHOCOLATE PEANUT BUTTER TRUFFLES

1 (8-oz.) pkg. Baker's semi-sweet
   baking chocolate
½ c. peanut butter

1 (8-oz.) tub Cool Whip whipped
   topping (thawed)

Suggested coatings:

Powdered sugar
Finely chopped Planter's pecans
Toasted Baker's Angel Flake
   coconut

Grated Baker's semi-sweet baking
   chocolate
Finely crushed Nabisco cookies
Colored sprinkles

Microwave chocolate in large microwavable bowl on high for 2 minutes or until chocolate is almost melted, stirring after 1 minute. Stir until chocolate is completely melted. Stir in peanut butter until well blended. Cool to room temperature. Gently stir in whipped topping. Refrigerate 1 hour. Scoop truffle mixture with melon baller or teaspoon, then shape into 1-inch balls. Roll in one of the suggested coatings. Store in refrigerator. Makes 3 dozen. **Super nutty chocolate truffles:** Mix and refrigerate truffle mixture as directed, using chunky peanut butter. Shape into balls. Roll in finely chopped Planter's peanuts.

Note: This is great for parties or gatherings and is out of this world. My favorite coating is coconut flakes and finely chopped pecans, mixed together and toasted to a chocolate brown.

Shirley Satterfield
Daisy, Oklahoma

"Never limit your view of life by any past experience."

Ernest Holmes

50191-03

BUCKEYES

3 c. creamy peanut butter
1 c. butter
8 c. (2 lbs.) powdered sugar
2 tsp. vanilla extract

2 lbs. Baker's semi-sweet
  chocolate blocks
1-in. sq. paraffin (cooking wax)

Mix peanut butter, butter, powdered sugar and vanilla in order given. Roll the mixture into quarter-size balls and freeze for about 60 minutes. You can keep them frozen for several weeks or until you are ready for dipping. Remove when ready for dipping. **Dip:** Melt chocolate and wax in a double boiler. Dip balls into chocolate using a toothpick in the center. Leave a dime-size spot of the ball undipped at the top. This is what makes it look like a buckeye! Immediately place the dipped balls on a cookie sheet, covered with wax paper. Refrigerate for 30 minutes before removing to the dipped balls from the wax paper. Keep refrigerated until ready to serve.

Note: Delicious!

Kimberlee Buter
Holloman Air Force Base, New Mexico

KENTUCKY COLONELS

1 (16-oz.) box powdered sugar (4
  c.)
½ c. butter

¼ c. bourbon
½ c. pecans (chopped)
8-oz. chocolate bar (melted)

Cream together sugar, butter, and bourbon. Add nuts. Shape into balls, place on wax paper. Place in refrigerator for at least 30 minutes until balls have set. Dip each ball into the melted chocolate and return to wax paper. Allow to cool and set again.

Louise Hickman
Morehead, Kentucky

CRUNCHY CANDY

18 oz. chocolate almond bark
2 c. Rice Krispies cereal

2 c. Cap 'N Crunch cereal
2 c. peanuts

Soften almond bark in microwave (about 2 minutes). Stopping to stir every 30 seconds. Remove and sir in Rice Krispies, Cap 'N Crunch and peanuts until all are coated well. Drop onto wax paper by spoonfuls. Allow to cool. Sets up quickly.

Note: This was brought in as a Christmas gift while I was working for the American Cancer Society. Thus, I call it my cancer crunchy candy!

Bonnie Eddy
Napoleon, Ohio

PRETZEL CANDY

2½ c. sm., skinny, stick pretzels
  (broken into pieces)
¾-1 c. dry roasted or any salted
  peanuts

12-14 oz. white chocolate candy
  melts or bark coating
2 T. oil

Place pretzels in plastic bag. Put a pinhole in the bag to let air out, and hit the bag with meat pounder, etc. to break into pieces. This is faster than breaking them individually. Mix with peanuts and set aside. Melt white candy melts and oil in a double boiler or microwave. Be careful if using microwave, melt for very short periods, stirring in between. Pour melted candy coating over pretzel mixture, mix well, and spread on cookie sheet to cool. When thoroughly cooled, break into pieces.

Note: Given to me by my dear friend Vern Hopewell. I love to bake Christmas cookies, but this is the item that is always a winner! Try to eat just one!

Mary Busse
Alexandria, Virginia

50191-03

UTTY-O'S

1 c. packed brown sugar	12 c. Cheerios
1 c. dark corn syrup	2 c. pecan halves
½ c. butter	1 c. whole almonds

In a large saucepan, heat brown sugar, corn syrup and butter until sugar is dissolved. Stir in cereal and nuts; mix well. Spread onto greased 15 x 10-inch baking pans. Bake 15 minutes at 325°. Cool 10 minutes; stir to loosen from the pan. After completely cooled, store in Ziploc bags or airtight container. Makes 16 cups.

Note: Great gift idea. In celebration of my survivor sister, Marcia Guenin.

Cheryl Bendix
Ridgefield, Connecticut

MICROWAVE PEANUT BRITTLE

1.5 c. raw, shelled Virginia peanuts (leave skins on)	1 tsp. butter
	1 tsp. vanilla
1 c. granulated sugar	1 tsp. baking soda
½ c. light corn syrup	⅛ tsp. salt

Mix the peanuts, sugar, corn syrup and salt together in a microwave-safe casserole dish until well mixed. Cook in microwave on high for 4 minutes; open and stir the mix well; then cook on high for another 4 minutes. Open, stir in the butter and vanilla, then microwave on high for a further 2 minutes. Finally, remove from the microwave, open the dish, add the baking soda and stir quickly until the mix is light and foamy. Immediately pour the mixture onto a lightly greased baking sheet, spreading it out thinly. Allow the mix to cool, then break it into small pieces and store in an airtight container.

Tip: The trick to making thin, tender peanut brittle is to keep the baking sheet(s) you use warm. I recommend heating them in a conventional oven at around 200° (about 95° C) before you spread the peanut brittle mix. This should allow you to spread the mix 1 cm to 2 cm thick without it setting up.

Charlene Seim
Issaquah, Washington

ANDIED PECANS

1 egg white	½ tsp. cinnamon
1 T. water	½ tsp. nutmeg
¾ c. sugar	2 c. pecans
1 tsp. salt	

Beat egg whites and water until stiff. Set aside. In another bowl, mix sugar, salt, cinnamon, and nutmeg. Toss pecans in egg white to coat, then toss in sugar mixture until covered. Place on greased cookie sheet at 275° for 30 minutes. Remove and stir on cookie sheet every 10 minutes during baking process. When finished, cool and separate.

Libby Cleves
Ft. Wright, Kentucky

Recipe Favorites

50191-03

Sauces & Snacks

Peter Randlov - Denmark

Frances Duncan (left) - Utah

Paul Leverett (left), family and friends - Texas

It Had Me But I Got Away

"I have been blessed. I feel like I have found my way. I thank God for all I have been given at the end of every day. I have been blessed."

-*Blessed*, Martina MacBride

In May 1999, I was diagnosed with a grade 4 glioblastoma multiforme in the brain stem. All stop. It was as if I'd been hit by a freight train. Overseas, I stopped working and came home.

I went to a cancer hospital in Houston, Texas, and was given less than a one percent chance of survival. This was devastating. Just married, and finally having a job I enjoyed, life was great. This was about to abruptly change.

After six weeks of radiation, my doctor and I couldn't agree on the chemotherapy treatment. They'd never had any success with my condition. Why use the same treatment that had never worked on anyone else?

Despite what they said, there had to be another option out there. I could not accept their one percent chance. After much prayer and constant research, I found a controversial doctor in Houston. There were stories on the web indicating he just "may" have something with some efficacy for my type of tumor.

I was put on an intravenous infusion of antineoplastons. These are synthesized proteins that act to turn off genes in your cells that cause cancer. The medicine attempts to promote natural cell death. Though not yet FDA approved, it worked for me.

Grade 4 glioblastomas double in size every 14 days. But, as treatment progressed, my tumor stopped growing and then began to shrink. By September 2000, I was in complete remission.

I am back to work now and it's February 2003. I have been blessed with a miracle. Pray. Research all options. Have faith. Do whatever it takes to survive and never give up.

Paul Leverett
Houston, Texas

For further details, see www.cancerguide.org/pleverett_story.html

Sauces & Snacks

BECKY'S SPAGHETTI SAUCE

1 lb. lean ground beef
1 lb. mild Italian sausage
2-3 cloves garlic (crushed)
½ med. onion
3 (28-oz.) cans tomato sauce
3 (8-oz.) cans tomato paste
2 tsp. basil

2 tsp. oregano
2 tsp. rosemary
2 tsp. thyme
2 tsp. salt
1 pinch sugar
2 c. sliced mushrooms

Brown beef, sausage, onion and garlic in sauté pan. Drain and put mixture into stockpot. Add tomato sauce, tomato paste, basil, oregano, rosemary, thyme, salt and sugar to pot. Simmer for at least 30 minutes. Add mushrooms and simmer for another 30 minutes. Water or more tomato paste may be added to adjust thickness. Serve over pasta noodles or use to make lasagne.

Note: So easy! Can be doubled or halved. Freezes great.

Loretta Duberow
Irvine, California

BARBECUE SAUCE

2 T. butter or margarine
1 med. onion (minced)
2 T. brown sugar
2 T. French's mustard

1 T. Worcestershire sauce
1 tsp. salt
¾ c. ketchup
1 green pepper (minced)

Combine butter, onion, brown sugar, mustard, Worcestershire sauce, salt, ketchup and green pepper in pan and simmer on stove for 15 minutes.

Note: Use this sauce with leftover beef or pork to make great sandwiches!

Martha Karch
Celina, Ohio

LIGHT HONEY/GARLIC VINAIGRETTE SALAD DRESSING

1 clove garlic (halved)
3 T. olive oil
2 T. Bragg's apple cider vinegar
1 T. fresh lemon juice
1/4 tsp. sea salt
Salt free seasoning containing no MSG or other chemicals (to taste)
Fresh ground black pepper, to taste (opt.)
1 tsp. honey (or to taste)

Place garlic, oil, vinegar, lemon juice, sea salt, salt free seasoning and honey in a measuring cup. Allow to sit for at least 15 minutes so garlic can fully flavor the oil. Pierce garlic with fork, and whip ingredients together with the same fork. Discard garlic. Pour dressing over salad, and toss well. Makes enough for 1 large salad or 2 small salads.

Note: Great quick dressing.

Alex Fraser
Courtenay, British Columbia, Canada

ITALIAN CHEESE DRESSING

1 (10 1/2-oz.) can tomato soup
1/2 c. salad or olive oil
1/4 c. vinegar
1/4 c. grated Parmesan cheese
1 tsp. basil leaves
1 tsp. oregano leaves
1/8 tsp. garlic salt

Blend soup, vinegar, cheese, basil, oregano, garlic. Add oil. Mix well. Chill. Shake well before using. Served with tossed green salad. Makes 2 cups. Keep refrigerated.

Sherri Quinn
Morehead, Kentucky

"*My constant prayer is for patience and wisdom; with these God will see me through.*"

N. Dunn

50191-03

ᴘASTO GENOVASSE

(Green Sauce of Genoa for Spaghetti)

2 lg. or 3 med. garlic cloves
2 c. basil leaves (packed) of fresh
  sweet basil
¼ c. butter
½ c. olive oil

⅛ c. pinole (pine nuts, may
  substitute walnuts)
¼ c. Parmesan or Romano cheese
  (may use a blend or both)
Salt & pepper to taste

In a blender, blend fresh basil for 5 minutes. Add garlic, butter, olive oil, nuts, cheese, salt and pepper to taste. Blend again and serve over hot spaghetti. It only takes a little of this sauce to enhance a large bowl of pasta. Therefore, use sparingly, two to three tablespoons is usually sufficient. The hot spaghetti will heat the sauce, so no sauce preheat is necessary. **To freeze:** Prepare sauce without the cheese and butter. It can be frozen to enjoy when fresh basil is not available. Just thaw, add the appropriate amounts of butter and cheese, and you are in business!

Note: Recipe received from Pepe (chef) in Naples, Italy, when I was stationed there with the Navy. It's delicious! **Author's note:** Mr. King passed on before this book was finished. He had a wonderful spirit and was a terrific storyteller!

Hal King
Winter Springs, Florida

ᴅAIRY FREE PESTO

½ c. walnuts or pine nuts
2 cloves garlic
1 tsp. salt

2 c. lightly packed basil
¼ c. olive oil

Grind walnuts and pine nuts and garlic in food processor. Add basil and salt. With the machine running gradually add oil. Serve over rice, pasta or salad.

Note: You won't be able to tell the difference between this version and the one with cheese. The fresher the basil, the tastier it is.

Dorene Campbell
Vancouver, Washington

$\mathcal{R}$ITA'S FAVORITE FREEZER PESTO

2 lg. cloves garlic
2 c. basil leaves (packed)
¾ c. Parmesan cheese or ½ c.
  Romano cheese
2 T. butter or margarine (opt.)

2 T. pine nuts (toasted if desired)
½ c. minced parsley (opt.)
½ c. extra virgin olive oil
Salt to taste

Place garlic in food processor and pulse to mince. Add basil leaves, Parmesan or Romano cheese, butter (optional), pine nuts, minced parsley (optional). Process until smooth. Add oil and process. Add salt to taste. Or you may mince all by hand and mix. Makes about 2 cups.

Note: When measuring herbs for recipes, pack the whole leaf tightly in whatever you're measuring in. Then mince. This should give you a fairly accurate measure. Go to taste on this recipe. You can always add more of the flavoring components.

Rita Heikenfeld
Batavia, Ohio

$\mathcal{A}$MAZING SEASONED OYSTER CRACKERS

1 c. vegetable oil
1 tsp. dill weed
1½ tsp. powdered Ranch salad
  dressing mix (original flavor)

2 (12-oz.) pkgs. oyster crackers

Place crackers in a large bowl. Sprinkle crackers with dill weed and dry Ranch dressing mix. Add vegetable oil and mix well. Cover and let sit for 1 hour.

Note: Great for something different with soup, or just by themselves! Delicious munchies!

Melanie Jump
Batavia, Ohio

"*Always laugh when you can. It's cheap medicine.*"

Lord Byron

50191-03

NUTS AND BOLTS

1 sm. (10-oz.) box Cheerios
1 sm. (12-oz.) box Corn Chex
  cereal
1 sm. (12-oz.) box Rice Chex cereal
1 (15-oz.) bag thin pretzels
  (broken)
12 oz. cashews
12 oz. Spanish nuts

3.25 (½ of 7-oz. bag) Bugles
5 oz. (½ of 10-oz. box) Cheez-Its
24 oz. mixed nuts
2 c. butter or margarine (melted)
4 T. garlic salt
2 T. garlic powder
4 T. onion salt
5 T. celery seed

Put Cheerios, Corn Chex, Rice Chex, pretzels, mixed nuts, cashews, Spanish nuts, Bugles and Cheez-Its in a large size roasting pan. Melt butter. Add spices to butter and let boil for 1 minute. Pour over cereal mixture. Stir well. Cover and bake at 300° for one hour. Take lid off and bake for 2½ hours. Stir every ½ hour.

Note: In dedication to my brother, Larry Allen. He came and lived with us until he passed away from cancer in 1978. We were very close and when he came home for Christmas we always made this mix.

Evelyn Adams
Barboursville, West Virginia

NUTTY CARAMEL POPCORN

6 qt. popped corn (about 1 c.
  uncooked) (be sure it's hot air
  popcorn)
1 c. cashews
1 c. pecans
1 c. butter/margarine

2 c. brown sugar
½ c. light corn syrup
1 tsp. salt
½ tsp. baking soda
1 tsp. vanilla

Pop corn, pour into large roasting pan. Add nuts to popcorn, set aside. Melt butter in large saucepan. Add brown sugar, corn syrup and salt. Stir over medium heat until it begins to boil. Let boil, without stirring, for 5 minutes. Remove from heat. Stir in baking soda and vanilla. Pour over popcorn and nuts. Stir. Bake for 1 hour at 225°, stirring every 15 minutes. Store in airtight container.

Chris Soranno
Flower Mound, Texas

THE BEST CARAMEL CORN

6-7 qt. popcorn, popped
1 c. butter (not margarine)
2 c. brown sugar
1/2 c. corn syrup

1 tsp. salt
1 tsp. baking soda
1 tsp. vanilla

Melt butter in a saucepan, add sugar, corn syrup and salt. Boil for 5 minutes. Take off heat and add soda and vanilla. Stir really well. Put popcorn in a large stainless steel bowl, pour mixture over popcorn and mix. (It is important to mix this very well.) Bake at 200° for 1 hour in a big metal bowl, stirring every 15 minutes. Pour on waxed paper to cool.

Note: Add gummy worms, candy corn, fall colored M & M's for the kids!

Teresa Bohner
Renton, Washington

BUTTERSCOTCH BROWNIE GIFT JAR

1/2 c. flaked coconut
3/4 c. chopped pecans
2 c. packed brown sugar

2 c. self rising flour
1-qt. wide mouth canning jar

In canning jar, layer coconut, pecans, brown sugar, and then flour. (Important to do this in order given.) Press each layer firmly in place before adding the next one. Put lid on jar. Can be given as a gift with the following directions: Empty contents of jar into large mixing bowl. Add 3/4 cup of margarine (softened), 2 eggs (slightly beaten), 2 teaspoons vanilla. Mix until completely blended. Spread into a sprayed 9 x 13-inch metal pan. Bake at 375° for 25 minutes. Cut brownies in 1 1/2-inch squares. Cool completely in pan. Makes 2 dozen.

Note: A great gift with a personal touch! Perfect for Christmas or anytime for friends, neighbors, teachers, etc!

Sheila Butler
Mt. Orab, Ohio

50191-03

INDEX OF RECIPES

VEGETABLES & SIDE DISHES

MAIN DISHES

DESSERTS

COOKIES & CANDY

SAUCES & SNACKS

How to Order

Get additional copies of this cookbook by returning an order form and your check or money order to:

Resolve Publishing
c/o Julie Scott
1820 Bell Tower Circle
Batavia, Ohio 45103-9758
E-mail: cookbookforcancer@juno.com
Web site: www.cookbookforcancer.com

✂ --

Please send me _____ copies of **Cookbook for Cancer** at **$14.95** per copy and **$3.00** for shipping and handling per book. **Ohio residents add 7% ($1.05) sales tax.** Enclosed is my check or money order for $_____.

Mail Books To:

Name _____

Address _____

City _____ State _____ Zip _____

✂ --

Please send me _____ copies of **Cookbook for Cancer** at **$14.95** per copy and **$3.00** for shipping and handling per book. **Ohio residents add 7% ($1.05) sales tax.** Enclosed is my check or money order for $_____.

Mail Books To:

Name _____

Address _____

City _____ State _____ Zip _____

Cooking Tips

1. After stewing a chicken, cool in broth before cutting into chunks; it will have twice the flavor.

2. To slice meat into thin strips, as for stir-fry dishes, partially freeze it so it will slice more easily.

3. A roast with the bone in will cook faster than a boneless roast. The bone carries the heat to the inside more quickly.

4. When making a roast, place dry onion soup mix in the bottom of your roaster pan. After removing the roast, add 1 can of mushroom soup and you will have a good brown gravy.

5. For a juicier hamburger, add cold water to the beef before grilling (½ cup to 1 pound of meat).

6. To freeze meatballs, place them on a cookie sheet until frozen. Place in plastic bags. They will stay separated so that you may remove as many as you want.

7. To keep cauliflower white while cooking, add a little milk to the water.

8. When boiling corn, add sugar to the water instead of salt. Salt will toughen the corn.

9. To ripen tomatoes, put them in a brown paper bag in a dark pantry, and they will ripen.

10. To keep celery crisp, stand it upright in a pitcher of cold, salted water and refrigerate.

11. When cooking cabbage, place a small tin cup or can half full of vinegar on the stove near the cabbage. It will absorb the odor.

12. Potatoes soaked in salt water for 20 minutes before baking will bake more rapidly.

13. Let raw potatoes stand in cold water for at least a half-hour before frying in order to improve the crispness of French-fried potatoes. Dry potatoes thoroughly before adding to oil.

14. Use greased muffin tins as molds when baking stuffed green peppers.

15. A few drops of lemon juice in the water will whiten boiled potatoes.

16. Buy mushrooms before they "open." When stems and caps are attached firmly, mushrooms are truly fresh.

17. Do not use metal bowls when mixing salads. Use wood, glass or china.

18. Lettuce keeps better if you store it in the refrigerator without washing it. Keep the leaves dry. Wash lettuce the day you are going to use it.

19. Do not use soda to keep vegetables green. It destroys Vitamin C.

20. Do not despair if you oversalt gravy. Stir in some instant mashed potatoes to repair the damage. Just add a little more liquid in order to offset the thickening.

Herbs & Spices

Acquaint yourself with herbs and spices. Add in small amounts, ¼ teaspoon for every 4 servings. Crush dried herbs or snip fresh ones before using. Use 3 times more fresh herbs if substituting fresh for dried.

Basil
Sweet, warm flavor with an aromatic odor. Use whole or ground. Good with lamb, fish, roast, stews, ground beef, vegetables, dressing and omelets.

Bay Leaves
Pungent flavor. Use whole leaf but remove before serving. Good in vegetable dishes, seafood, stews and pickles.

Caraway
Spicy taste and aromatic smell. Use in cakes, breads, soups, cheese and sauerkraut.

Chives
Sweet, mild flavor like that of onion. Excellent in salads, fish, soups and potatoes.

Cilantro
Use fresh. Excellent in salads, fish, chicken, rice, beans and Mexican dishes.

Curry Powder
Spices are combined to proper proportions to give a distinct flavor to meat, poultry, fish and vegetables.

Dill
Both seeds and leaves are flavorful. Leaves may be used as a garnish or cooked with fish, soup, dressings, potatoes and beans. Leaves or the whole plant may be used to flavor pickles.

Fennel
Sweet, hot flavor. Both seeds and leaves are used. Use in small quantities in pies and baked goods. Leaves can be boiled with fish.

Ginger
A pungent root, this aromatic spice is sold fresh, dried or ground. Use in pickles, preserves, cakes, cookies, soups and meat dishes.

Herbs & Spices

Marjoram May be used both dried or green. Use to flavor fish, poultry, omelets, lamb, stew, stuffing and tomato juice.

Mint Aromatic with a cool flavor. Excellent in beverages, fish, lamb, cheese, soup, peas, carrots, and fruit desserts.

Oregano Strong, aromatic odor. Use whole or ground in tomato juice, fish, eggs, pizza, omelets, chili, stew, gravy, poultry and vegetables.

Paprika A bright red pepper, this spice is used in meat, vegetables and soups or as a garnish for potatoes, salads or eggs.

Parsley Best when used fresh, but can be used dried as a garnish or as a seasoning. Try in fish, omelets, soup, meat, stuffing and mixed greens.

Rosemary Very aromatic. Can be used fresh or dried. Season fish, stuffing, beef, lamb, poultry, onions, eggs, bread and potatoes. Great in dressings.

Saffron Orange-yellow in color, this spice flavors or colors foods. Use in soup, chicken, rice and breads.

Sage Use fresh or dried. The flowers are sometimes used in salads. May be used in tomato juice, fish, omelets, beef, poultry, stuffing, cheese spreads and breads.

Tarragon Leaves have a pungent, hot taste. Use to flavor sauces, salads, fish, poultry, tomatoes, eggs, green beans, carrots and dressings.

Thyme Sprinkle leaves on fish or poultry before broiling or baking. Throw a few sprigs directly on coals shortly before meat is finished grilling.

Baking Breads

Hints for Baking Breads

1. Kneading dough for 30 seconds after mixing improves the texture of baking powder biscuits.

2. Instead of shortening, use cooking or salad oil in waffles and hot cakes.

3. When bread is baking, a small dish of water in the oven will help keep the crust from hardening.

4. Dip a spoon in hot water to measure shortening, butter, etc., and the fat will slip out more easily.

5. Small amounts of leftover corn may be added to pancake batter for variety.

6. To make bread crumbs, use the fine cutter of a food grinder and tie a large paper bag over the spout in order to prevent flying crumbs.

7. When you are doing any sort of baking, you get better results if you remember to preheat your cookie sheet, muffin tins or cake pans.

Rules for Use of Leavening Agents

1. In simple flour mixtures, use 2 teaspoons baking powder to leaven 1 cup flour. Reduce this amount 1/2 teaspoon for each egg used.

2. To 1 teaspoon soda use 2 1/4 teaspoons cream of tartar, 2 cups freshly soured milk, or 1 cup molasses.

3. To substitute soda and an acid for baking powder, divide the amount of baking powder by 4. Take that as your measure and add acid according to rule 2.

Proportions of Baking Powder to Flour

biscuits	....	to 1 cup flour use 1 1/4 tsp. baking powder
cake with oil	....	to 1 cup flour use 1 tsp. baking powder
muffins	....	to 1 cup flour use 1 1/2 tsp. baking powder
popovers	....	to 1 cup flour use 1 1/4 tsp. baking powder
waffles	....	to 1 cup flour use 1 1/4 tsp. baking powder

Proportions of Liquid to Flour

drop batter	....	to 1 cup liquid use 2 to 2 1/2 cups flour
pour batter	....	to 1 cup liquid use 1 cup flour
soft dough	....	to 1 cup liquid use 3 to 3 1/2 cups flour
stiff dough	....	to 1 cup liquid use 4 cups flour

Time and Temperature Chart

Breads	Minutes	Temperature
biscuits	12 - 15	400° - 450°
cornbread	25 - 30	400° - 425°
gingerbread	40 - 50	350° - 370°
loaf	50 - 60	350° - 400°
nut bread	50 - 75	350°
popovers	30 - 40	425° - 450°
rolls	20 - 30	400° - 450°

Baking Desserts

Perfect Cookies

Cookie dough that is to be rolled is much easier to handle after it has been refrigerated for 10 to 30 minutes. This keeps the dough from sticking, even though it may be soft. If not done, the soft dough may require more flour and too much flour makes cookies hard and brittle. Place on a floured board only as much dough as can be easily managed. Flour the rolling pin slightly and roll lightly to desired thickness. Cut shapes close together and add trimmings to dough that needs to be rolled. Place pans or sheets in upper third of oven. Watch cookies carefully while baking in order to avoid burned edges. When sprinkling sugar on cookies, try putting it into a salt shaker in order to save time.

Perfect Pies

1. Pie crust will be better and easier to make if all the ingredients are cool.

2. The lower crust should be placed in the pan so that it covers the surface smoothly. Air pockets beneath the surface will push the crust out of shape while baking.

3. Folding the top crust over the lower crust before crimping will keep juices in the pie.

4. In making custard pie, bake at a high temperature for about ten minutes to prevent a soggy crust. Then finish baking at a low temperature.

5. When making cream pie, sprinkle crust with powdered sugar in order to prevent it from becoming soggy.

Perfect Cakes

1. Fill cake pans two-thirds full and spread batter into corners and sides, leaving a slight hollow in the center.

2. Cake is done when it shrinks from the sides of the pan or if it springs back when touched lightly with the finger.

3. After removing a cake from the oven, place it on a rack for about five minutes. Then, the sides should be loosened and the cake turned out on a rack in order to finish cooling.

4. Do not frost cakes until thoroughly cool.

5. Icing will remain where you put it if you sprinkle cake with powdered sugar first.

Time and Temperature Chart

Dessert	Time	Temperature
butter cake, layer	20-40 min.	380° - 400°
butter cake, loaf	40-60 min.	360° - 400°
cake, angel	50-60 min.	300° - 360°
cake, fruit	3-4 hrs.	275° - 325°
cake, sponge	40-60 min.	300° - 350°
cookies, molasses	18-20 min.	350° - 375°
cookies, thin	10-12 min.	380° - 390°
cream puffs	45-60 min.	300° - 350°
meringue	40-60 min.	250° - 300°
pie crust	20-40 min.	400° - 500°

Vegetables & Fruits

Vegetable	Cooking Method	Time
artichokes	boiled	40 min.
	steamed	45-60 min.
asparagus tips	boiled	10-15 min.
beans, lima	boiled	20-40 min.
	steamed	60 min.
beans, string	boiled	15-35 min.
	steamed	60 min.
beets, old	boiled or steamed	1-2 hours
beets, young with skin	boiled	30 min.
	steamed	60 min.
	baked	70-90 min.
broccoli, flowerets	boiled	5-10 min.
broccoli, stems	boiled	20-30 min.
brussels sprouts	boiled	20-30 min.
cabbage, chopped	boiled	10-20 min.
	steamed	25 min.
carrots, cut across	boiled	8-10 min.
	steamed	40 min.
cauliflower, flowerets	boiled	8-10 min.
cauliflower, stem down	boiled	20-30 min.
corn, green, tender	boiled	5-10 min.
	steamed	15 min.
	baked	20 min.
corn on the cob	boiled	8-10 min.
	steamed	15 min.
eggplant, whole	boiled	30 min.
	steamed	40 min.
	baked	45 min.
parsnips	boiled	25-40 min.
	steamed	60 min.
	baked	60-75 min.
peas, green	boiled or steamed	5-15 min.
potatoes	boiled	20-40 min.
	steamed	60 min.
	baked	45-60 min.
pumpkin or squash	boiled	20-40 min.
	steamed	45 min.
	baked	60 min.
tomatoes	boiled	5-15 min.
turnips	boiled	25-40 min.

Drying Time Table

Fruit	Sugar or Honey	Cooking Time
apricots	¼ c. for each cup of fruit	about 40 min.
figs	1 T. for each cup of fruit	about 30 min.
peaches	¼ c. for each cup of fruit	about 45 min.
prunes	2 T. for each cup of fruit	about 45 min.

Vegetables & Fruits

Buying Fresh Vegetables

Artichokes: Look for compact, tightly closed heads with green, clean-looking leaves. Avoid those with leaves that are brown or separated.

Asparagus: Stalks should be tender and firm; tips should be close and compact. Choose the stalks with very little white; they are more tender. Use asparagus soon because it toughens rapidly.

Beans, Snap: Those with small seeds inside the pods are best. Avoid beans with dry-looking pods.

Broccoli, Brussels Sprouts and Cauliflower: Flower clusters on broccoli and cauliflower should be tight and close together. Brussels sprouts should be firm and compact. Smudgy, dirty spots may indicate pests or disease.

Cabbage and Head Lettuce: Choose heads that are heavy for their size. Avoid cabbage with worm holes and lettuce with discoloration or soft rot.

Cucumbers: Choose long, slender cucumbers for best quality. May be dark or medium green, but yellow ones are undesirable.

Mushrooms: Caps should be closed around the stems. Avoid black or brown gills.

Peas and Lima Beans: Select pods that are well-filled but not bulging. Avoid dried, spotted, yellow, or flabby pods.

Buying Fresh Fruits

Bananas: Skin should be free of bruises and black or brown spots. Purchase them green and allow them to ripen at home at room temperature.

Berries: Select plump, solid berries with good color. Avoid stained containers which indicate wet or leaky berries. Berries with clinging caps, such as blackberries and raspberries, may be unripe. Strawberries without caps may be overripe.

Melons: In cantaloupes, thick, close netting on the rind indicates best quality. Cantaloupes are ripe when the stem scar is smooth and the space between the netting is yellow or yellow-green. They are best when fully ripe with fruity odor.

Honeydews are ripe when rind has creamy to yellowish color and velvety texture. Immature honeydews are whitish-green.

Ripe watermelons have some yellow color on one side. If melons are white or pale green on one side, they are not ripe.

Oranges, Grapefruit and Lemons: Choose those heavy for their size. Smoother, thinner skins usually indicate more juice. Most skin markings do not affect quality. Oranges with a slight greenish tinge may be just as ripe as fully colored ones. Light or greenish-yellow lemons are more tart than deep yellow ones. Avoid citrus fruits showing withered, sunken or soft areas.

Napkin Folding

Shield

Easy fold. Elegant with monogram in corner.

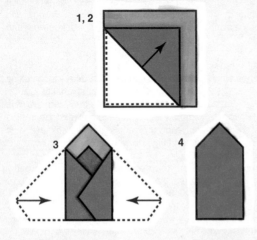

Instructions:
1. Fold into quarter size. If monogrammed, ornate corner should face down.
2. Turn up folded corner three-quarters.
3. Overlap right side and left side points.
4. Turn over; adjust sides so that they are even, single point in center.
5. Place point up or down on plate, or left of plate.

Rosette

Elegant on plate.

Instructions:
1. Fold left and right edges to center, leaving ½" opening along center.
2. Pleat firmly from top edge to bottom edge. Sharpen edges with hot iron.
3. Pinch center together. If necessary, use small piece of pipe cleaner to secure and top with single flower.
4. Spread out rosette.

Napkin Folding

Candle

Easy to do; can be decorated.

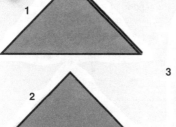

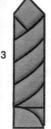

Instructions:
1. Fold into triangle, point at top.
2. Turn lower edge up 1".
3. Turn over, folded edge down.
4. Roll tightly from left to right.
5. Tuck in corner. Stand upright.

Fan

Pretty in napkin ring or on plate.

Instructions:
1. Fold top and bottom edges to center.
2. Fold top and bottom edges to center a second time.
3. Pleat firmly from the left edge. Sharpen edges with hot iron.
4. Spread out fan. Balance flat folds of each side on table. Well-starched napkins will hold shape.

Lily

Effective and pretty on table.

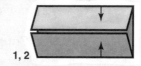

Instructions:
1. Fold napkin into quarters.
2. Fold into triangle, closed corner to open points.
3. Turn two points over to other side. (Two points are on either side of closed point.)
4. Pleat.
5. Place closed end in glass. Pull down two points on each side and shape.

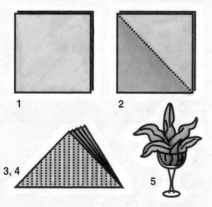

Measurements & Substitutions

Measurements

a pinch	1/8 teaspoon or less
3 teaspoons	1 tablespoon
4 tablespoons	1/4 cup
8 tablespoons	1/2 cup
12 tablespoons	3/4 cup
16 tablespoons	1 cup
2 cups	1 pint
4 cups	1 quart
4 quarts	1 gallon
8 quarts	1 peck
4 pecks	1 bushel
16 ounces	1 pound
32 ounces	1 quart
1 ounce liquid	2 tablespoons
8 ounces liquid	1 cup

**Use standard measuring spoons and cups.
All measurements are level.**

Substitutions

Ingredient	Quantity	Substitute
baking powder	1 teaspoon	1/4 tsp. baking soda plus 1/2 tsp. cream of tartar
catsup or chili sauce	1 cup	1 c. tomato sauce plus 1/2 c. sugar and 2 T. vinegar (for use in cooking)
chocolate	1 square (1 oz.)	3 or 4 T. cocoa plus 1 T. butter
cornstarch	1 tablespoon	2 T. flour or 2 tsp. quick-cooking tapioca
cracker crumbs	3/4 cup	1 c. bread crumbs
dates	1 lb.	1 1/2 c. dates, pitted and cut
dry mustard	1 teaspoon	1 T. prepared mustard
flour, self-rising	1 cup	1 c. all-purpose flour, 1/2 tsp. salt, and 1 tsp. baking powder
herbs, fresh	1 tablespoon	1 tsp. dried herbs
milk, sour	1 cup	1 T. lemon juice or vinegar plus sweet milk to make 1 c. (let stand 5 minutes)
whole	1 cup	1/2 c. evaporated milk plus 1/2 c. water
min. marshmallows	10	1 lg. marshmallow
onion, fresh	1 small	1 T. instant minced onion, rehydrated
sugar, brown	1/2 cup	2 T. molasses in 1/2 c. granulated sugar
powdered	1 cup	1 c. granulated sugar plus 1 tsp. cornstarch
tomato juice	1 cup	1/2 c. tomato sauce plus 1/2 c. water

**When substituting cocoa for chocolate in cakes, the amount of flour must
be reduced. Brown and white sugars usually can be interchanged.**

Equivalency Chart

Food	Quantity	Yield
apple	1 medium	1 cup
banana, mashed	1 medium	1/3 cup
bread	1 1/2 slices	1 cup soft crumbs
bread	1 slice	1/4 cup fine, dry crumbs
butter	1 stick or 1/4 pound	1/2 cup
cheese, American, cubed	1 pound	2 2/3 cups
American, grated	1 pound	5 cups
cream cheese	3-ounce package	6 2/3 tablespoons
chocolate, bitter	1 square	1 ounce
cocoa	1 pound	4 cups
coconut	1 1/2 pound package	2 2/3 cups
coffee, ground	1 pound	5 cups
cornmeal	1 pound	3 cups
cornstarch	1 pound	3 cups
crackers, graham	14 squares	1 cup fine crumbs
saltine	28 crackers	1 cup fine crumbs
egg	4-5 whole	1 cup
whites	8-10	1 cup
yolks	10-12	1 cup
evaporated milk	1 cup	3 cups whipped
flour, cake, sifted	1 pound	4 1/2 cups
rye	1 pound	5 cups
white, sifted	1 pound	4 cups
white, unsifted	1 pound	3 3/4 cups
gelatin, flavored	3 1/4 ounces	1/2 cup
unflavored	1/4 ounce	1 tablespoon
lemon	1 medium	3 tablespoon juice
marshmallows	16	1/4 pound
noodles, cooked	8-ounce package	7 cups
uncooked	4 ounces (1 1/2 cups)	2-3 cups cooked
macaroni, cooked	8-ounce package	6 cups
macaroni, uncooked	4 ounces (1 1/4 cups)	2 1/4 cups cooked
spaghetti, uncooked	7 ounces	4 cups cooked
nuts, chopped	1/4 pound	1 cup
almonds	1 pound	3 1/2 cups
walnuts, broken	1 pound	3 cups
walnuts, unshelled	1 pound	1 1/2 to 1 3/4 cups
onion	1 medium	1/2 cup
orange	3-4 medium	1 cup juice
raisins	1 pound	3 1/2 cups
rice, brown	1 cup	4 cups cooked
converted	1 cup	3 1/2 cups cooked
regular	1 cup	3 cups cooked
wild	1 cup	4 cups cooked
sugar, brown	1 pound	2 1/2 cups
powdered	1 pound	3 1/2 cups
white	1 pound	2 cups
vanilla wafers	22	1 cup fine crumbs
zwieback, crumbled	4	1 cups

Food Quantities
For Large Servings

	25 Servings	50 Servings	100 Servings
Beverages:			
coffee	½ pound and 1 ½ gallons water	1 pound and 3 gallons water	2 pounds and 6 gallons water
lemonade	10-15 lemons and 1 ½ gallons water	20-30 lemons and 3 gallons water	40-60 lemons and 6 gallons water
tea	¹/₁₂ pound and 1 ½ gallons water	¹/₆ pound and 3 gallons water	¹/₃ pound and 6 gallons water
Desserts:			
layered cake	1 12" cake	3 10" cakes	6 10" cakes
sheet cake	1 10" x 12" cake	1 12" x 20" cake	2 12" x 20" cakes
watermelon	37 ½ pounds	75 pounds	150 pounds
whipping cream	¾ pint	1 ½ to 2 pints	3-4 pints
Ice cream:			
brick	3 ¼ quarts	6 ½ quarts	13 quarts
bulk	2 ¼ quarts	4 ½ quarts or 1 ¼ gallons	9 quarts or 2 ½ gallons
Meat, poultry or fish:			
fish	13 pounds	25 pounds	50 pounds
fish, fillets or steak	7 ½ pounds	15 pounds	30 pounds
hamburger	9 pounds	18 pounds	35 pounds
turkey or chicken	13 pounds	25 to 35 pounds	50 to 75 pounds
wieners (beef)	6 ½ pounds	13 pounds	25 pounds
Salads, casseroles:			
baked beans	¾ gallon	1 ¼ gallons	2 ½ gallons
jello salad	¾ gallon	1 ¼ gallons	2 ½ gallons
potato salad	4 ¼ quarts	2 ¼ gallons	4 ½ gallons
scalloped potatoes	4 ½ quarts or 1 12" x 20" pan	9 quarts or 2 ¼ gallons	18 quarts 4 ½ gallons
spaghetti	1 ¼ gallons	2 ½ gallons	5 gallons
Sandwiches:			
bread	50 slices or 3 1-pound loaves	100 slices or 6 1-pound loaves	200 slices or 12 1-pound loaves
butter	½ pound	1 pound	2 pounds
lettuce	1 ½ heads	3 heads	6 heads
mayonnaise	1 cup	2 cups	4 cups
mixed filling			
meat, eggs, fish	1 ½ quarts	3 quarts	6 quarts
jam, jelly	1 quart	2 quarts	4 quarts

Microwave Hints

1. Place an open box of hardened brown sugar in the microwave oven with 1 cup hot water. Microwave on high for 1 1/2 to 2 minutes for 1/2 pound or 2 to 3 minutes for 1 pound.

2. Soften hard ice cream by microwaving at 30% power. One pint will take 15 to 30 seconds; one quart, 30-45 seconds; and one-half gallon, 45-60 seconds.

3. To melt chocolate, place 1/2 pound in glass bowl or measuring cup. Melt uncovered at 50% power for 3-4 minutes; stir after 2 minutes.

4. Soften one 8-ounce package of cream cheese by microwaving at 30% power for 2 to 2 1/2 minutes. One 3-ounce package of cream cheese will soften in 1 1/2 to 2 minutes.

5. A 4 1/2 ounce carton of whipped topping will thaw in 1 minute on the defrost setting. Whipped topping should be slightly firm in the center, but it will blend well when stirred. Do not over thaw!

6. Soften jello that has set up too hard - perhaps you were to chill it until slightly thickened and forgot it. Heat on a low power setting for a very short time.

7. Heat hot packs. A wet fingertip towel will take about 25 seconds. It depends on the temperature of the water used to wet the towel.

8. To scald milk, cook 1 cup for 2 to 2 1/2 minutes, stirring once each minute.

9. To make dry bread crumbs, cut 6 slices of bread into 1/2-inch cubes. Microwave in 3-quart casserole 6-7 minutes, or until dry, stirring after 3 minutes. Crush in blender.

10. Refresh stale potato chips, crackers or other snacks of such type by putting a plateful in the microwave for 30-45 seconds. Let stand for 1 minute to crisp. Cereals can also be crisped.

11. Nuts will be easier to shell if you place 2 cups of nuts in a 1-quart casserole with 1 cup of water. Cook for 4 to 5 minutes and the nutmeats will slip out whole after cracking the shell.

12. Stamp collectors can place a few drops of water on a stamp to remove it from an envelope. Heat in the microwave for 20 seconds, and the stamp will come off.

13. Using a round dish instead of a square one eliminates overcooked corners in baking cakes.

14. Sprinkle a layer of medium, finely chopped walnuts evenly onto the bottom and side of a ring pan or bundt cake pan to enhances the looks and eating quality. Pour in batter and microwave as recipe directs.

15. Do not salt foods on the surface as it causes dehydration and toughens food. Salt after you remove from the oven unless the recipe calls for using salt in the mixture.

16. Heat left-over custard and use it as frosting for a cake.

17. Melt marshmallow creme. Half of a 7-ounce jar will melt in 35-40 seconds on high. Stir to blend.

18. To toast coconut, spread 1/2 cup coconut in a pie plate and cook for 3-4 minutes, stirring every 30 seconds after 2 minutes. Watch closely, as it quickly browns.

19. To melt crystallized honey, heat uncovered jar on high for 30-45 seconds. If jar is large, repeat.

20. One stick of butter or margarine will soften in 1 minute when microwaved at 20% power.

Calorie Counter

Beverages

apple juice, 6 oz.	90
coffee (black)	0
cola type, 12 oz.	115
cranberry juice, 6 oz.	115
ginger ale, 12 oz.	115
grape juice, (prepared from frozen concentrate), 6 oz.	142
lemonade, (prepared from frozen concentrate), 6 oz.	85
milk, protein fortified, 1 c.	105
skim, 1 c.	90
whole, 1 c.	160
orange juice, 6 oz.	85
pineapple juice, unsweetened, 6 oz.	95
root beer, 12 oz.	150
tonic (quinine water) 12 oz.	132

Breads

cornbread, 1 sm. square	130
dumplings, 1 med.	70
French toast, 1 slice	135
melba toast, 1 slice	25
muffins, blueberry, 1 muffin	110
bran, 1 muffin	106
corn, 1 muffin	125
English, 1 muffin	280
pancakes, 1 (4-in.)	60
pumpernickel, 1 slice	75
rye, 1 slice	60
waffle, 1	216
white, 1 slice	60-70
whole wheat, 1 slice	55-65

Cereals

cornflakes, 1 c.	105
cream of wheat, 1 c.	120
oatmeal, 1 c.	148
rice flakes, 1 c.	105
shredded wheat, 1 biscuit	100
sugar krisps, ¾ c.	110

Crackers

graham, 1 cracker	15-30
rye crisp, 1 cracker	35
saltine, 1 cracker	17-20
wheat thins, 1 cracker	9

Dairy Products

butter or margarine, 1 T.	100
cheese, American, 1 oz.	100
camembert, 1 oz.	85
cheddar, 1 oz.	115
cottage cheese, 1 oz.	30
mozzarella, 1 oz.	90
parmesan, 1 oz.	130
ricotta, 1 oz.	50
roquefort, 1 oz.	105
Swiss, 1 oz.	105
cream, light, 1 T.	30
heavy, 1 T.	55
sour, 1 T.	45
hot chocolate, with milk, 1 c.	277
milk chocolate, 1 oz.	145-155
yogurt	
made w/ whole milk, 1 c.	150-165
made w/ skimmed milk, 1 c.	125

Eggs

fried, 1 lg.	100
poached or boiled, 1 lg.	75-80
scrambled or in omelet, 1 lg.	110-130

Fish and Seafood

bass, 4 oz.	105
salmon, broiled or baked, 3 oz.	155
sardines, canned in oil, 3 oz.	170
trout, fried, 3 ½ oz.	220
tuna, in oil, 3 oz.	170
in water, 3 oz.	110

Calorie Counter

Fruits

apple, 1 med.	80-100
applesauce, sweetened, 1/2 c.	90-115
unsweetened, 1/2 c.	50
banana, 1 med.	85
blueberries, 1/2 c.	45
cantaloupe, 1/2 c.	24
cherries (pitted), raw, 1/2 c.	40
grapefruit, 1/2 med.	55
grapes, 1/2 c.	35-55
honeydew, 1/2 c.	55
mango, 1 med.	90
orange, 1 med.	65-75
peach, 1 med.	35
pear, 1 med.	60-100
pineapple, fresh, 1/2 c.	40
canned in syrup, 1/2 c.	95
plum, 1 med.	30
strawberries, fresh, 1/2 c.	30
frozen and sweetened, 1/2 c.	120-140
tangerine, 1 lg.	39
watermelon, 1/2 c.	42

Meat and Poultry

beef, ground (lean), 3 oz.	185
roast, 3 oz.	185
chicken, broiled, 3 oz.	115
lamb chop (lean), 3 oz.	175-200
steak, sirloin, 3 oz.	175
tenderloin, 3 oz.	174
top round, 3 oz.	162
turkey, dark meat, 3 oz.	175
white meat, 3 oz.	150
veal, cutlet, 3 oz.	156
roast, 3 oz.	76

Nuts

almonds, 2 T.	105
cashews, 2 T.	100
peanuts, 2 T.	105
peanut butter, 1 T.	95
pecans, 2 T.	95
pistachios, 2 T.	92
walnuts, 2 T.	80

Pasta

macaroni or spaghetti, cooked, 3/4 c.	115

Salad Dressings

blue cheese, 1 T.	70
French, 1 T.	65
Italian, 1 T.	80
mayonnaise, 1 T.	100
olive oil, 1 T.	124
Russian, 1 T.	70
salad oil, 1 T.	120

Soups

bean, 1 c.	130-180
beef noodle, 1 c.	70
bouillon and consomme, 1 c.	30
chicken noodle, 1 c.	65
chicken with rice, 1 c.	50
minestrone, 1 c.	80-150
split pea, 1 c.	145-170
tomato with milk, 1 c.	170
vegetable, 1 c.	80-100

Vegetables

asparagus, 1 c.	35
broccoli, cooked, 1/2 c.	25
cabbage, cooked, 1/2 c.	15-20
carrots, cooked, 1/2 c	25-30
cauliflower, 1/2 c.	10-15
corn (kernels), 1/2 c.	70
green beans, 1 c.	30
lettuce, shredded, 1/2 c.	5
mushrooms, canned, 1/2 c.	20
onions, cooked, 1/2 c.	30
peas, cooked, 1/2 c.	60
potato, baked, 1 med.	90
chips, 8-10	100
mashed, w/milk & butter, 1 c.	200-300
spinach, 1 c.	40
tomato, raw, 1 med.	25
cooked, 1/2 c.	30

Cooking Terms

Au gratin: Topped with crumbs and/or cheese and browned in oven or under broiler.

Au jus: Served in its own juices.

Baste: To moisten foods during cooking with pan drippings or special sauce in order to add flavor and prevent drying.

Bisque: A thick cream soup.

Blanch: To immerse in rapidly boiling water and allow to cook slightly.

Cream: To soften a fat, especially butter, by beating it at room temperature. Butter and sugar are often creamed together, making a smooth, soft paste.

Crimp: To seal the edges of a two-crust pie either by pinching them at intervals with the fingers or by pressing them together with the tines of a fork.

Crudites: An assortment of raw vegetables (i.e. carrots, broccoli, celery, mushrooms) that is served as an hors d'oeuvre, often accompanied by a dip.

Degrease: To remove fat from the surface of stews, soups, or stock. Usually cooled in the refrigerator so that fat hardens and is easily removed.

Dredge: To coat lightly with flour, cornmeal, etc.

Entree: The main course.

Fold: To incorporate a delicate substance, such as whipped cream or beaten egg whites, into another substance without releasing air bubbles. A spatula is used to gently bring part of the mixture from the bottom of the bowl to the top. The process is repeated, while slowly rotating the bowl, until the ingredients are thoroughly blended.

Glaze: To cover with a glossy coating, such as a melted and somewhat diluted jelly for fruit desserts.

Julienne: To cut vegetables, fruits, or cheeses into match-shaped slivers.

Marinate: To allow food to stand in a liquid in order to tenderize or to add flavor.

Meuniére: Dredged with flour and sautéed in butter.

Mince: To chop food into very small pieces.

Parboil: To boil until partially cooked; to blanch. Usually final cooking in a seasoned sauce follows this procedure.

Pare: To remove the outermost skin of a fruit or vegetable.

Poach: To cook gently in hot liquid kept just below the boiling point.

Purée: To mash foods by hand by rubbing through a sieve or food mill, or by whirling in a blender or food processor until perfectly smooth.

Refresh: To run cold water over food that has been parboiled in order to stop the cooking process quickly.

Sauté: To cook and/or brown food in a small quantity of hot shortening.

Scald: To heat to just below the boiling point, when tiny bubbles appear at the edge of the saucepan.

Simmer: To cook in liquid just below the boiling point. The surface of the liquid should be barely moving, broken from time to time by slowly rising bubbles.

Steep: To let food stand in hot liquid in order to extract or to enhance flavor, like tea in hot water or poached fruit in sugar syrup.

Toss: To combine ingredients with a repeated lifting motion.

Whip: To beat rapidly in order to incorporate air and produce expansion, as in heavy cream or egg whites.

Morris Press Cookbooks has the right ingredients to make a really great cookbook. Contact us for our **FREE** step-by-step *Cookbook Publishing Guide*. It's so easy.

You Supply
the recipes
we'll do
the Rest!™

Three ways to contact us:
- Complete and return the **postage paid reply card** below.
- Order from our web site at **www.morriscookbooks.com**.
- Call us at **800-445-6621, ext. CB**.